APOCALYPTIC ANXIETY

APOCALYPTIC ANXIETY

Religion, Science, and America's Obsession with the End of the World

ANTHONY AVENI

UNIVERSITY PRESS OF COLORADO
Boulder

Published by University Press of Colorado
5589 Arapahoe Avenue, Suite 206C
Boulder, Colorado 80303

Printed in the United States of America

The University Press of Colorado is a proud member of
The Association of American University Presses.

The University Press of Colorado is a cooperative publishing enterprise supported, in part, by Adams State University, Colorado State University, Fort Lewis College, Metropolitan State University of Denver, Regis University, University of Colorado, University of Northern Colorado, Utah State University, and Western State Colorado University.

∞ This paper meets the requirements of the ANSI/NISO Z39.48-1992 (Permanence of Paper).

ISBN: 978-1-60732-470-6 (pbk)
ISBN: 978-1-60732-471-3 (ebook)
DOI: 10.5876/9781607324713

Library of Congress Cataloging-in-Publication Data

Names: Aveni, Anthony F.
Title: Apocalyptic anxiety : religion, science and America's obsession with the end of the world / Anthony F. Aveni.
Description: Boulder : University Press of Colorado, 2016. | Includes index.
Identifiers: LCCN 2015030348 | ISBN 9781607324706 (pbk.) | ISBN 9781607324713 (ebook)
Subjects: LCSH: Eschatology. | Apocalyptic literature—History and criticism. | Prophecies. | End of the world. | Religion and science—United States. | United States—Religion—History.
Classification: LCC BL501 .A94 2016 | DDC 001.9—dc23
LC record available at http://lccn.loc.gov/2015030348

Cover illustrations: from Albert and Shirley Small Special Collections Library, University of Virginia (front); © Bettmann/Corbis (back). Author photograph by John Hubbard.

For Lorraine . . . always.

Contents

Part III: New Age Religion and Science

Part IV: Episode 2, December 21, 2012

Figures

Preface

In the decade leading up to it, there were more than 3,400 books written on the Maya 2012 end of the world episode. I wrote one among a handful—none of them best sellers—arguing that if you really probe what the Maya were telling us, there's no need to worry.[1] A panoply of rival authors proffered that on December 21, 2012, the world would experience either total destruction or the sudden elevation of human consciousness to a higher plane—in either case the end of the world as we know it.

It was only after I pitched my wares at book signings, on the lecture circuit, in interviews, short essays, and op-eds that I realized just how obsessed contemporary American culture has been with apocalyptic thinking in general; for example, in the years since the turn of the millennium, the number of feature films focusing on apocalyptic themes has outnumbered those produced in the preceding four decades. As I explored further it became clear to me that mainstream America's preoccupation with the imminent end of the world goes all the way back to Columbus, who foresaw as part of his mission of discovery nothing less than preparing a distant land across the sea as a place worthy to receive the City of Zion here on Earth—the Second Coming of Jesus.

In *Apocalyptic Anxiety: Religion, Science, and America's Obsession with the End of the World* I trace the sources of this undying popular obsession with precisely predicting and preparing for time's end. Most of what has been written on apocalyptic thinking in America is academic stuff, embedded in disciplines such as the history of religion, US history, and subdisciplinary studies in utopianism, mysticism, esotericism, and the New Age movement. Among the most influential examples I've consulted in my research are Catherine Albanese's *A Republic of Mind and Spirit,* John Hall's *Apocalypse,* Paul Boyer's *When Time Shall Be No More,* Norman Cohn's *Cosmos, Chaos, and the World to Come* and *Pursuit of the Millennium*, and the works of Michael Barkun, *Culture of Conspiracy* among them. Books authored by members of the scientific community focus largely on debunking popular end of the world myths; for example, Michael Schermer's *Why People Believe Weird Things*, William Stiebing's *Ancient Astronauts, Cosmic Collisions*, and many works by James ("The Amazing") Randi.

I found that in many of the religion-based treatments, too little was said about relevant developments in the history of science. I also realized that the much-discussed conflict between conventional science and religion—that is, the difference between belief in acquiring truth by reason versus by revelation—is a major part of the history of mysticism, out of which so many end of the world scenarios are fashioned.

My intention here is to trace the history of contemporary predictions about the 2012 Maya end of the world phenomenon, which I dealt with only briefly in my previous work. I plant my comparative feet in the nineteenth-century Millerite episode in which a pastor on the American frontier claimed the setting of the end of time clock, October 22, 1844, was encoded in biblical Scripture. Though more secular in nature, the Maya 2012 phenomenon is woven out of a thread that connects to the fabric of its predecessor two centuries earlier. Both are motivated by the search for a divine cosmos capable of lifting humanity out of its corrupted existence. 2012 was entirely predictable. I seek not to debunk the seemingly never-ending American stories of the end of the world, only a handful of which I have the space to narrate, but rather to understand them and place them in the context of history.

I found this a particularly difficult book to write because I have biases. Let me confess that, as a scientist, my way of acquiring knowledge is predicated upon reason and the examination of evidence that converges with what we already know about the human condition. History shows that this shared methodology can often err; but even at the risk of bruising the egos of those who might have committed them, errors need to be corrected, a body of knowledge reinterpreted. In the scientific quest for getting at the truth of things, let me go further: we each must be our own, most critical skeptic. We should never cease to look for inconsistencies in or exceptions to truths we feel certain we have arrived at. Finally, we must always be open to new ideas—ideas that can be examined close up and put to the test of evidence. This is my *faith*. Despite my positivistic leanings I have tried extra hard not to use pejorative language, nor to prejudge or disrespect the ideologies of those with whom I disagree.

My pathway to acquiring truth through reason stands in stark contrast to an alternative way of knowing that I continually confronted in creating my narrative, one based on a claimed gift of intuition—a sudden grasp of the revealed truth—often regarded as accessible only to an elect few. This way of comprehending the world, which consistently serves up an entirely different account of human history, has been characterized by some historians as *occult*, or esoteric, a kind of shadow history that deals with clandestine, secret, or hidden knowledge, embedded in a deeper spiritual reality that extends beyond the rational. As I charted it in *Behind the Crystal Ball*, the history of the occult is braided together with what might be called mainstream history, or history established by the convergence of fact.[2] Sometimes the shadowy part of the fabric of history becomes thin and worn, but at other times its weave tightens—it can even become more prominent than the main part of the fabric. In contemporary mainstream America, despite what transpires in the halls of academia, occult history may well take precedence. Surveys demonstrate that more people believe in astrology than not and almost as many think the world began a few thousand rather than several billion years ago. Those who study comparative religion may justifiably view the foregoing as a slight oversimplification. Contemporary questions about the origin of religion are highly contentious within the discipline. For example, Tomoko Masuzawa notes that postmodern scholars have largely abandoned the quest for origins and the interpretations given in the works of nineteenth-century scholars, like Durkheim, who dealt with such questions.[3] Her critical rereading of these sources challenges the very notion of what we mean by historicity and temporality.

If I have learned anything from my research, it is that the two basic ways of knowing—reason versus revelation—are irreconcilable. I believe there can be no dialog, no real meeting ground between these versions of how to get at the truth of things. Though I've made clear in which camp I have chosen to pitch my tent, I am well aware that there is a lot of attractive appeal in the turf that makes up the campground on the other side of the chasm. As one of my students recently told me: "I know you don't believe in aliens coming down to enlighten us, but wouldn't it be cool if it were true?" Books, videos, and websites about lost Atlantis attract a vast audience—much larger than that tuned into what was happening in the world of classical Greece. As historian of the occult Joscelyn Godwin writes in answer to the question of why there are so many books on Atlantis. "It is because of an idea, a dream, a theory that will not let go: that there was a high culture in prehistoric times."[4] Godwin points out that the least interesting books on Atlantis to lay readers are those that make the myth rational—and less human-centered—for example, by attributing it to a relatively recent volcanic eruption that created the island of Santorini sometime around 1500 BCE. More intriguing and attractive are works that reject the scientific time barrier. They are more open to speculation. Why not a pre-prehistory as advanced or even more advanced than classical Athens? Especially if its proponents can marshal evidence, as they claim. Wouldn't *that* be cool?

I find that the same appeal holds for contemporary theorizers about time's end. A deep optimism resides in their hearts—the same optimism the post–New Age 2012ers shared with the Millerites on the eve of the anticipated Advent of 1844. Imagine: here we all are—situated on the very doorstep of kingdom come! There is transpersonal force in the passion exuded by nineteenth-century occultists Helena Blavatsky and William Miller and their later counterparts Daniel Pinchbeck and José Argüelles, all of whom we will meet—a confident, personal connectedness they claim to experience. What a big draw *that* is in a contemporary generation that has come to believe that, after all is said and done, things are really all about *me*.

Acknowledgments

I thank my many colleagues—scientists, historians of art and religion, archaeologists, anthropologists, classicists—for helpful discussions at various stages of this work: Victoria Bricker, Davíd Carrasco, David Freidel, Robert Garland, Joscelyn Godwin, Tim Knowlton, Gil Raz, Scott Sessions, Chris Vecsey, Alexei Vranich, John Watanabe, and especially John Hoopes, whose studies of the history of New Age phenomena have directly influenced my writing.

I am further grateful to the entire staff of the University Press of Colorado for their careful attention to successive stages of this manuscript and for the thought they put into selecting referees in the disciplines I, as an outsider, have converged upon. I thank those readers as well.

Finally, I owe the biggest thank you to Diane Janney, my assistant, who has unfailingly helped me cobble the pieces together, and Lorraine Aveni, my muse, who always reads and responds to my first thoughts.

APOCALYPTIC ANXIETY

INTRODUCTION

December 21, 2012—It Didn't Happen

And the Gospel of the Kingdom shall be preached in all the world for a witness unto all nations; and then shall the end come.

—*Matthew 24:14*

December 21, 2012—game over! The end of the world as we know it—the big blowup! The sun's magnetic field will suddenly reverse, emitting damaging electromagnetic particles that will short-circuit the Earth in a matter of minutes, destroying every piece of electronic equipment and wiping out all the knowledge stored in our computers. Massive solar flares will shoot out of the sun, each capable of generating the energy of a hundred billion nuclear bombs. The Earth's magnetic field will also abruptly reverse. Volcanoes will erupt and earthquakes will increase a hundred-fold as the Earth's crust experiences a sudden shift. Whatever architecture is left standing on the globe will be leveled and the oil released from damaged storage facilities will be carried over every sea and ocean by huge tides, contaminating every watery surface. Demolished nuclear plants will release hazardous materials into the environment and the world will be thrust into a sudden ice age, leaving few places habitable.

One 2012 prophet of doom pictured this alarming scenario: there's a black hole at the center of our Milky Way Galaxy; it protects us (like the ozone layer) by sucking up matter and energy. But when blocked for the first time in 26,000 years, on December 21, 2012 (at 11:11 p.m. Universal Time), our bodies and our world will be thrown out of kilter—just as the ancient Maya had predicted.[1]

Other head-turning 2012 prognostications proclaimed an end to the world caused by sunspots, a planetary lineup, the passage of our planet through an energetically hostile region of our Galaxy, a chain of simultaneous volcanic eruptions, collision with a giant asteroid, and suction of the entire terrestrial globe into a passing black hole. The sun will reach its extreme migratory point from the plane of the Milky Way, producing a tide in the galactic disk that will release millions of comets from outside the solar system to rain down on us. The cometary swarm will destroy the Earth, or what's left of it. Some visionaries of Armageddon blamed it all on God. He's the one pitching those swarms of comets earthward as punishment for the evil deeds of humanity. And that's only the short list.

Regardless of how the 2012 Doomsday clock was set, there were plenty of people—especially young people—deeply concerned about it. Responding to the public embrace of world's end (more than two-thirds of all Americans believe it will happen during their lifetime), the scientific community set up guides for classroom use, such as "Astronomy Answers, 21 Dec 2012" and Astronomical Society of the Pacific astronomer Andrew Fraknoi's "Resources for Responding to Doomsday 2012." Over 5,000 messages, many of them from teens, appeared on NASA's website Ask an Astrobiologist in response to the 2012 phenomenon, among them:

- "Last winter, I got extremely depressed because of my fears of December 21, 2012."
- "Every day would be filled with fear. Every little noise I heard I thought something was happening. I wouldn't watch the news for fear of seeing something bad or scary. I am seventeen years old, and I actually did contemplate suicide because of all the rumors."
- "I'm fifteen, and I'm terrified of all these rumors, and I don't know how to get over it. I keep hearing about the fifth sun and how it affects the North and South Poles."
- "If you could honestly tell me there is no danger, whatsoever to Earth on December 21, 2012, that would make me feel a lot better, because sometimes I think suicide would help."

- "I'm a twelve-year-old boy. The Moon hasn't been rising this past week and the Sun was rising and setting in different places each night. I'm freaked and my parents don't believe me. I can't even focus on my schoolwork. Please tell me the truth about the end."[2]

My initial motivation for writing *The End of Time: The Maya Mystery of 2012* grew out of e-mail correspondence with a concerned Canadian high school student. I dedicated that book to him.

Apocalypse means revelation or the unveiling of an underlying plan or design. It posits that fate rules and that there is unity in the predetermined structure of history. We usually associate apocalypse with worldwide cataclysm, but historians of religion differentiate between the end of the world by total destruction (catastrophic millennialism) and avertive apocalypticism, the belief that we can avoid catastrophe by, for example, conducting religious rites or engaging in practical activity.[3] Both forms of apocalypticism were present in 2012.

In addition to the doomsayers were just as many prophets who foresaw a blissful 2012 outcome. Instead of a planetary holocaust, they sensed a transcendental breakthrough. According to one prediction, resonances between the grand "eschaton time wave," about which the cycle of the lunar year, the sunspot cycle, and the *I Ching* divination system peak, pointed to the winter solstice of 2012 as the time when reality would be transformed instantaneously via the joining together of matter and mind in a higher dimension. But the collective rebirth of planetary consciousness would be experienced only by those who assembled at the acupuncture points of Mother Earth—places like Machu Picchu, Mt. Shasta, Maya Chichén Itzá, and the Egyptian pyramids—where they would be most likely to get beamed by the cosmic vibes. Speaking in scientific-sounding language, one prophet wrote that we shall attain new revelations, for only in that moment will we reconnect with "a major evolutionary upgrading of the light-life radiogenetic-process," a wave harmonic that constitutes an "exquisitely proportioned fractal of the galactic evolutionary process" that will "connect us to the heliotropic octaves in the solar activated magnetic field."[4] The cosmic lineup with the galactic center will open a different sort of entryway—a doorway of opportunity for a "conscious relationship with each other and a creative participation with the Earth process that gives birth to our higher selves."[5] Wrote another: we will reclaim the "grand galactic cosmovision" once experienced in ancient times.[6] We'll recover the long-lost philosophy whose demise has left modern consciousness a prisoner of the "values of self-serving egoism."[7]

Some biblically oriented prophets combined both doom and bliss scenarios. Long ago they foretold that December 21, 2012, would be the beginning of the Great Tribulation. On that day the sixth seal in the book of Revelation will be opened.[8] This will be the day of the Lord's Wrath: when the great earthquake will occur, when the sun will become black and the moon bathed in blood. The aftermath of 2012 will see God's rapture. Only he can save from eternal hell those who repent.

December 21, 2012: blow up, bliss out; planet Earth torn apart, human consciousness transformed; Jesus descended—none of it happened. Nor had it happened on May 21, 2011, the foreordained date of the taking up into heaven of God's elect people, according to an eighty-nine-year-old self-styled evangelical preacher from California. Nor on March 23, 2003, May 15, 2003, January 25, 2006, or any of the more than 100 dates since the beginning of the third millennium pegged by some prophet or another who had set the clock for the end of time. There were ten warnings in 2008 alone; fifteen were broadcast in 2006. Among the latter were the "Big One" targeting Los Angeles, a 650-foot tsunami caused by a wayward asteroid diving into the ocean, striking and wiping out the Atlantic Coast; Israel being erased from the map; a nuclear bomb destroying the United Nations building; a nuclear war—starting either in Iraq or North Korea—and the Second Coming of Jesus in Puerto Rico.

Thanks to the legitimizing effect of the Internet, the commerce-hungry media, and a spiritually starved society cringing in perpetual fear over one calamitous world event after another, predicting time's end has become big business—especially in America. After a breather following Y2K, the frequency of predictions has been on the rise. End of the world novels, computer games, TV programs, and films have become all the rage. The number of apocalyptic-themed feature-length films produced since the turn of the millennium has topped totals over the four decades ending in 2000.[9] Projected totals for 2011–2020 are expected to at least double the count for 2001–2010. The secular framework of these works and the sadistic violence exhibited in most of them have been characterized as a kind of "sanctified Darwinism" based on the "survival of the most weaponized."[10]

Millennialism—strictly speaking, the belief in a transition to salvation in which well-being will replace the unpleasant limitations of the human condition—is not unique to Y2K and Y12.[11] There were ominous end of time forecasts spread about the last century, too: 1914, 1918, 1920, 1925, 1941, 1975, and 1994 were banner years for the Second Coming based on biblical mathematics; for example, according to one account, 1975 was the 6,000th anniversary of the creation of Adam, which happened in 4026 BCE (provided you adopt the definition of a generation given in Psalms 90:10). And we mustn't leave out 1910, when the world was scheduled to be poisoned by noxious gases as our home planet passed through the tail of the returning Halley's Comet.

Among the most noteworthy of the 1970s Doomsdays were the predicted collision of Earth with Comet Kohoutek in 1973 and death by killer bees in 1977. In the 1960s the assassinations of the Kennedys and Martin Luther King Jr. and the Arab-Israeli war of 1967, in which Jerusalem was reclaimed by the state of Israel, prompted a host of dire world-ending predictions.

The Cold War 1950s were rife with UFO sightings. Equally prevalent were predictions of time's end generated by UFO observations. The case of Marian Keech, a Chicago housewife, became the subject of a social psychological study of cognitive dissonance.[12] Basically, we think up explanations that shape reality to fit what we believe. This is how we resolve the problem of living with conflicting ideas—or so goes the theory. Messages received by Keech via automatic writing from inhabitants of the planet Clarion revealed that the world would end in a great flood on December 21, 1954. She and a small band of followers were so convinced of the impending disaster that they quit their jobs and gave away their life savings in order to devote time to prepare for an anticipated terrestrial departure via the flying saucer the Clarionites promised to send down to transport them. The alien saviors never appeared. According to Keech, on the day of their anticipated arrival, Earth redeemers decided to withhold the flood and preserve the world. Marian Keech explained that it was because her group had behaved heroically in trying to get the word out.

Backing up further, the nineteenth century also had its share of endgamers. Adepts from the Hermetic Brotherhood of Luxor calculated that a Great Solar Period, over which each of the seven angels would rule the universe twelve times, was due to end in 1881, or alternatively 1879, 1880, and 1882, depending on whose math you followed.

If you were around in the 1840s you certainly would have been aware of the big end of the world scare sweeping across middle America. The well-publicized Second Coming of Christ, slated for October 22, 1844, according to country preacher William Miller, was part of a long anticipated premillennial event that people had begun talking about as early as the 1830s in the charged religious atmosphere of upstate New York and western New England. Toward the end of the decade, by which time the idea had spread to Boston, New York City, and Philadelphia, and then on to the frontier cities of Cleveland, Cincinnati and even Montreal, "Advent near" preaching had won more than 50,000 solid believers and an estimated 1 million skeptical, but nonetheless watchful, followers—a hefty number in a US population that bordered on 17 million.

I found remarkable parallels between the phenomena of 1844 and 2012; this is why I decided to choose the Millerite movement as a way of exploring past and present attitudes about American versions of apocalypse. In *The End of Time: The Maya Mystery of 2012*, I suggested that the end of the world craze that closed the twelfth year of the new millennium had a peculiarly American ring to it. Likewise, no time was more fevered and no place more inflamed with anticipation about the end of the world than the mid-nineteenth-century American hinterland. Frontier America became a safe haven for diverse religious groups to act out their own versions of the Second Coming writ in the New Testament book of Revelation. Apocalyptic prophesying and the building of utopian communities were an integral part of what religious historians regard as peak in a series of social awakenings that make up American history.

I begin part I, "Episode 1, October 22, 1844," in chapter 1 by telling the story of the Millerite movement in some detail. I show how Pastor William Miller arrived at his prophetic Doomsday clock setting by performing biblical arithmetic, which has a long history of its own. Understanding Millerism necessitates at least a brief encounter with the roots of Western apocalyptic thinking, which I trace back to Middle East antiquity in chapter 2. It began in the fourteenth century BCE, when the prophet Zoroaster outlined the apocalyptic battle fought in heaven between Mazda, god of light, and Ahriman, god of darkness. These dual deities would become the precursors of the forms of good and evil that grew up in early Christianity and took on various aspects throughout the Middle Ages, the Renaissance, and the

Reformation. God's promised end of time and the schedule of dispensations, or events that would lead up to it, was thought to be secreted in the Old and New Testaments, awaiting close readings by those capable of deciphering the message.

Part II, "American Apocalypse," is made up of three chapters. There I provide further background and begin to forge a link to present-day apocalypticism in America. chapter 3, "From Columbus to the Great Awakenings," follows the germination and growth on American soil of the seed heralding the imminent end of the world planted by Columbus and nurtured by the English Puritans. Both imagined the pristine New World as the setting for God's kingdom come.

Chapter 4 deals with how Christian millennialism went mainstream toward the end of the nineteenth century, when it acquired a strong secular component. Historians call it the "New Thought" movement, the predecessor of the "New Age" of the 1960s. In this sort of progressive millennialism you could perfect yourself in preparation for whatever the transcendent powers might have in store for you by using the power of your will—aided by the products of modern science.

In chapter 5 I explore the curious love-hate relationship between science and religion that grew out of the American theosophical or spiritualist movement. Here was a tension quite different from the conventional clash—what I call the irreconcilable dialog—that characterizes contemporary ways of arriving at truth. I focus especially on the influential Helena Blavatsky's esoteric writings, which embraced even as they contorted scientific concepts. She posited a history dispensed via a series of rounds of existence characterized by rest periods punctuated by action episodes in which life's energy is redistributed. For the so-called theosophist, revealed deep truth, whether scientific or religious—or both—lay in the "monomyth," or divine wisdom related to a single, shared past that we are capable of recovering in the present life by studying the myths of the ancients.

The four chapters comprising part III, "New Age Religion and Science," have to do with the concatenation of rational and wishful ideologies and practices that grew out of New Thought and nineteenth-century spiritualism, which developed alongside traditional Christian millennialism. I begin with the anticipation of the astrologically timed "Age of Aquarius" in chapter 6, followed by additional signs in the sky, in the form (following Jung) of what I call the "Techno-Angels of the Alien Advent" (chapter 7). These space age secular replacements for the descending Christ were sent here as part of the divine cosmic plan to help the world avoid the catastrophic mess we've made of our planetary home. Alongside this avertive form of millennialism, Christian dispensationalism continued to thrive, as I relate in chapter 8, where I explore the end of time articulated in the popular media. Chapter 9, on "world age" theories surfacing in the 1960s, breathes new life into the astronomically based version of the monomyth, the notion that cyclic world history is fixed in the stars and dispensed in large temporal doses marked by transitions in the shifting of the world's axis due to the precession of the equinoxes.

This sets the stage for part VI, "Episode 2, December 21, 2012." Having laid down the basis for the New Age version of an astronomically derived apocalypse, in chapter 10 I discuss the most influential early 2012-related prophecies about the end of the world as we know it. These include the nativist writings of Frank Waters in the 1960s, the LSD-induced trance revelations of the McKenna brothers in the 1970s, and José Argüelles's "Harmonic Convergence" of 1987—all focused on seeking spiritual refuge in the lost knowledge of a once unified indigenous American past.

In the 1970s and 1980s the ancient Maya of Central America enter the picture, having attracted popular attention owing to advances in the decipherment of their ancient texts, new knowledge of their exceptional astronomical achievements, increased archaeological excavations of their cities, and the promotion of sacred tourism. Chapter 11 deals specifically with Mayanism, which anthropologist John Hoopes identifies as an eclectic collection of New Age, Western-derived beliefs projected on the Maya civilization. Among the most notable is the theory that the ancient Maya had timed the end of their 5,125-year-long count cycle to end on December 21, 2012, and that they predicted that the world as we know it would then come to an end—either in catastrophe or via the escalation of humanity to a higher level of consciousness.

Chapter 12 closes the Maya 2012 narrative with a summation of the "perennial philosophy," which envelops most monomythical 2012 time's-end predictions. This is the notion that all humanity—Homo religiosus—shares in a longing to return to a more perfect past, a primordial condition superior to the corrupted present-day world and, most important, that this condition can be achieved here and now. Anthropologists and historians of religion contrast this sui generis theory of the origin of religion with the more gradualist-based hypothesis that religion arose out of a need for societies, rather than individuals, to understand who they were, such as to make sense of transcendent forces by developing an ideology that accounted for their condition.

Finally, in the closing, comparative conclusion, I look back at the 1844 Millerite episode, which emerges as a seemingly less complex inquiry into the drama of the end of human existence, drawn largely from biblical text, placed alongside 2012 Mayanism, a largely secular, highly individualistic episode. The media are different and so are the social settings out of which each apocalyptic movement grew, but the fervent need to peer around time's corner is shared over the 168-year span that separates 1844 and 2012.

A 2002 Time/CNN poll revealed that 59 percent of Americans believed the world would soon come to an end—about the same proportion (62 percent) as those who expressed this belief in a 1983 Gallup poll and a 1994 US News and World Report poll (60 percent).[13] The story of where beliefs about the impending end of the world come from is worth tracing through history not only because such a large segment of the contemporary population thinks we are living out our last days, but also because such an exercise helps us understand the sources of the unsated nature of the American appetite for world endings. We need to know: what is it about *us* that fuels our never-ending hunger for time's end?

PART I

Episode 1

October 22, 1844

1

Millerites and the Biblical End of the World

A man with a conviction is a hard man to change. Tell him you disagree and he turns away. Show him facts or figures and he questions your sources. Appeal to logic and he fails to see your point.

—*Psychologist Leon Festinger*

It began in the "Burned-over District," a funnel-shaped conduit of turf between New York's Adirondack and Catskill Mountains that opens into the Great Lakes and connects the Midwest to New England and colonial America's eastern coastal cities. Early in the nineteenth century, during a period of intense religious revivalism known as the Second Great Awakening, religious dissenters, along with adventurers and opportunists, trekked their way out of the established territory of the Northeast toward the open frontier via the newly constructed Erie Canal.[1] The fervor of unorthodox Yankee social and religious practices that swept over the area like fire in a dry cornfield would bestow the char on the territorial label this region would come to acquire. Here Adventism, a belief in the imminent Second Coming of Christ, would become the birth child of Pastor William Miller (figure 1.1).

Miller was born at the end of the American Revolutionary War in 1782. Typical of the New England "Yorkers," his pioneer family, like that of Mormon founder Joseph Smith, had migrated across the wilderness line from settled

FIGURE 1.1. Pastor William Miller, leader of a religious fringe group that would become the Seventh-day Adventist movement, preaches to a popular audience. (© Review & Herald Publishing / GoodSalt.com.)

communities in western New England. By modern standards, you could call the Miller family middle class. William's frugal parents held a mortgage on a small farm in upstate Yates County, New York. The Millers were well read, politically involved, and deeply religious—the mother pious, the father descended from a long line of preachers.

Young William was bookish and he kept a diary. An early entry reads: "I was early educated and taught to pray the lord."[2] He was fifteen at the time. Miller later married, served a stint in the militia, then fought in the War of 1812. Once discharged, he worked his way up in county government, became established financially, and settled into the life of a gentleman farmer. It is worth noting that before he became an interpreter of biblical passages, Miller was a deist, one who believes that, though a supreme being created the world, reason and the observation of nature alone can be used to determine the relationship between people and God. Skeptical of ideas tied to his Baptist upbringing, Miller became immersed in his own study of the Scriptures. He also developed into a devout apostle of apocalyptic eschatology, the belief that God has disclosed, in the Scriptures and other forms of revelation, secret knowledge of a particular kind about the end of the world—the "mysteries of heaven and earth." Young Miller managed to convince himself not only that the word of the Bible was absolutely pure revelation, but also that its prophetic messages pointed to an imminent event of world-shaking proportions. Far from appearing a religious fanatic, Miller was characterized by his contemporaries not so much as an inspired prophet but rather as a humble logician driven to conduct patient research, a man with a resourceful and imaginative mind and a literal-minded soul.[3]

His principal early biographer, the Adventist historian Francis Nichol, traces Miller's first specification of a date for the end of the world as we know it back to 1818, when he recorded in his diary that in about twenty-five years "our present state would be wound up."[4] Four years later Miller wrote out his detailed justification for timing the event as well as the method for arriving at it, though initially he refused to go public.

Precisely what biblical passages pointed to a premillennial Advent circa 1843? Miller displays his number-crunching logic in a famous numerological chart frequently used to illustrate his lectures (figure 1.2). He based his argument on prophecies in the Old Testament book of Daniel and in New Testament Revelation, together with the long-held key assumption that numbers specified in Scripture as *days* are to be interpreted instead as *years*; for example, Numbers 14:34 tells us: "According to the number of the days . . . each day you shall bear your guilt, namely forty years." Miller started with the decree of Artaxerxes, given in the seventh year of his reign, to rebuild Jerusalem, written in Daniel 8:14: "For two thousand and three hundred evenings and mornings; then shall the sanctuary be restored to its rightful state." He took this to mean that 2,300 years after 457 BCE, the date he assigned to the commandment issued to the prophet Daniel by the angel Gabriel, the sanctuary will be cleansed of all sin by the Second Coming of Christ.

What else could the sanctuary be but the church? reasoned Miller. And surely the cleansing must refer to total redemption from sin in the aftermath of Christ's Second Coming. A second passage, also from Daniel (9:24–27), reads: "Seventy weeks are determined upon thy people . . . to make reconciliation for iniquity, and to bring in everlasting righteousness, and to seal up the vision and prophecy, and to anoint the most holy." Miller thought this prophesied that seventy weeks, or 490 days—equal to 490 *years*—were already cut off from the first part of the long period in Daniel 8:14. So the math is simple: 2,300 – 457 = 1843 CE.

Figure 1.2. Pastor Miller used this chart (an enlargement of that shown in the background of figure 1.1) in his lectures to sketch out the biblical mathematics that portended the end of the world, which he predicted would come in 1843—later revised to 1844. (P. G. Damsteegt, *Foundations of the Seventh-day Adventist Message and Mission* [Grand Rapids, MI: Eerdmans, 1977], 310.)

But, notes historian Ruth Alden Doan, Miller didn't stop there.[5] Dedicated to the principle that no portion of Scripture involving number coincidence should be overlooked, he interpreted the number 1,335 (Daniel 12:12) to be the number of days (again, years) between the establishment of papal supremacy (he sets that at 508 CE) and end-time: 508 + 1,335 = 1843 (see the bottom of the chart in figure 1.2). Later Miller reset the first date at 538 CE, added it to the 1,260 days (years) of the woman in the wilderness mentioned in Revelation 12:14, and landed on 1798, the date the papacy fell to Napoleon. In this case the last days made up the 45 years between 1798 and 1843. By subtracting the 70 weeks in Daniel (490 years) from 2,300 years and tacking on the 33-year life of Christ, the pastor again arrived at 1843—another coincidence.

What would happen? How would it end? To address these questions Miller turned to the New Testament's last chapter, the Revelation according to John. Revelation 6:13–17 paints a frightening portent:

> And the stars of heaven fell unto the earth, even as a fig tree casteth her untimely figs, when she is shaken of a mighty wind.
>
> And the heaven departed as a scroll when it is rolled together; and her mountain and island were moved out of their places.
>
> And the kinds of the earth, and the great men, and the rich men, and the chief captains, and the mighty men, and every bondman, and every free man, hid themselves in the dens and in the rocks of the mountains;
>
> And said to the mountains and rocks, Fall on us, and hide us from the face of him that sitteth on the throne, and from the wrath of the Lamb:
>
> For the great day of his wrath is come; and who shall be able to stand?
>
> Armageddon will be the place where God's and Satan's army will confront one another at the end of the world. All sin and sinners will perish and a New Jerusalem will rule for eternity.

Interestingly, some of Miller's detractors foresaw not the physical catastrophic conflagration—the doom of fiery judgment cast upon sinners—but rather the more blissful Advent of a moral regeneration for those who would redeem themselves. Rule by physical force and demonstration of power is surely not God's way, they reasoned. It sounded, as historian Michael Barkun characterizes it, too much like "a sad last resort inadequate for a God capable of triumph through nobler means."[6]

Some viewed the Advent as gradual rather than sudden—the coming of an age of God's mercy. But everyone, theologian and prophet alike, agreed: something *big*—or at least the beginning of it—lay just over the horizon; biblical prophecies, however interpreted, were on the verge of being fulfilled.

If the end was near, then the world would need to know it—and Miller would be the one to tell it. And so in 1831 he made himself over from farmer to preacher, moving from pew to pulpit. Once the harvest was in Miller would mount the dais wherever and whenever he had the opportunity. "There was nothing halfway about Miller. He reminds one a little of the Apostle Paul," Francis Nichol describes him. "He thought and acted intensely. He used in abundance those hand maidens of the fervid—colorful adjectives and superlatives."[7] However, Michael Barkun's less biased, more recent assessment tells us that Miller did not attract followers because of his oratorical skills. He pictures Miller as a rather bland individual who, though sincere in his personal commitment, was a colorless figure "utterly lacking in glamour and magnetism."[8] Barkun attributes Miller's efficacy to his persistence at a time when his message seemed appetizing to those in the communities where he preached.

Miller's sphere of influence quickly began to expand well beyond remote rural towns as he acquired a band of followers from adjacent Massachusetts and even more distant Connecticut. The messenger became as important as the message. In 1835 he wrote to one disciple, the Reverend Truman Hendryx, "I now have four or five ministers to hear me in every place I lecture. I tell you it is making no small stir in these regions."[9] The media fueled his fire: in 1832 a Vermont newspaper spread the word by publishing Miller's lectures. Evidently the preacher himself shared what he interpreted to be his audience's high opinion of his skills as a persuasive speaker. As Miller's diary reports: "As soon as I commenced speaking . . . I felt impressed only with the greatness of the subject, which, by the providence of God, I was enabled to present."[10]

Aggressive promotion by the organization that grew around Miller also had a profound effect on the movement's success. Pamphlets detailing the pastor's sermons published in lots of a thousand or more quickly sold out. His diary informs us that between October 1, 1834, and June 9, 1839, Miller delivered 800 lectures, some with as many as 1,800 in attendance, on the "Advent near" theme. In a span of eight weeks in 1836 he gave a total of 82 lectures, sold $300 worth of pamphlets, and received an undisclosed number of small financial donations. By his own estimate Miller preached more than 600 sermons in 1841 alone.

By the early 1840s Miller had acquired a cadre of fellow preachers who sowed his prophetic seeds all across the northeastern United States and Canada. They journeyed as far east as Bangor, Maine, and west to Oberlin, Ohio. Millerite sermonizing organizations even turned up in England and Australia.

Not only in politics does the person behind the scenes have as much to do with the success of the message as the one who delivers it. Joshua Himes, pastor of the Chardon St. Chapel in Boston, is credited with spreading Miller's word beyond the Burned-over District. Himes was a take-charge promotional genius who knew how to handle the media of his day.[11] He employed camp meetings, a Presbyterian innovation. And he chose sites that were easily accessible by rail, thus urbanizing the effort. Himes set up outposts and staffed them with able and enthusiastic disciples; he founded newspapers and issued books and pamphlets along with periodicals. He raised funds. Religious historian David Arthur, who traces Himes's enthusiastic involvement in a number of contemporary social causes, including the antislavery movement, notes that without him, Miller "might have remained simply another obscure figure predicting the end of the world."[12] It was Joshua Himes who added the *ism* to Miller's name, he who made Miller's ideas a movement. Though without a church, the fledging Millerites organized a commission, conducted meetings, and examined and passed judgment on the knowledge and skills of those who sought lectureships as a means of spreading the word.

As head of the movement, Miller welcomed not only those who would preach his 1843 day of doom doctrine but also those who believed the Advent was near without necessarily specifying an exact time. To keep followers up to date, detailed accounts of the whereabouts and content of meetings were published in *Signs of the Times,* a Boston newspaper dedicated exclusively to Millerite news. The vigorous Himes also expanded the publishing effort from semimonthly to weekly in 1838. The *Midnight Cry,* a publication out of New York City, also flourished. In the first half of 1843 an estimated 600,000 copies of Millerite publications were distributed in that city alone.

Of signs, Matthew (24:29) writes that after the tribulation the sun will go dark and the moon will cease to give light. Stars will fall from the sky.

Religious historian David Rowe has traced the abundant literature said to link signs that an angry God was already beginning to sound the trumpets' apocalyptic blast.[13] Millerites searched out past records of astronomical prophecy, for example, the darkening of the sky on May 19, 1780 (later attributed to smoke from forest fires), spectacular northern lights displays, especially in 1827 (a peak year in the solar magnetic cycle), and the June 16, 1806, total eclipse of the sun, visible throughout New England. Newspapers reported that wonders in the sky were becoming more common as the year of the end of the world loomed near. "Every meteor that flashes in the heavens is imagined to have some portentous meaning and seen to take some extraordinary form," read a commentary in the *Kennebec Journal*.[14] The more the editors searched their files, the greater the number of spectacular phenomena they were able to discover; for example, the Leonid meteor shower, which occurs with unusual intensity every thirty-three years, had put on a spectacular sky show in October 1833, and 1837 witnessed an extraordinary display of the northern lights.

Then in February 1843 a great comet, the most brilliant of the nineteenth century, appeared in the evening sky (figure 1.3). By early March it was visible in broad daylight and sported a luminous tail that stretched nearly halfway across the heavens. Because of their unpredictable nature, comets have long been viewed as negative portents. Julius Caesar's assassination was attended by one such celestial phenomenon. Though the media teemed with descriptions of spectacular signs in the heavens, Miller himself was reluctant to attach apocalyptic connotations to them, only remarking that he patiently looked forward, unmoved, to the glorious appearance of the savior. Such things are not needed to confirm the word of God, he explained.

An extraordinary number of terrestrial disasters coincided with the Second Great Awakening, thus fueling the Millerite movement. There were climatic disturbances in the Northeast, such as the "year without a summer" (1816), when repeated frosts decimated crops; there were flash floods in 1811 and 1826. An outbreak of meningitis in 1810 killed 6,000 people; and cholera, originally carried by European immigrants, reached epidemic proportions in New England and New York in 1832. How to account for so much misery being visited upon a people devoted to their God? As Michael Barkun explains: "Disasters must not only be survived; they also need to be fitted into a picture of the world as an ordered place, where moral purpose

Figure 1.3. The Great Comet of 1843 made a timely appearance—a sign in the heavens foretelling what would soon befall us all. (Albert and Shirley Small Special Collections Library, University of Virginia.)

informs even apparently arbitrary events."[15] The more attention given to the problem of moral order, the greater the reception to alternative ways of framing it, including a tendency to question orthodoxy. Barkun reads this as a

FIGURE 1.4. Another comet fueled thoughts of Armageddon in 1857. (© Bettmann/ CORBIS.)

circular process: believing themselves to be punished for their sins, the deeply devout redoubled their efforts to rejuvenate themselves. In an atmosphere of religious enthusiasm their shared attitude of victimization by disaster led to more religious revivals.

As revivalist fervor built, Millerite tent camp meetings became more widespread, especially in the summers of 1841, 1842, and 1843. Like a traveling circus, the great tent, a 120-foot-wide canvas 50-feet high at the center and with a seating capacity of 4,000, migrated from city to city across upstate New York and on to the Midwest. People from the surrounding countryside flocked to hear up to eight hours of continuous preaching on the promised appearance of Christ. Meanwhile, public camp meetings spread up and down the East Coast. Millerite newssheets put the estimate of attendees at an 1842 tent assemblage in southern New Hampshire at 15,000—an impressive number given the sparse population (280,000) of that state. People from all over New England and Canada gathered there

FIGURE 1.5. Popular cartoons were critical of William Miller's predictions of the end of the world. Comfortably couched in the forerunner of the modern Doomsday shelter, the man in the "salamander safe," named after an animal thought to be able to endure fire, is equipped with, among other items, a ham to eat and a fan to keep cool. (Prints and Photographs Division, Library of Congress, LC-USZ62-23784.)

in groups, clasping hands and surrounding a minister who reaffirmed the group's conviction in the Advent foretold. Over an eight-day period surrounding the Fourth of July, they listened to a series of lectures by the man himself. Many became emotionally charged converts on the spot. As the Doomsday clock ticked down, campground events followed in Newark, Portland, Concord, and Albany.

The most influential media of the day—newspapers, broadsides, and pamphlets—fueled the enthusiasm of both detractors and believers. One cartoon showed Miller ascending to heaven with followers clinging to his

FIGURE 1.6. Caricature of preacher Miller (seated on the roof of the house) being carried off to heaven while stragglers desperately hang on. Those below have missed their chance and are doomed to burn in the fires of hell. (Photography © New York Historical Society.)

heels. Obese individuals are pictured being drawn up into the afterworld on tow chains. One satirically minded editor told of seeing an old dog with a deformed tail in the shape of a "three." That it ran on four legs and looked to be about eighteen years old led to the conclusion that the number of the beast signified "1843."

The scientific community also weighed in. Since the 1830s, British geologist Sir Charles Lyell's textbook *Principles of Geology* had popularized the concept of uniformitarianism, or gradualism. Thus, critics from the vanguard of the scientific establishment argued that the present world had come about as a result of slow geologic change via the action of natural processes that would continue for the foreseeable future. The editorials of those who held the scientific position noted that claims made by the predictors of destruction were physically impossible. Neither could the whole world break out in fire, nor could volcanoes or colliding stones produce spontaneous combustion.

Harsher critics proclaimed Miller a monomaniac and his preachings narrow-minded humbug. City newspapers following the movement explained that Millerism was not affiliated with any organized Protestant denomination but seemed instead to stand as an independent enterprise. Though most conventional sects did sense the revivalist fervor, church leaders forbade the Advent-near doctrine acquired from camp forays indulged in by their worshippers, who might bring the message back to the church.

Far from the crazed eagerness increasingly attributed to them, however, most Millerites remained controlled and sober in their demeanor, bound by an awareness of the "nine dangers" Miller had warned about: avoid a censorious spirit toward nonbelievers, eschew extravagant notions and everything that might tend to fanaticism, do not test others' experience by your own, for all men's experiences differ, and so on.[16]

When 1843 turned to 1844 and time's journey went on uninterrupted, Millerite enthusiasm began to wane as criticism waxed. Wrote one scoffer: "What!—not gone up yet?—We thought you'd gone up! Aren't you going up soon?—Wife didn't go up and leave you behind to burn, did she?"[17]

Miller retorted that maybe God was delaying his plan to test his adherents' faith, or possibly there had been a small chronological error in interpretation of the ancient Jewish calendar to which the Old Testament adheres. Pastor and disciples pored over the data, calculating and recalculating. One of them, the Reverend Samuel Snow, found the problem: the decree of Artaxerxes was issued not at the beginning but rather late in the year 457 BCE. Revised expectations focused on a single fixed date: the tenth day of the seventh month of the Karaite Jewish sacred calendar (the so-called seventh month movement), which worked out to October 22, 1844.

As the revised Advent appointment approached, tent revivals and camp meetings became reinvigorated with increased numbers of attendees. Eager anticipation returned: "Many are leaving all, to go out to warn the brethren of the world," read one news item.[18] Farmers abandoned their crops in the fields. Many hadn't even bothered to plow the land. Merchandise stores held clearance sales. Customers rushed to settle their debts. "This shop is closed in honor of the king of kings, who will appear about the 20th of October.

Get ready to crown Him Lord of All," read a sign in a Philadelphia store window.[19] A man named Henry Bear wrote: "I got rid of all my money except eighty dollars; this I laid on the table . . . we now left, as we believed, never to return to that house; and went to one of the Advent believer's about three miles distant, where all the Millerites had agreed to meet and await the coming of the Lord within twenty-four hours."[20]

Wild stories appeared in the press on the eve of the scheduled day of the descent of Christ and his angels. One family was said to have crouched in laundry baskets awaiting the heavenly pick up. Another story told of a woman who packed her entire wardrobe in a trunk and strapped herself to it. In Boston, New York, and Philadelphia, ardent followers dressed in white ascension robes were reported to be streaming out into the countryside for their rendezvous with the denizens of the firmament. One robe-clad woman was said to have calmly jumped out her third-story apartment window, intending to fly to heaven. A man donned a pair of turkey wings to the same end. Many of these stories were later discredited, the product of proactive media eager to peddle newssheets.[21]

Exaggerated reports notwithstanding, on the eve of the awaited event anxious Millerites gathered in public meeting places and in private homes to pray. Preachers and followers alike remained sincere in their convictions, recounted one reporter in attendance. They were filled with hope, elated at the prospect of gazing upon the face of the One to whom they had prayed all their lives. But as the new day dawned, high expectations plummeted to the depths of what would come to be known as the Great Disappointment. The pathway to disconfirmation exacted a heavy emotional toll: "Our fondest hopes and expectations were blasted, and such a spirit of weeping came over us as I had never experienced before . . . We wept and wept till the day dawned."[22]

For many, the Advent experience represented the culmination of a Christian life misled. What would belief in Jesus as savior now be worth? Why had the Bible failed us? Was there indeed no God? As a social movement Millerism seemed dead in the water—but it wasn't.

Maybe there were reasons to explain why nothing had happened? Perhaps the sanctuary referred to in Daniel was in heaven and not on Earth? Could it be that's where the Second Coming took place, instead of here below? Or perhaps the Lord would provide only light on the Advent day, rather than appearing physically? Others channeled their passion toward an already revealed outcome they believe they had experienced: "Heaven was open to my view," wrote one farmer who stood in his field as the rising sun heralded a new day. "The Lord was answering our morning prayer by giving light with regard to our disappointment."[23]

Two months of seclusion followed before Miller emerged to address his followers. When he did, he seemed surprisingly unperturbed. There might be an error of a few years in the computation of the 2,300-year part of the prophecy, he said, but: "We must patiently wait the time in dispute, before we can honestly confess we are wrong in time."[24] And even if Providence overruled the ultimate act, he went on, look at all the good that has come of our efforts. "Many thousands . . . have been made to study the Scriptures by the preaching of the time," and so the faith has been spread.[25]

I opened this chapter with an epigraph drawn from a famous case study of cognitive dissonance—the social movement initiated by Marian Keech referred to in the introduction. In the face of the disconfirmation of her prediction, which had been informed by automatic writing from extraterrestrials, that the world would end on the winter solstice of 1954, Keech became even more convinced of the truth of her beliefs. Her passion about convincing others that the event she predicted would happen because of the action she and her followers undertook was redoubled. A team of social psychologists led by Leon Festinger that documented and analyzed the case concluded that a number of factors contributed to Keech's insistence, among them the acquisition of strong support from a group of believers. In addition, her conviction was deeply held; she had taken action that was difficult to undo; and, most important of all, the timing of the event was specific and directly concerned with precisely what would take place in the real world. These are the same sort of conditions and outcome, Festinger et al. argue, that we find in the Millerite movement.[26]

Cognitive dissonance arises when opinions or beliefs do not fit together, such as if they are inconsistent. Take a cigarette smoker who believes smoking is bad for his health. His opinion is dissonant with the knowledge that is consonant with his continuing to smoke; for example, smoking relaxes him. Now, the smoker can ease the tension that comes with cognitive dissonance by seeking new information that will increase the existing consonance (smoking is cool: it gives me higher status among those with whom

I associate—remember this *was* the 1950s); or he can disregard or diminish the importance of the cognitions that increase dissonance: my parents lived into their nineties so why should I worry?—I've got good genes.[27] Applied to the most devout Millerites, the shared belief that Christ's appearance was imminent was bolstered by the support of fellowship in the social movement and the many activities the group conducted that were consonant with the prediction of the Advent. Notwithstanding, the nonoccurrence of the event intervened as a sudden, sharp discordant chord, not only with the ideology but also with the social action that attended it.

So how did the Millerites eliminate dissonance short of quitting the movement? They could shed the belief that the truth of their faith *was* disconfirmed. This is precisely what happened as repeated attempts were made to revise the predicted date. It happened at least three times. Recall that Miller's first prediction, arrived at in 1818, indicated that things would be "wound up" in about twenty-five years.[28] On New Year's Day in 1843 he revised his prediction (by making a shift from solstice to equinox in his calculations): "And I am fully convinced that sometime between March 21, 1843, and March 21, 1844, Christ will come and bring all his Saints with Him, and that then He will reward every man as his work shall be."[29] Then followed the October 22, 1844, prediction.[30]

Some preferred to live with the pain of the Great Disappointment by refusing to admit they were incorrect about the Lord's intent to return from heaven simply by extending the date indefinitely. The most devout Adventists, incapable of accepting any alternative, stubbornly clung to their faith. Eventually some were reclaimed by their churches; others picked up the pieces of the Millerite movement and began to organize it into an enterprise that refocused on where their reckonings had once again erred. They would come to be known as the readers of precise reckonings in biblical text, the Second Advent Believers. What of Miller himself? He quickly lost his eminence, though up to his death four years later he firmly held to the belief that the Second Coming could not be far off. Shortly before his death, he wrote, almost in seeming desperation, that "anything which will prove Christ near, and the nearer the better [would satisfy me]."[31]

In the decade following 1844, revised end of the world target dates based on new interpretations of the 2.300-day prophecy, among them the autumn of 1853 and the spring of 1854, were forecast by persistent followers of Millerism.

Various prophets who descended from the movement would later place time's end at 1866, 1914, 1987, and 2015, the last coinciding with a string of four eclipses on key Christian holy days—more signs in the sky. Eventually the doctrine of the Advent Christian Church would declare that "biblical prophecy indicates the approximate time of Christ's return" and "believers should proclaim that redemption will come soon."[32]

Some disappointed Millerites, who had experienced a wonderful communal experience in belonging to the movement, sought to build on rather than abandon what they had achieved. One key to their transformation to a less volatile form of apocalypticism lay in what historian Jonathan Butler calls an "elongation of the eschatological timetable."[33] They achieved this by establishing a doctrine based on the revised belief that Miller had misinterpreted the *event* rather than the date—which actually signified not that Christ was to come to Earth but rather that he had moved to the most holy place in the heavenly sanctuary. Accordingly, 1844 was not the end of the world. It was the time of "the investigation of the sins of God's people *in preparation for the end of the world*" (my italics).[34] The new Adventists rationalized the delay and set up a mechanism for stability by advocating that more time was needed for moral introspection and improvement. Equally important, throughout the 1850s the new church opened itself to non-Millerites and other evangelicals. They developed a missionary outreach program to save souls and established new rules for observing the seventh-day Sabbath and a system for ordaining clergy. The 1850s saw membership increase tenfold. By 1863 the Adventist church claimed 3,500 members.

If Adventism is thought of as a stage of life, remarks Butler, "Millerism provided a creative, if quixotic, adolescence that a more mature, stable sect outgrew but still recalled with nostalgia."[35] As long as it retained some aspect of the spirit of boundlessness it had acquired as a child, the movement would survive.

Today, the Seventh-day Adventist Church, a modern outgrowth of the Millerite movement, claims 16 million members around the world. As psychologists Festinger et al. concluded, the greater the number of people who are persuaded that a system of belief is correct, the more likely it is they will come to believe that the belief is, indeed, correct. In an interesting study of responses to prophecy failure, historian Gordon Melton argues that acceptance of failure just isn't an option, and that the most common way millennial proponents deal with disconfirmation involves cultural spiritualization (a reinterpretation of the event as an invisible, spiritual occurrence rather than a happening in the real world) and social reaffirmation (an inward-directed attempt to reestablish group solidarity in the face of dissonance).[36] So, what outsiders call prophecy failure insiders see as success—once the prophecy is reinterpreted.[37]

Apocalyptic social movements tend to thrive in hard times. What conditions obtained in America in the 1830s when Millerism became popular? Added to the natural disasters mentioned earlier, there were social and political instabilities of national and international significance. Even though two decades of peace and relative prosperity had followed the War of 1812, historians still characterize mid-nineteenth-century America as a time of pessimism pervaded by deep desire for social change. Newspapers stoked the fires of a financial reform movement by relating stories of excessive poverty among the masses, as monopolies added to their already considerable wealth. Abolitionism reached violent proportions in the 1830s. The first temperance reform organization was formed in Haverhill, Massachusetts, in 1828. Other moral refashionings of the day encompassed education, diet, and dress codes. Parsimonious habits of the way we dress and furnish our homes can save more than $35 million a year, which could be devoted to benevolent causes, preached one social reformer.

Mid-nineteenth-century America was also a hotbed of polarized viewpoints. Sylvester Graham, inventor of the famous health cracker, railed against sexual promiscuity as part of his widespread campaign to change American lifestyles and stamp out every form of evil. Wherever Graham preached on his vegetarian whole grain diet, butchers and bakers held hostile demonstrations, attempting to block his passage into the lecture hall. At one such event in 1837 organizers resorted to dumping powdered lime on protestors from a second-story window above the speaker's venue.

The condition of the US economy fanned sparks of the activist mentality. The years 1837–1842 saw widespread unemployment. The Panic of 1837, a financial crisis that produced five years of runaway inflation, was fueled by land speculation during the economic boom that had preceded it. Completion of the Erie Canal in 1825 had opened up the vast natural resources of the West. Even in the newly built cities, public land could be purchased for as little as $1.25 an acre. Real estate values soared by a factor of twenty between

1831 and 1837. Commerce and trade grew, as tonnage carried by steamboats on the rivers of mid-America quadrupled during that same period. The country felt prosperous and few state banks were reluctant to extend credit, even as prices of both land and goods escalated, while wages remained fixed. All of the so-called wealth had been paid for in bank paper. As a way of curbing wild speculation, President Andrew Jackson ordered land offices to accept payment in gold and silver only. But the state banks lacked adequate backup and a deflationary backlash ensued. Bankruptcies and commercial failures followed, accompanied by protests against the monopolists and extortionists accused of perpetrating it all. One protest conducted at city hall in New York City in February 1837 marshaled several thousand people. Between 1837 and 1842 nearly half the banks in the United States failed. Tough times—and tough times call for moral reconstitution.

Like other communal groups dissenting from orthodoxy, the Millerites were particularly sensitive to aberrations in the economic status quo. Michael Barkun notes that their value structure was built around security and equality; there was to be no poverty.[38] Nor was there a place for boom-and-bust in their way of coping with the world—only alarm. Though Millerite writings have little to say directly about the national malaise, they do address its local effects, among them rural poverty—no money, too little grain, barely enough bread on the table—sure signs that we are entering our last days.

News of imminent war abroad also colored Millerite apocalyptic predictions. In 1840 England and its Russian, Austrian, and Prussian allies were about to intervene, on the Ottoman side, in a conflict between Turkey and Egypt that threatened to drag the United States into an all-out war. Pondering the numbers in Revelation, Adventist preacher Josiah Litch set the beginning of the apocalyptic war at August 11, 1840, with rebellious Egypt's victory. Michael Barkun traces a number of related alarming messages appearing in *Signs of the Times:* "a change has again spread a cloud over the world's civil and political horizon, which, at each recurrence has become more dark and foreboding" and "What a prospect! Nothing short of one universal blaze of war all over the world can be anticipated."[39] As Barkun notes, once the date passed, peace having been restored, the publication continued to rationalize by arguing that this had been only a warning and crisis still loomed.

Historians regard the mid-nineteenth-century revival in religion that lay at the foundation of moral reform as part of a combination of attitudes and activities that fostered the idea of social experimentation. Some escapists from social norms ventured into communal living, which advocated the sharing of labor and its fruits, all under a single multifamily roof. One of the earliest such ventures was Brook Farm, developed in the environs of Boston in 1831. It was endorsed by Ralph Waldo Emerson and headed by notables such as journalist Charles Dana and Bronson Alcott, father of author Louisa May. But to many traditional Christians, including Pastor William Miller, social activism was both dangerous and self-serving. If people had more Bibles, he once said, "they would tell more truth and learn more than dependence on God."[40] Millerism was "the summation of all the reforms of the age," the Millerites' great expectations an escape mechanism, a reactionary movement against positive human action aimed at solving society's problems.[41]

Active participation via mass meetings of the kind Miller would convene under the great tent suited the climate of the times; for example, a very active political campaign had preceded the presidential election of 1840, in which incumbent Martin Van Buren sought a second term. William Henry Harrison, a military general, and his running mate, John Tyler, who would assume the presidency following the untimely death of the victor, stood in opposition. Both sides organized mass meetings, soul-stirring parades, and displays. Fiery oratory accompanied by patriotic music drew tens of thousands. Opined one skeptical newspaper account of a New York assembly proceeding: "Its enchanting power . . . and scenic effect is far better than its moral effect."[42]

Disillusionment with the efficacy of reform, combined with a new generation of religious enthusiasm, greatly aided the ascent of Millerism in the early 1840s. That it based its ideology on the same Bible shared by all organized Protestant religions, which dominated the country at the time, strengthened its origins in deep tradition. Only their extreme literal-mindedness and excess imagination differentiated the Millerites from the established Protestant sects.

Writing a century later, in the 1940s, Francis Nichol noted that by 1914 most intellectuals had subscribed to the notion that the world is undergoing gradual progress, either by the slow upward surge of evolution or via the mysterious workings of the divine—a far cry from the widely preached fatalistic doctrine of half a century earlier, when the only solution to the world's ills had been sought in the imminent reappearance of Jesus on Earth. Only then could the wicked be done away with and the righteous redeemed. On the times of the Millerite social movement, Nichol concludes: "The idea of a sudden and supernatural end to our present world is neither incredible nor irrational, and it is eminently scriptural."[43] Nichol's biography is admittedly that of an apologist. Modern historians Jonathan Butler and Ronald Numbers have pointed out that other earlier historians, like Whitney Cross, tended to canonize their subjects.[44]

Only following the 1970s, when a revival of interest in American millenarianism took place, did professional historians begin to reexamine the role of Millerism, which is regarded now less as a fringe phenomenon and more as a development that belongs in the mainstream of the history of religious reform movements. In their volume of collected essays on Millerism, which began with a 1984 conference, Butler and Numbers offer a concise summary of the literature leading up to that meeting.[45]

In this chapter I recounted the Millerite episode in some detail because I will argue later that it resonates strongly with recent end of the world narratives, also framed in a time when so much public interest seems to be invested in apocalyptic ideology. But before we move forward too swiftly into the present, we need to back up further in history than mid-nineteenth-century America to trace, if only briefly, the wellspring of what turns out to be an unbroken stream of consciousness that led to the sort of apocalyptic theorizing that poured out onto American soil in the aftermath of European contact. The source of that stream, which has ebbed and flowed for at least three millennia, takes us back to stories of creation once told in the ancient Middle East.

2
A Brief History of Apocalyptic Thinking in the West

Apocalyptic fervor, whether engaged in by Christians or Muslims, allows no neutral ground between God's kingdom and the lake of fire, and no room for compromise, much less for human—or humane interaction.

—*Historian Elaine Pagels*

Food and sex—life's raw necessities. Homo sapiens depends on the proliferation of other species because they lie at the root of our ability to sustain ourselves. They guarantee our success. This is why our ancestors tracked the buffalo and followed the migration patterns of herds of caribou. They learned by careful observation when the blossoming and ripening of edible plants took place. They structured what they observed to create the first calendars, which they pecked on stone or carved on bone in the form of tally marks. The more closely they watched the world around them the more they began to realize that the power of fertility waxes and wanes: abundance turns to scarcity as heat changes to cold, rain to drought; vegetation withers and dies only to be born anew. Our human ancestors learned that the cycle of life, death, and rebirth of all things operates by extremes, each entity with its own turning point—all in harmony with a symphony whose notes are made up of nature's visible cues: when the thistles sprout, the birds come back, the leaves change color and frost appears, each in its *time due*, or "season," as the English, after the Greeks, would later come to call it. The more precisely people became acquainted with environmental time signals, the greater the adaptive advantage they would come to possess over their rivals.

Our will to live and to extend our kind transformed the fundamental things in life into objects of veneration. Our forebears began to punctuate the seasons with formal rituals, or religious ceremonies, each assigned its appropriate time in the cycle—times when they could anticipate and celebrate each of nature's gifts they believed were imminent. Why did our Paleolithic ancestors draw figures of bison on the walls of the caves they inhabited? Did they don the mask of the animal to impersonate its essence—its spirit? Anticipating the hunt, did they ceremonially "kill" the animal, believing a rehearsal would bring about the act itself? Might they have conceived of ritual performance as a way of harnessing and controlling the power of nature?

If religion is a product of cultural development, when did it begin? To judge from the material record—the paintings and carved figurines, the extraordinary care taken in the disposal of the dead—it seems clear that people were concerned with the extension of human identity into the afterlife at least as early as Paleolithic times. Once our ancient ancestors became sedentary, the seasonal rituals got more precisely fixed in the yearly cycle—rainmaking and irrigation ceremonies, plowing, sowing, and reaping festivals, and rites associated with fasting, purifying, purging, and expelling disease. As I have argued elsewhere, these sacred occasions were the forerunners of our seasonal holidays, such as Thanksgiving, Christmas, May Day, Groundhog Day, and Halloween.[1] We can think of them as stress points in the temporal framework of the seasons, moments of intense spiritual experience tied to specific times in a cycle of events in which celebrants came to believe they *must* participate in order to make things happen. As small villages grew into large cities, the modest hearths around which people gathered to pay their debt to the sustaining powers of fertility became temples. There resided the priests—a special class of people who focused on the precise timing and increasingly complex observances of the holy days; they were the ones who saw to it that all segments of diverse, growing urban populations could engage.

In 1912 one of the founders of social science, Émile Durkheim, put these ideas together in an influential book entitled *The Elementary Forms of the Religious Life*.[2] In it he argued that religion rose out of a need for people to experience who they were—not as individuals but as part of a group. Being alive takes on greater meaning if it goes beyond oneself. To make sense of that essence greater than themselves, people developed diverse ideologies, or ways of assigning meaning to transcendent forces.

This is one theory of how organized religion came to be. Durkheim's idea of cultural change follows in the footsteps of Lyell's theory of gradual processual change in establishing the Earth's geologic history. It is the theory most widely accepted today by cultural anthropologists. But there is another theory—a competing one—popularly known as the sui generis theory. It posits that religion has no historical connections. It emerged not out of *collective* but rather *personal* experience, and especially from an inherent need in ancient people to become free of the recollection of sin. According to the sui generis theory, mythic, or cosmic, time is a transcendent reality; it existed in its purest form and was best understood by our ancient ancestors, who lived closer to nature. You could say that those who resided in the past were way ahead of us. According to historian of religion Mircea Eliade, we suffer from an inability to escape from the "terror of history," a false history made up of the materialism and rationality that has accompanied modernity.[3] Modern culture has simply lost touch with the reality of our ancestors.

If religious myths and rituals are not culturally or historically created, but rather are reflections of a higher universal reality shared by all of humanity, might our species then be more appropriately named Homo religiosus; that is, are we not all religious by nature? Do we all exhibit a latent, shared spirituality that compels us to return to our origins? Is there a "collective consciousness," a deeper layer of universal comprehension that envelops all psychic structures in humanity throughout the ages? The sui generis theory answers yes to all.

As we will learn, the battle waged between the processual and monomythical theories about the origin and nature of religion plays a key role in contemporary ideas about how and when the world will come to an end. The latter—the eternal return theory—of the origin of religion has had a profound effect in promoting the popular belief that there once was a world of greater value in the past, a world with a pristine history far grander than that taught us in most textbooks—a world we can access directly. The sui generis theory has emerged as a driving force in many of the New Age millennial beliefs that continue to command our attention. This was the essence of our beginning, declare its proponents. We *must* rediscover it and learn from it, for it is the key to understanding how it all will end. In my own view there is no meeting point, no room for agreement in the debate about the origin of religion and what constitutes history.

Apocalypse—the word comes from the Greek *apocalypsis* and it means *uncovering*. The Christian meaning of apocalypse was largely conveyed to modern culture via the last chapter of the New Testament, the book of Revelation. In its narrative the uncovering of the truth about human destiny along the road of time is brought to the world by a transcendent being who promises to save those who believe in him by transporting them to a higher form of existence in the world to come after the present one is destroyed. This form of apocalypse is deeply rooted in an ancient pan–Middle Eastern worldview wherein various accounts of history tell of a highly polarized division between the inherently chaotic evil world we live in and the pristine forces of transcendent good. Together they occupy a battlefield on which a cosmic war is waged—a war destined to end in a final battle, with the forces of good triumphing.

Historian of religion Jamel Velji succinctly outlines a common time scale in stories of the apocalypse.[4] The elect, those with special access to the transcendent, variously termed prophets or gurus of apocalypse, know that the end of the world is upon us. There is a sense of urgency in the community of believers that binds members of the group together, exalts them, isolates them, and makes them impervious to outside influence. It places them uniquely at the focal point of history's most important event—an event long promised that has finally arrived at their doorstep. Signs of the times, either on Earth—in the form of floods, earthquakes, and volcanic eruptions—or in heaven—via apparitions of comets, eclipses, and planetary conjunctions—mark the course of human degeneration. These are the temporal mileposts en route to the final battle. To understand the way these attributes of apocalyptic narrative work and how they were handed down to us, we need to trace the story through texts and other remains bequeathed us by the old storytellers.

The threat to an ordered existence lies at the root of all cosmologies. What society has not experienced some form of nature's perilous power? Hurricane, flood, tsunami, earthquake, fire, pestilence—all are forces capable of disrupting the fragile equilibrium of the world we live in. The ancient Egyptians called that delicate state of balance *ma'at*, an all-embracing principle that covered every aspect of existence. The gods established ma'at in the form of nourishment to Ra, the sun god, when they first caused him to rise over the primordial desert hills. Ever since, Ra's daily reappearance has mirrored that first occasion, offering a guarantee that he would always retain the power to sustain humanity. Pharaoh, his divine representative on Earth, would prescribe the manner in which society could repay the debt incurred for the nurturing of humanity by making offerings to Ra and the other deities who embodied ma'at. This notion is part of what historians of religion call the "redemptive process." With redemption come certain assumptions about the nature of transcendent power and the moral rules of behavior taken on faith—a kind of faith that guarantees believers that they understand the truth of things.

Warding off danger, be it flood, famine, or foreign intrusion, and restoring order in the face of it required a collaboration between people and their gods. When Egyptian citizens entered the temple to offer sacrifice to the gods, they were, in effect, reenacting that first sunrise. Their victories in battle were a reaffirmation of ma'at; and when the seed they planted in the rich soil of the Nile valley sprouted, they were witnessing the rebirth of life. As one Egyptian inscription puts it, "The span of earthly things is as a dream, but a fair welcome is given him who has reached the west [where] all our kinfolk rest within it since the earliest day of time."[5] Only in the west, the land of the dead, would pristine order be realized for all eternity. Only those who have never killed, robbed, or exploited others, only those who have dutifully made their offerings to the gods, only those who have lived a life of ma'at, are capable of achieving a blissful afterlife.

As in many water-bound cultures, flood constituted the major destructive power in the Tigris-Euphrates river valleys of ancient Mesopotamia. Every winter heavy rains disrupted the orderly flow of the twin rivers, which transcended their banks and inundated the fields. In the spring that followed, strong winds dried out the land and made it fertile again, so that planting could commence. Legend held that the Babylonian god Marduk, personification of both wind and storm, had descended from an earlier generation of gods of both salt and fresh water. For eons the gods had lived in constant conflict until this brave, young warrior-deity managed to consolidate the forces of nature. He invented irrigation and he separated the waters above from those below. The Babylonian creation myth known as Enuma Elish tells how Marduk used brute strength to defeat his principal foe, Tiamat, goddess of saltwater.

He split her open like a (mussel) into two (parts);
Half of her he set in place and formed the sky (therewith) as a roof.
He fixed the crossbar (and) posted guards;
He commanded them not to let her waters escape.[6]

The annual New Year *akitu* festival celebrated Marduk's victory in battle over Tiamat. In that ceremony the people were reminded that even though Marduk had restored order to the world, the essence of Tiamat as a disruptive force capable of plunging the world into sudden famine would be ever present. To sustain order, worshippers must never cease to come to the temple of Esagila with offerings as debt payment. There they would listen to a priest's recitation in front of the seven tablets on which the Enuma Elish was inscribed. Only human action could assure that the crop cycle would be renewed for another year.

Great mythological works found in other cultures of the world also tell of apocalyptic endings, and a brief diversion into some of them is worthwhile for the sake of comparison. The Inca of South America evolved a creation myth that consisted of four ages. We find it described in the Spanish chronicler Juan de Betanzos's opening to the final chapter of the creation story:

1. In ancient times they say the earth and the province of Peru were in darkness, and that there was neither light nor day upon it. 2. And that in those times this earth was entirely night, they say that Con Titi Viracocha came forth from a lake. 3. That he went to Tiaguanaco . . . He made the sun and the moon, and that he sent the sun to go along the course which it follows; and then they say that he made the stars and the moon. 4. Previously, he had already created another people at that time when he made heaven and earth. This people had done a certain disservice to him, and in punishment for this annoyance which they did, he ordained that they be turned into stone on the spot. 5. In Tiaguanaco he made a certain number of peoples from stone and a chief who governed and ruled them and many pregnant women and others who had lately given birth; and that the children have their cradles, as is the custom; all this made of stone. 6. He ordained that they disperse, except for two who stayed with him, and whom he instructed. 7. "These will be called such and such and will come forth from such and such a province and will live in it and there they will grow in number and these others will come forth from such and such a cave and will call themselves such and such, and will

> inhabit such and such a place, and just as I keep them here painted and made of stone, so much they come forth from the springs and rivers and caves and mountains, in the provinces which I thus tell you and which I name to you and you will go straightway to this place (pointing toward where the sun rises) separating them, each one unto itself, and making known to them the law they must observe (literally: 'showing them the direction they must take . . .')."[7]

The place was Cuzco, destined to become the Inca capital.

Some Spanish chroniclers tell of earlier creation-destructions from the high Andes that sound vaguely similar to an Aztec creation story, at least similar enough for some scholars to question whether the basic narrative might have been imported from their distant neighbors to the north. In both versions, between each cyclical orderly epoch chaos and destruction reigned. In the Inca story one age ended when people were turned to stone; another race was destroyed by earthquakes, still another by fire. Finally the storm god, Viracocha, rose to the occasion. He created a race of men who emerged from caves. The Inca would become their rightful heirs. Imitating the raging storm, they would be destined to conquer the world by warfare.

Both the Aztec and Inca creation stories emphasize a better world to come. In both, earlier fabrications of the world left something to be desired. The present world may be better, but it is not without flaws. We, the chosen ones, are its stewards and we have been mandated to maintain it; but the price to pay for failing to do so shall be enormous. This situation really is not so different from what religions in the Western Judeo-Christian tradition offer.

While the myths of Native America may be tainted by their European conquerors, those that come to us from Asia were more likely invented independently. In many instances they exhibit apocalyptic overtones. For example, to explain the interlocking rhythms they believed made up their world, ancient Chinese philosophers originated the concept of Tao (or Dao), meaning "Way." Everything has its own Tao, or cycle of birth, growth, death, and rebirth. All of these cycles build upon one another to form larger cycles, or world ages—23,639,040 years, according to one reckoning—when all of the elements that made up the smaller cycles become resynchronized.

The Lingbao texts from the early centuries CE of Taoist China contain an abundance of prophecies from the Celestial Masters pertaining to cyclic world renewal. The end of the present cycle is variously marked by fire, flood, or pestilence. To help ward off such disasters, people are given certain prescriptions. Some texts tell of supernatural beings, messianic figures who intervene on behalf of humanity and secure its salvation.

Historian of religion Gil Raz describes the period of the development of Taoism as one of political chaos and social turmoil, with epidemics and natural disasters perceived as signs of disordered harmonies in cosmic cycles.[8] Once again, humans were exhorted to play an active role in shaping their cosmology; those who convert to the correct moral/ethical path and who conduct the proper rituals hold the potential to restore universal harmony—they are the ones who will be saved. So wrote the teachers of Tao.

Some Taoist prescriptions for ritual action were precisely timed and quite detailed, for example: "On the fifth *yin* day of the vernal equinox, pick orchids and, in the center [of the ritual arena] make an infusion [with the flowers]. Wash [yourself with this]. On the fifth *mao* day take the brewed chrysanthemum and boil it to a broth, at the place of *yin* and *mao*. On the next day pick the *zhangju* stalks. Just as you are about to pick them, purify the [ground at their] side. Of small mats make fourteen seats for them. Light incense, and worship each with wine and dried meat. Bow repeatedly and say the incantation."[9] Another reads: "Whenever the cycles of heaven and earth come to an end, you should practice retreats, presenting incense and this scripture."[10]

Recently reinvented, post–New Age American Taoism promotes the power of the individual as a way to achieve enlightenment in the form of the body-self. Macrobiotics is one of its most popular outcomes. The macrobiotic Zen diet is said to offer one way to join the yin and yang in a single unifying principle by balancing two basic energies: the cool, expansive, moist, upward-going and the warm, contractive, drying, downward-going. If the mind resides within the body, then the body must be nourished by ingestion of the proper yin versus yang foods. Yin foods include apples, bananas, broccoli, mushrooms, fish, honey, beer, and peppermint tea, while the yang list is comprised of beef, butter, chicken liver and fat, leeks, onions, turkey, whiskey, and wine, all of which should be locally, organically grown, and pesticide free.

Indian Buddhism, which rose to prominence during the medieval era, drew on Taoist millenarian beliefs.[11] Time and history were cyclical and the universe alternated between "manifestation" and "nothingness," each subdivided into *kalpas* (phases) and subphases. One text tells us that at the beginning of every manifestation, people are well fed; they live long lives (up to 80,000 years), and world peace prevails. Then the pendulum swings in the other direction and life spans shrink to a mere ten years. Even these brief lives are plagued by disasters and end in warfare.[12] Then comes nothingness, followed by a rebeginning in the next cycle.

Of all the world religions that feature Armageddon, the one given most attention by contemporary American popular culture belongs to radical Islam. Islamic religion is a close cousin of Christianity with a different time scale for Armageddon. In the Sunni version, the Mahdi is the successor of Muhammad, the Prophet. He, like Jesus, is destined to arrive in the world at some unspecified future date to set things right. According to the Mujaddid tradition, a branch of the Shi'ite Muslim faith, the Mahdi is a divinely inspired individual, the so-called good one, who will appear in different guise every century to usher in a new age.[13] At the beginning of each century that follows the period of the Prophet, one or more individuals rise to make the claim of Mahdi, which may be endorsed or rejected by different Muslim communities. Regardless of claims, only the intersection of the Mahdi with history can set the stage for the Second Coming of the Muslim version of Christ. So reads the Qur'an, the 114-chapter sacred book of the Muslim faith revealed to the Prophet Muhammad in the early seventh century CE.

Again, politics factor strongly into apocalyptic thinking. Historian Jean-Pierre Filiu attributes the contemporary Muslim apocalyptic militancy and anti-Semitism that have attracted so much world attention to entrepreneur populists who have taken extreme liberties in their interpretation of Islamic literature. He finds among the most influential works Said Ayyub's *The Antichrist*, the central theme of which is that most of the history of humanity is made up of attempts by the Jews, who have placed themselves in the hands of Antichrist, to control the world. According to Ayyub, America has become the new enemy in the Jewish plan to perpetrate a third world war as a way of eliminating their last barrier to rule the world—the Islamic world. As Filiu documents in detail, the Qur'an actually says little about the end of the world.[14] Such narratives, which offer strong appeal to revolutionaries in times of tumult and violence, actually emanated from later Muslim campaigns against the Byzantine Empire. Moreover, there is no Antichrist in the Qur'an.

Interestingly, Filiu argues that Ayyub's apocalyptic leanings were heavily influenced by millenarian conspiracist writings of the 1950s, which we will discuss in chapter 8. Some US neoconservative acolytes think one Muslim motive behind attacking other countries, such as Iraq in the 1980s, and repeatedly threating to attack Israel, is that such action would hasten the return of the Mahdi, thus setting the stage for final judgment and the end of time.[15]

Historian John Hall theorizes that all apocalyptic thinking is part of a "transcendental here-and-now ecstasy" that comes out of a consciousness that exists in the absolute present. It becomes activated during the most intensely experienced periods of historical time in the minds of those who have held hopes and experienced disappointment, felt subjugated, disenfranchised, and seen themselves as part of a community of fate. One of the manifold possibilities of such a state of mind becomes an end to all history followed by a timeless eternity. This unstable "apocalyptic time axis," braided together with the more stable unfolding, historicized here-and-now axis, "defines the sacred and fosters solidarity through ritual."[16]

Like most cultures in the ancient world, those of the ancient Middle East, from Egypt to India, in one way or another shared the belief that an ordered world was set up by the gods deep in the past. Though basically unchangeable, the world was constantly subjected to threats—flood, drought, famine, hostile enemies. But the gods, repaid via offerings, could and did restore the balance. Then, just as rain follows drought, the cycle would be repeated. In the Middle East, reenactment of the combat myth in Enuma Elish and similar stories certified the perpetuity of the creation cycle. But late in the second millennium BCE, a different form of the creation narrative would appear there. In that story, time's cycle would be replaced by time's final end.

The Persian name of Zoroaster (also called Zarathustra) is commonly linked in Middle Eastern antiquity to the practice of magic. No one is sure exactly when he lived. Some say it was sometime around the reign of Ashurbanipal (a ninth-century BCE king of Assyria). Others place him a few centuries earlier. Zoroaster seems to have been the first to preach about the dualistic nature of forces in the universe. Life is a struggle, and just as darkness opposes light, evil exists in the world alongside good—thus spake Zoroaster. He and the kings who would follow him were personified in the form of the male deities Ormazd (also called Mazda), the god of light, and Ahriman, the god of darkness. One was accompanied by a retinue of angels, the other by demon helpers; they would battle one another, like the black and white figures on a chessboard, for control of the binary world they had created.

Zoroaster's worldview predicted that even though the war between the powers of light and darkness would be waged for a long time, ultimately it would come to an end, the forces of light emerging victorious. This is the so-called Apocalypse, the uncovering, unraveling, or revelation of the hidden truth of things. When this happens the day of redemption will be at hand. At the end of time everyone who has ever lived will be brought together and asked to reveal all their good and evil deeds. Those judged to be saved will see their spirits, or souls, live eternally in the luminous mansion of the sky in the presence of Mazda. But the spirits of the damned will pass through rivers of molten metal, reaching confinement and perpetual torment in the dark world below, also known as the Abode of the Lie, where Ahriman dwells. The invention of hell is among the many attributes Christianity owes to Zoroastrianism, which would become the official religion of the Persian Empire through the reigns of the great sixth- and fifth-century BCE kings Darius, Xerxes, and Artaxerxes.

The essence of the Christian story of the nativity is also a product of Zoroastrianism. Devised at the height of the empire, the tale told of a time when Mazda brought fire into the body of the prophet's grandmother, which caused her to give birth to a daughter with a body as radiant as fire. After drinking a special mixture of milk and grain, consisting of Mazda's body and soul, she gave birth to the divine prophet, Zoroaster himself. This is how the idea of a natural order under constant threat and needing to be continually redeemed—call it cyclic history—gave way to the belief that the world is bound to face consummation and total transformation at time's end—linear history. We could call Zoroaster the world's first millenarian prophet; that is, one who claims access to a future condition in which collective salvation, or permanent well-being for the faithful, will come about.

Just to clarify, the terms *millennialism* (or *millenarianism*) and *apocalypticism* are often used interchangeably. Strictly speaking, millennialism, which derives from Christianity, refers to the belief that a transformation to collective salvation is about to occur. Apocalypticism applies to the end of the world via cataclysm. Scholars regard it as but one form of millennialism—namely, catastrophic millennialism. This contrasts with other forms, for example, avertive millennialism, whereby catastrophe on the way to salvation may be avoided via concentrated spiritualistic behavior; or progressive millennialism, a forward-looking attitude that views society as becoming more purified, or perfected, through time.[17]

Given his familiar-sounding philosophy, why has Zoroaster been negatively viewed by the organized religions to which his ideas gave birth? Maybe it's because there is an uncomfortably dark side to his tenets, for along with his story of creation comes a whole retinue of rituals that advocate dealing with angels and demons by magical means. Quite distinct from organized religion, magic implies the existence of a power held in human hands to connect directly with the gods. Ordinarily magic makes use of material objects—charms or fetishes—as conduits of power through which to communicate with and influence the gods. The idea that it is an *occult* practice, a shadow religion that followed the course of conventional religious practice through history, didn't take hold until the sixteenth century, when the notion of worshipping idols declined. This accompanied a trend toward more abstract forms of supernatural belief and scientific experimentation, the latter involving testing the behavior of nature for cause and effect. Thus, Zoroaster's teachings included using secret words and transformations and employing personal effects, such as amulets and talismans, as a way of communicating with—even exerting a measure of control over—the higher powers.

Zoroaster's cosmology, by then ancient, acquired wide appeal among at least two religious communities in the land of Israel between 200 BCE and 100 CE, a period referred to by historian Bernard McGinn as classical apocalypticism. Texts from this period share three attributes: history is a divinely preconceived totality; an imminent crisis lies ahead; and in the judgment to follow, the triumph of good over evil will vindicate us all.[18] One of those communities was the Qumran cult, associated with the authors of the Dead Sea Scrolls. The War Scroll, for example, tells of the end of time in an imminent battle between the "sons of light," commanded by the archangel Michael, and the "sons of darkness," under the leadership of his adversary, Belial. It describes the violent battle between the forces of light and darkness: trumpets summon the foot soldiers, who advance on the enemy as the gates of war are opened. "The formations shall consist of one thousand men ranked seven lines deep, each man standing behind the other. They shall all hold shields of bronze burnished like mirrors . . . All these [formations] shall pursue the enemy to destroy him in an everlasting destruction in the battle for God."[19]

Though their connection with more established Judaism is not clear, we do know that the Qumran cult practiced a rigorous set of rituals that required its members to pray exactly at sunrise and sunset as well as keep a precise liturgical calendar. Members of the sect regarded themselves as the sons of light; they were the patient and the good and they would triumph in the battle. But the identity of the proud, haughty, and impious children of darkness changed with the times, being first identified with the establishment Jerusalem priesthood, and later with the Romans who ruled over them.

This idea of apocalypse appealed to fringe cults. Convinced of the word of the prophets derived from texts only they were capable of decoding, believers looked forward to God's promised end of time and the annihilation of all the evil forces that had oppressed them. For a persecuted minority such an idea held great appeal. But victory would not be won easily, warned the prophets. The war on earth would last forty years, with battles being won successively by the two evenly matched foes. In the end God would intervene and destroy all evil, and that would lead to a new age—the age of the Messiah.

The Jesus sect, which would ultimately blossom into Christianity, was another religious group that latched onto Zoroastrian apocalyptic thinking. The good news of Jesus's teachings, as told through the New Testament Gospels, is all about what the kingdom of God will be like and how to prepare for it. "'Thy kingdom come, Thy will be done, on Earth as it is in heaven" offers the promise that the Garden of Eden in Genesis will be restored here on Earth. Jesus's miracles are signs of it. Satan is losing his power. The moment is at hand: "For the Lord himself will descend from heaven with a cry of command, with the archangels' call, and with the sound of the trumpet of God. And the dead in Christ will rise first; then we who are alive, who are left, shall be caught up together with them in the clouds to meet the Lord in the air; and so we shall always be with the Lord."[20]

As it turned out, the world didn't end as scheduled. But, said the most steadfast among Jesus's followers, those who would later come to be known as Christians, he was resurrected with the promise that the one who would preside over the world restored would come down from heaven only after his death—and this would happen in the very near future. Details of the hour of fulfillment of Apocalypse are told in the one New Testament book more frequently cited than any other in both the early years of the development of Christianity and today—the book of Revelation according to the prophet John. Bernard McGinn defines a prophet as "an inspired person who believes himself to have been sent by his god with a message to tell." In wider usage the term refers to one who foretells the future or wishes to alter the misguided course of history "in the light of an ideal past or glorious future."[21]

John's Revelation was modeled along the lines of the Old Testament book of Daniel. Whoever wrote it could scarcely have imagined how influential it would become, even if the prophet might have been a bit surprised to see us all still alive here below to read it. Credit the striking imagery—the vivid, colorful, and especially violent descriptions in the narrative—whose messages would be interpreted and reinterpreted over the 2,000 years since it was first written. Revelation tells in dramatic detail, via a series of visions experienced by its author, exactly what will transpire on Judgment Day, as well as the signs to look for in anticipation of it.

Revelation's vivid scenes qualify as anybody's worst nightmare. The story line opens with a loud voice. When the man named John turns to confront its source, he sees Jesus disguised as the prophet Daniel, who tells him that God's kingdom on earth is soon to be revealed. He then sweeps John up and lifts him to the court of heaven for a preview of how things will unfold. As the voice narrates, John witnesses the participants in a nascent cosmic war. Angels appear alongside four monsters with many eyes; one has the face of a lion, another a bull, another an eagle, the last a human face. Seated on God's throne, a fire-faced effigy holds a scroll closed by seven seals detailing the plan. Then, in front of the throne appears a strange-looking lamb. It stands upright and its countenance displays seven eyes and seven horns—the seven spirits of God, John is told. The voice tells John that the lamb is Jesus, slaughtered by the very followers who had previously declared him their Messiah. As the lamb begins to open the seven seals, John realizes that each carries a message of the coming disasters that will befall the world—war, famine, death, martyrdom, earthquake . . .

The cosmic drama continues as angels sound trumpets announcing the Four Horsemen, who emerge, each riding a horse of a different color and carrying swords portending, respectively, death, famine, plague, and wild animals (figure 2.1). Then, as in a discontinuous nightmare, come more

FIGURE 2.1. The Four Horsemen of the Apocalypse and the disasters they prophesy change with the times. Here they are pictured in an 1887 painting by Viktor Vasnetsov, *Conquest, War, Famine, and Death*. (Wikimedia Commons.)

prophesied disasters, each one announced by trumpeting angels: hail and fire will destroy the Earth's trees; the seas will turn to blood; a wayward star will fall to Earth, poisoning people; an eclipse will darken the sky. Out of a bottomless pit emerges a swarm of locusts with human faces. A pregnant woman screaming in labor and about to give birth to the Messiah is terrorized by a giant dragon whose name is Satan; he lies in wait to devour her child. The archangel Michael and his cadre enter and defeat the monster, but not before another Satanic dragon with multiple heads and horns comes out of the sea to wage war on the faithful. The Satanic dragon, who will come to rule the Earth, is called Antichrist. He blasphemes God and requires all to carry his mark on their right hand and on their forehead. Then the seven angels pour out the contents of seven bowls containing the wrath of God upon those here below—more death, plagues, rivers of blood, lightning . . . The battles continue, both in heaven and on Earth, until Jesus himself, garbed in warrior's armor, leads the angels down from heaven in the decisive battle between the forces of light and darkness—á la Zoroaster. The forces of Satan are either destroyed or imprisoned; the dead who were faithful to the one true God are restored to life. What begins as a nightmare laced with unimaginable horror ends in ecstasy.

FIGURE 2.2. The Four Horsemen depicted on a poster advocating water conservation in the American Southwest. (Santa Ana Watershed Project Authority.)

No high-tech cinematographic rendition of the many manifest forms of evil can do justice to the prophet's words in Revelation:

> And I stood upon the sand of the sea, and saw a beast rise up out of the sea, having seven heads and ten horns, and upon his horns ten crowns, and upon his heads the name of blasphemy.
>
> And the beast which I saw was like unto a leopard, and his feet were as the feet of a bear, and his mouth as the mouth of a lion: and the dragon gave him his power, and his seat, and great authority.
>
> And I saw one of his heads as it were wounded to death; and his deadly wound was healed: and all the world wondered after the beast.[22]

Long thought to be laden with hidden meaning, Revelation has often been regarded as a dangerous book, especially because it erupts with the vengefulness of a Christ who is portrayed quite differently from the one we read about in the Gospels. The Christ of Revelation displays fire in his eyes: "He is clad in a robe dipped in blood . . . From his mouth issues a sharp sword with which to smite the nations: and he will rule them with a rod of iron."[23] He is the violent Christ portrayed in so many extreme narratives about the future of the world, stories that tell of a fierce encounter between good and evil—opposing forces that are irreconcilable (see this chapter's epigraph).

The enflamed rhetoric of the book of Revelation has inspired other prophets throughout history to witness visions of their own. For example, the wrath of God to be unleashed on the offending Romans was once thought to have been intended to apply to the Seleucid Empire in an earlier version of Apocalypse written in the Old Testament book of Daniel. In the hands of imaginative latter-day prophets, some of whom took the fantastic descriptions in Revelation quite literally, the scenario described could be applied generically to *any* oppressor.

One passage in Revelation that has proven especially durable when it comes to historical interpretation is the secret name of Antichrist. The cryptic statement reads: "It causes all, both small and great, both rich and poor, both free and slave, to be marked on the right hand or the forehead, so that no one can buy or sell unless he has the mark, that is, *the name of the beast or the number of its name*. This calls for wisdom: let him who has understanding reckon the number of the beast, for it is a human number, its number is *six hundred and sixty-six* [my italics]."[24]

Just who is this beast—this false prophet of pagan worship? Every age offers its own solution to the number puzzle. One answer identifies the beast with the Emperor Nero, first to persecute Christians. Why? Because 666 = DCLXVI in Roman numerals; this was thought to be a secret Latin code, provided each number is read as the first letter of a word. The words make the sentence: *Domitius Caesar Legatos Xti Violenter Interfecit*, or "Nero violently killed the envoys of Christ." At the inception of the European nation-state in the early nineteenth century one puzzle solver deduced the beast of Revelation to be none other than Napoleon, because the letters that make up his name can be grouped NAPOLE-ONBUON-APARTE, each segment consisting of six letters. Other historical figures dubbed Antichrist have included Mussolini, Hitler, any number of popes, and Judas Iscariot. Among post–World War II candidates were Popes Pius XII, John XXIII, and John Paul II, John F. Kennedy, Henry Kissinger, Jimmy Carter, Ronald Reagan, Pat Robertson, Saddam Hussein, and Barack Obama. Ronald Reagan got singled out because there are six letters in his first, middle (Wilson), and last names—and he lived at a 666 house address in California. A sarcastic twentieth-century British code buster identified the blasphemous horned one with the House of Commons, which consisted of 658 members, three clerks, a sergeant, a deputy, a chaplain, a door keeper, and a librarian, totaling 666. Indeed, every age reveals its own beast.

Matching real people and events in contemporary time with descriptions of characters and happenings in Revelation—a game author Jonathan Kirsch calls pin-the-tail-on-the-Antichrist—has become a cottage industry.[25] It propagates the enticing notion that the real truth about time's end has yet to be deciphered. Basically, the code remains unbroken, so the world hasn't ended because we haven't figured out precisely when it will.

Historian Elaine Pagels documents the likelihood that apocalyptic literature has always carried political ramifications and that this was particularly so with Revelation, in its own time.[26] She theorizes that the John who wrote the book of Revelation, not to be confused with either John the apostle or the one who wrote the Gospel of John, was an elderly Jewish person who had lived during the war with Rome at the time the Temple of Jerusalem was destroyed in 70 CE. Having seen many of his people killed or dragged into slavery, John left the city as a war refugee and wandered about the Middle East, finally settling in Patmos, an island off the coast of Turkey. There he met relatively well-off Christians who, some while earlier, had been converted by the apostle Paul. Bothered by the tolerant attitude exhibited by these people toward Rome, with images of the decimation of his people still burning in his soul, John felt the need to rail against what he saw as the "Evil Empire." He preached about a vision he had recently experienced, which prophesied a great cosmic war that would result in the violent destruction of Rome by an army of angels. He promised that those who remained faithful would be saved. This, according to Pagels, was pure anti-Roman propaganda and wartime literature.

Pagels narrates how apocalyptic literature has often been used to incite fear and promote hatred of the establishment. The same phenomenon occurred two centuries earlier when, in 164 CE, Old Testament prophet Daniel told of a series of visions with the intention of raising the consciousness of his people against the rule of Antiochus IV, king of Jerusalem and ruler of the Seleucid Empire of Greece and Syria. She also cites an example from the American Civil War, when Confederates portrayed Lincoln being strangled by the Union, which is pictured as a giant dragon, even as the North chose the "Battle Hymn of the Republic" for its anthem; thus the Civil War is portrayed as the Tribulation that gives way to Judgment Day:

> Mine eyes have seen the glory of the coming of the Lord,
> He is trampling out the vintage where the grapes of wrath are stored;
> He hath loosed the fateful lightning of His terrible, swift sword;
> Our God is marching on.

One of the early literalists to draw on Revelation was the second-century CE prophet Montanus of Phrygia in Asia Minor. He interpreted the vision of New Jerusalem descending from the sky in chapter 21 of Revelation—"And I saw the holy city, new Jerusalem, coming down out of heaven"—not as a symbol of Jerusalem in heaven, but rather as the very city itself, fashioned of gold and precious gems, which would actually drop down from the sky and land, conveniently, in a small town not far from where Montanus happened to preach.[27] He claimed he saw it all in a vision and he held no reservations about broadcasting its message: cease to give birth to children; abandon your homes and your jobs and make your way to heaven on Earth. For the time to witness these "things which must shortly come to pass" is upon us.[28] Despite emanating from a fringe group situated in a remote region of Asia Minor, the Montanist message managed to attract a famous convert, the Roman emperor Tertullian. He tells us that his soldiers stationed in the area had already made early sightings of the gleaming turrets and spires above the horizon in the faint predawn light.[29]

Oddly enough, when New Jerusalem failed to materialize, Montanus's followers, far from demoralized, only redoubled their fervency. Like the members of the Qumran cult, they spoke confidently of *their* unique gift: not only could they visualize the imagery in Revelation, they also could pass on that ability to anointed followers.

Another aspect of the inherited apocalyptic philosophy is the habit of date setting. Precise arithmetic has always played a role in the occult interpretation of the Scriptures. For example, the text in Revelation specifies that the "Beast from the Sea" will reign for forty-two months, or three and a half years, which jibes with other passages that speak of 1,200 and threescore (1,260) days and of "a time and times, and half a time."[30] (It works out to three and a half years if you assume a "time" to be one year, "times" to be two, and "half a time" to be one-half.) This interval is frequently invoked in end-time calculations. Also, such counts can be extended by tacking zeroes onto the numbers—the way Pastor William Miller and (as we shall see) later prophets did.

The idea that the winding down of the world clock is meted out in cyclic intervals of ten to the power of three, what we generally mean when we refer to millenarianism in its strictest sense, has long been a part of Western history. Historian of astrology Nicholas Campion summarizes the basic features of millenarian beliefs, which include reference to the aforementioned sui generis theory of the origin of religion: "There is a strong belief that historical time is cyclical and wavelike, with peaks of tension culminating in the occurrence of catastrophic events; at a cultural level there is a preoccupation with moral collapse accompanied by an alienation from nature or the divine. There is also a nostalgia for a long lost time in the past when humanity was closer to God or nature (the so-called Golden Age)."[31] As we'll see in later chapters, these aspects of millenarianism are deeply ingrained in contemporary portrayals of end of the world scenarios. Moreover, most millenarians share the belief that prophesied events are repetitive and that they can be forecast by astronomical means; in other words, the timing of such events can be determined via calculations based on observed celestial phenomena. Millenarianism is especially familiar to us today because we happen to be living during a rare overturn of the millennial odometer.

Revelation has also played a significant role in encouraging believers in the millennial apocalypse to bide their time. For example, the first mention of such an apocalypse, that is, one based on a count of 1,000 years, appears in the book of Revelation. It tells of the devil being bound for 1,000 years, when the victorious angel "cast him into the bottomless pit, and shut him up, and set a seal upon him, that he should deceive the nations no more, till the thousand years should be fulfilled: and after that he must be loosed a little season."[32]

Why choose millennia? In addition to Revelation, the apostle Peter wrote that "one day is with the Lord as a thousand years, and a thousand years as one day."[33] Thus, he set up the 1,000-year mileposts that would pave the road to apocalyptic prophecy. Fourth-century CE Christian sages reasoned that since the work of creation took six days, the present state of the world cannot be altered until 6,000 years have passed. In the fifth century St. Augustine parsed out a historical chronology for the Second Coming that divided time into six successive stages. First came the period between the creation of Adam and the great flood; second the post-flood epoch to the founding of all nations by Abraham; then from Abraham to King David; and from David to the Babylonian captivity of the Jews. The fifth epoch began with the migration out of Babylonia leading up to the birth of Jesus. According to Augustinian chronology we live in the sixth age, which is reckoned from Jesus's birth to the Second Coming. This will lead to the seventh (as in Genesis) and final stage of eternal rest with God in heaven.

Now, in order to know precisely when to anticipate the Second Coming, chronologists have long wrangled over the issue of setting the start time for the creation process. It took until the middle of the seventeenth century for biblical computists to settle on the determination of Archbishop James Ussher. He rigorously tabulated all the begats written in the Old Testament and projected them backward from the birth of Jesus, which he reckoned as having occurred in 4 BCE. Thus, in his *Annals of the Old Testament, Deduced from the First Origin of the World*, Ussher made his widely quoted proclamation that God created the world in 4004 BCE. In rounded-off terms, the ticking clock that metes out the six millennia of all mortal existence covers the period from 4000 BCE to 2000 CE. No wonder some futurists considered Y2K such a big deal. Interestingly, Y1K (1000 CE) was not such a time, owing largely to the church campaigning for a spiritual as opposed to a literal reading of Scriptures.

While the social atmosphere in later ninth- and early tenth-century Europe has been described as one of "mingled hope and fear," it was driven far more by the former.[34] Writes historian Richard Landes: "The millennial enthusiast looks forward eagerly to Judgment Day as a day of pleasure," filled with "the hope for a release from the sufferings of this world, the hope for a place in the coming millennial kingdom."[35] Not so during the medieval period that followed, when hope tilted significantly in the direction of despair, thus allowing apocalyptic thinking to pervade all levels of society. Catastrophic events such as the Great Plague, famine, widespread warfare, and natural disasters made the language of Revelation a refuge for the desperate. One sage calculated that 1326 would be the year of the end of the millennial kingdom of the church—the 1,000-year anniversary of the inauguration of Constantine, the first Christian emperor.

So, after a quiescent period following the millenarian Montanist sect, occasioned largely by the church's strong opposition to apocalypticism, things began to change. "The juxtaposition of terror and bliss is one of the most important features of apocalyptic believers in the Middle Ages," writes contemporary historian Damian Thompson—then he adds the telling phrase "as in our day."[36] The prophecies detailed in the book of Revelation were once again very much alive in the minds of medieval Christians. You can also witness the tension in medieval paintings that depict terrified people experiencing Judgment.

At the close of the eleventh century Pope Urban II called for a crusade to free Jerusalem from Saracen rule. Spurred on by having experienced a series of droughts and a devastating plague that killed significant portions of the population, hordes of peasants, their Christian crosses sewed on their clothing, joined the appointed military forces. As they made the pilgrimage eastward, the uneducated masses thought Jerusalem to be the New Jerusalem they had heard about in biblical Scripture—a place where they would finally gain all of which they had been deprived and live in paradise. In their eagerness they would slaughter thousands of Jewish occupants of the Holy Land, whom they saw as the enemy of Satanic nonbelievers needing to be removed for the prophecy of Revelation to be fulfilled.

Apocalyptic prophet Joachim of Fiore (1135–1202) pegged the termination date of all worldly affairs at 1260. He experienced a vision of Christ, who clued him in about how to read Revelation. According to Joachim there were, echoing the Trinity, only three ages, each of 1,000 years. The first ended with the Crucifixion, the second was due to end with the appearance of Antichrist, and the third would end only after Antichrist had been defeated. The second age, he predicted, would end not in the time of our grandchildren or even our children, but in our own days. Joachim reasoned that the age of the Son, the second in the Trinity time schedule, was coming to an end; but since he calculated that forty-two generations had existed between Adam and Jesus, forty-two more generations must pass before the new age would dawn. Since 1200 CE marked forty generations, the third age was due to arrive in 1260. But it wouldn't happen all at once. First there would be a struggle—the battle with Antichrist. Only the truly spiritual people who would evolve out of that crisis would consolidate the good. They would herald the beginning of a new age.

For Joachim of Fiore and many other prophets of his age, Antichrist resided in the church itself, whose clergy stole from the coffers and indulged in sexual excess, or even in the pope, who had persecuted their sect. Joachim predicted that the pope's true identity would be exposed in 1325, 1330, or 1335. He was also aware of the Islamic resurgence under Saladin, whom he cast as yet another version of Antichrist. Norman Cohn notes that the sort of revolutionary messianism proffered by Joachim and others in the eleventh and twelfth centuries appealed to hard-struggling agricultural peasants who survived at the whims of nature on the edge of famine.[37] Their condition of serfdom by birth in a social environment that offered them little security and protection opened the way for many to the possibility of a radical transformation of society. And they were especially tuned to revolutionary millennialism when disaster befell them. Cohn cites the widespread famines preceding the First and Second Crusades and the Black Death plague.[38]

In effect, Joachim converted the symbolic Trinity into an evolutionary progressive historical process, as philosopher Michael Grosso characterizes it. The age of fear (the Father of the Old Testament) gives way to the age of faith, an attitude developed in the New Testament (the Son). Faith then develops into the highest stage of history, that of the Holy Spirit, which is characterized by love among a people who would possess a faculty of intelligence and reason above the ordinary. The law of history is thus understood as a law of progress from slavery toward freedom.[39] As we shall see, the notion of a future unifying spiritual consciousness experienced here on Earth has an appeal that is alive today in New Age philosophy. Despite the disapproval of the church, the *how* and *when* aspects of Joachim's prophesying have had an impact on theories of the course of history even down to the present, according to Norman Cohn; for example, we see it resonate in Marx's three stages of the evolution of communism and, he contends, in the Third Reich, originally a new order intended to last 1,000 years.[40]

Joachim's ideas caught fire in Protestant circles, especially when Martin Luther used Revelation as a weapon against the Roman Catholic Church. Many Protestants interpreted Antichrist to be the papacy itself. They thought of Apocalypse as a revenge mechanism against the evildoing religious establishment. Lutheran followers even computed the date: Michael Stifel, a German mathematician, worked it out to be October 19, 1533—at 8:00 a.m.

The world certainly did seem to be unraveling in the early fourteenth century. The Little Ice Age, three decades of unprecedented frigid weather in northern Europe, followed on the heels of the famine of 1315 and the Great Plague (1347–1351), which wiped out one-third of the population of Europe. Halley's Comet, which appeared in 1301, was one of many signs of the times (figure 2.3). So were shooting stars, earthquakes, and volcanic eruptions—or any unusual natural phenomenon, such as the birth of a two-headed calf or a deformed child. Dante spoke of signs of the impending doom in the *Inferno*: "For I see surely . . . stars already close at hand . . . that shall bring us a time when a Five Hundred, Ten, and Five, sent by God shall slay the thievish woman and that giant who sins with her."[41] The cryptic numerological code identifies Henry VII, king of Luxembourg, as the culprit. But then, Shakespeare in *Henry VI* later pegged a different Henry, sans numbers: "O, let the vile world end, / And the premised flames of the last day / Knit earth and heaven together!"[42]

The vernacular translation of the Bible, that is, in the lingua franca rather than Latin, and the concomitant rise of Protestantism in sixteenth-century Germany, weakened the authority of the church and its sole right to interpret what the Bible said. Accompanied by social tension, this theological sea change helped unleash a host of radical apocalyptic sects, each led by its own charismatic ruler. One sect that grew up in Münster, Germany, worked out that 1534 was the last year of history. Its leader declared that city to be the foundation on which descending New Jerusalem would rest. In a state of frenzy he ran naked in the streets to spread the news, adding this mandate: that all citizens were required to give up their precious goods and thereafter practice abstinence in order to gear up for the big day by purifying themselves. After advocating the death penalty for adulterers, the group leader abruptly and inexplicably reversed his doctrine in favor of free sex for all his followers. He switched his role, too, proclaiming himself king of the Last Days. Accompanied by a cadre of young wives, he paraded around town clad in jeweled robes. Those who refused his will were beheaded. Only when the town was besieged by orders from the bishop was rule of the city returned to its people.

FIGURE 2.3. When Halley's Comet appeared in 1301, it was likened to the Star of Bethlehem in this painting of the Nativity by Giotto. (Comune di Padova—Assessorato Cultural e Turismo.)

Historian Ruth Bloch thinks Protestantism increased apocalyptic thinking by bringing Christianity's ambiguity about the nature of the experiential world out into the open.[43] Devoted to righteousness and hard work as an expression of grace carried out in the real world, believers came to understand their lives as part of the process of transforming an inherently Satanic world into a place worthy of the return of Christ. No longer passive participants waiting for an organized priesthood to tell them when the end of time would occur, they saw themselves as actors in the unfolding drama.

Flickering to light in northern Europe, the torch of the Apocalypse would be passed to England. There, during the reign of Elizabeth I (1558–1603), the designation of the pope as Antichrist would become the defining mark of the Protestant religion. For the hard-line English Puritans, linking the papacy with Antichrist was not enough. They believed that even the bishops of the Church of England were tinged with Satan and they held his evil spirit responsible for the government that supported it. In the wake of political upheaval and an impending civil war (1642–1660), mid-sixteenth-century England became saturated with attempts to reset Doomsday. Many predictions settled on the mid-1650s; 1656 was the most popular choice because many prophets agreed that the great flood had occurred 1,656 years after creation. One Puritan prophetess predicted the conversion of the Jews in 1656 to be followed, in five, ten, or twenty years, by an earthly utopia.[44] But mainstream England managed to shake off its apocalyptic trends in favor of a progressive ideology—what historian Christopher Hill has identified as a secular form of millennialism.[45]

Rational thought and scientific investigation as means to attain God's and nature's truths were beginning to develop in seventeenth-century Europe, and so were technological advances. With this came the optimistic notion that these new ways of knowing could be applied to solve many of society's problems—this thanks to a new force intervening. According to progressive millennialism, the golden age is put off into the future, where it will be attained by an optimistic, materially based culture. This would set the stage for the conservative Puritan minority to seek out a faraway utopia where they could set their own stage of self-perfection leading up to a more immediate Second Coming.

PART II

American Apocalypse

3

From Columbus to the Great Awakenings

[And this] has ever been received as a Truth in the churches of New England.
—*Seventeenth-century Puritan minister Cotton Mather*

Annuit Coeptis Novus Ordo Seclorum—so read the words on the reverse side of the Great Seal of the United States, which has appeared on the back of US $1 bills since the 1930s. The words come from the Latin poet Virgil's *Eclogues* and they mean, "He [God] has Favored our Undertakings [of] A New Order of the Ages."[1] This early statement about American exceptionalism, viewed in the visionary context of America as heaven on Earth, can be taken as a prophecy that refers to Jesus's promised descent from heaven. That is certainly the way many early Christians in America understood it, though Charles Thomson, designer of the Great Seal, who proposed the motto in 1782, had in mind a reference to the new American freedom proclaimed in the signing of the Declaration of Independence.

Later interpreters would mistranslate the second half of the Great Seal motto as "New World Order," interpreting *seclorum* to mean "secular," and believing this was the secret declaration of a conspiracy among certain elites bent on destroying the sovereign states and creating a godless world government under dictatorial rule. Conspiracy theorists interpreted these cultural globalizers, among them Woodrow Wilson and Winston Churchill, to be latter-day Antichrist candidates because they used the term to suggest that great changes in international politics and the balance of world power would follow each of the two world wars. The creation of NATO and the United Nations was regarded by some as the first steps toward this New Order, which antiglobalists feared. Later, Soviet communists, Wall Street capitalists and, as we'll learn in chapter 8, the government-controlled scientific-technological establishment would replace the imagined cabal of elites in the new secular order, hell-bent on turning America into a tyrannical one-world government.

The Great Seal (figure 3.1), with its hypnotic eye and unfinished pyramid, has been connected with (though it did not derive from) the Freemason philosophy. The mysticism inherent in it would remain one of the foundations of the theosophical movement (to be discussed in chapter 5) that would flourish in the United States in the late nineteenth century. Freemasonry holds that a special bond exists between man and God, part of the secret search for lost universal truths harbored in ancient civilizations—the *monomyth* again—that finds its mandate in the American Masonic brotherhood.

European Freemasonry began as a late seventeenth-century organization of well-to-do, educated gentlemen who drew upon visionary prognostications derived from alchemy, astrology, and other occult practices during the Renaissance. At that time it was known as Rosenkreuz (Rose Cross), or the Rosicrucians (Brothers of the Rose Cross), after a quasi-mythical scholar, Christian Rosenkreuz, who traveled throughout the Holy Land gathering knowledge and writing fundamental texts. Rosenkreuz was said to have been found alive in his tomb, where he continued to declaim his philosophy of metaphysical spirituality.

The early eighteenth-century English transplant version of Freemasonry connected Freemasons' lodges, or clubs, with the building trade in the form of the medieval guilds of masons who had built the great cathedrals, thereby achieving high social status. The raising of a temple to glorify God had its parallel in human development, wherein the improvement of the body and mind was thought to build a more durable temple for the soul. Freemasons regarded their collective as speculative societies, an invisible college of specially qualified adepts who, drawing from the philosophy of Joachim of Fiore, sought from their learning the prophetic pathway to the dawn of a new age of enlightenment.

FIGURE 3.1. The Great Seal of the United States on the back of the $1 bill depicts the country's metaphysical origins. (Library of Congress Rare Book and Special Collections Division, LC-US62-45509.)

The Masonic rite of self-perfection most well known to those outside the secret brotherhood is the ascent through the thirty-three degrees of higher consciousness toward true union with the Great Architect. These oddly named degrees—among them Secret Master (4), Intimate Sanctuary (6), Venerable Grand Master (20), Knight of the Brazen Serpent (25), Sublime Prince of the Royal Secret (32), and the culmination, Grand Inspector General (33)—were conferred on Freemasons based on their level of understanding of secret texts and mystical processes, the accompanying ceremonies featuring an elaborate dress code.[2]

To give an example of the rites of reenactment of a myth by initiates, one of the degrees tells of the vision of Enoch the Prophet, who had beheld a triangular plate carved with hieroglyphic characters of the never-to-be-pronounced name of the one true God.[3] (Later this plate would find a parallel in Joseph Smith's gift of the Golden Tablets from the angel Moroni that would lead to the foundation of Mormonism.) So Enoch built an underground temple consisting of nine arches atop one another, in the bottom of which he placed an exact replica of the plate he had envisioned, along with two carved pillars containing additional lost knowledge. After many thousands of years, knights engaged in the building of the temple of King Solomon happened upon these ruins. When they reported their find to the king, who somehow had already known about the engraved plate, he promised that he would accord them access to knowledge of the true pronunciation of the name of God. Meanwhile, others who had been refused this mysterious knowledge by the king took it upon themselves to descend into the excavated passage. But they were crushed in a terrible accident when the arches collapsed on them. Enough of the text remained, however, for at least a partial decipherment, and Solomon had it all deposited in a secret vault. Thus the story goes, if you think of it metaphorically, that you can reach the secret and privileged truth of God only by repeatedly descending a deep, dark passageway, an endeavor requiring arduous labor and fraught with considerable danger.

Freemasonry became very popular once it was introduced in the colonies in the 1730s. Within a decade every city had at least one lodge. George Washington was a member and Benjamin Franklin an enthusiastic promoter. Franklin published the definitive work on Masonic practice. Sixteen US presidents, including Madison, Monroe, Jackson, both Roosevelts, Johnson, Ford, and Reagan, were members—all of them Protestants. Freemasonry was inherently anti-Catholic; with the arrival of Jews and other eastern and southern Europeans on the eastern seaboard in the mid-late 1800s, its members became even more strongly nationalistic and suspicious of any foreign ideology or practice that departed from their Anglo-Saxon heritage, a habit developed, according to Michael Barkun, out of the "insecurities of a newly independent state."[4] In America, writes historian Catherine Albanese, the Masonic philosophy would be encoded "in a mysticism that could easily lend itself to the worship of nature . . . this alongside its elaborate grand master initiation ceremonies featuring symbolic scientific/technological elements, such as the square and the compass." As a consequence: "It was this combination of the clear light of reason and the dark shadow of secrecy out of which American metaphysical religion was poised to emerge, even as it transformed darkness into light."[5]

The roots of American exceptionalism and its ties to Christianity can be traced all the way back to the time of European contact. Even as he sailed west across the Atlantic, Columbus was convinced he had discovered the entrance to paradise. For him, the compass pointed the way to heaven: "Each time I sailed from Spain to the Indies, I found that when I reached a point a hundred leagues [about 300 miles] west of the Azores, the heavens, the stars, the temperature of the air and the waters of the sea abruptly changed. It was as if the seas sloped upward."[6] The source of the downhill flowing water, he believed, was unreachable; but he felt sure paradise lay just beyond the gushing rivers he had glimpsed on the mainland. As biographer Laurence Bergreen characterizes it, Columbus "believed he was on the doorstep of the Indies, as well as the threshold of paradise."[7]

Columbus even wrote a book about the Apocalypse. He was heavily influenced by the writings of Joachim of Fiore, whose *Book of Prophecies* had laid out the dispensation of events he believed were about to take place that would pave the way to history's end: first, world recognition of Christianity; second, the discovery of the biblical Garden of Eden; third, a final crusade that would expel Muslims from the Holy Land; and fourth, the inauguration of the last World Emperor. The third event is where the Americas, or "Terra Nova," as he called it, figured in the plan. Columbus envisioned the "New World" as the Garden and he appointed himself the agent of the great happening about to dawn in history's progressive evolution: "Of the new heaven and the new earth which the Lord made, and of which St. John writes in the Apocalypse, . . . he made me the messenger and he showed me the way."[8]

Columbus's son and biographer Ferdinand symbolically connects his father's name with the image of a man of providential destiny. He tells us that *Ypo Ferens* or Christoferens, as Columbus was baptized, means "bearer of Christ," and *Columba* is the Latin word for "dove," symbol of the third part of the Trinity, which Joachim of Fiore had predicted would come forth to climax world history in the final age following the age of the Father and the age of the Son—the age of the Holy Spirit.[9]

Columbus tacked on a clever corollary to the Second Coming scenario designed to enhance the proposals he submitted to the young monarchs Ferdinand and Isabella in hopes they would fund his voyages. It had been their mission to make Roman Catholicism the exclusive religion in the Spanish Empire. Columbus would give over the gold and other treasures of the New World to finance the final crusade, which would include rebuilding the Temple of Jerusalem. This would set the stage for Christ's descent. The devout monarchs, who had recently expelled the Muslims from their kingdom, would be the Last World Emperors leading the crusade. Columbus, then, was more than just a daring adventurer and profiteer—to judge from his own words, he was a prophet of Apocalypse.

Oddly enough, Protestants rather than Catholics would become the actors who would set the stage for fulfillment of the great Columbian prophecy. The English Puritans, among the first New World settlers, who set out for the New England wilderness five generations after Columbus landed, believed that the act of doing so would lead to the Second Coming. Earlier, in 1609, a London promoter of the colonization of Virginia wrote that "God hath reserved in this last age of the world, an infinite number of those lost and scattered sheep, to be won and recovered by our means."[10]

Colonial historian Perry Miller once confessed that he found it hard to imagine how the Puritan colonists, who were constantly surrounded by grotesque, realistic imagery within and without the churches where they worshiped, and who were repeatedly reminded in the sermons they heard and in the literature they read that the anticipated sound of Gabriel's trumpet was already in the air, could possibly ever have been cheerful.[11] The founders of the Massachusetts Bay Colony certainly harbored a fear-laden frame of mind. Every Puritan household was familiar with minister Michael

Wigglesworth's characterization of the awakening dead in his poem *The Day of Doom* (1662):

For at midnight brake forth a Light
Which turn'd the night to day,
And speedily an hideous cry
Did all the world dismay.
Sinners awake, their hearts do ake.
Trembling their loynes surprizeth;
Amazed with fear, by what they hear,
Each one of them ariseth.[12]

The Puritans were among the most radical Protestant reformers. Their very name indicates an ideology of perfecting oneself as the best way to prepare for the heaven on Earth that lay just around the bend in the road of time. But self-perfection also involved recognizing and purging themselves of evil in all forms. Many Puritans regarded the king of England (James I, who followed Elizabeth to the throne in 1603) as the Antichrist of the book of Revelation. They thought the English population in general so detestable—with its extravagant dress, excessive drinking and eating habits, its scandalous poetry—that the farther they could remove themselves from such blatant manifestations of evil the better. Even the unknown wilds of New England would offer a superior place to *live* their apocalyptic ideology by practicing morally clean, frugal habits. Little wonder, then, that the first governor of the Massachusetts Bay Colony called his settlement the "City on a Hill"—New Jerusalem. Late fifteenth- and early sixteenth-century England experienced plague and smallpox along with financial problems and a shortage of land. Convinced that all this misfortune, which they attributed to England's sins, portended the Apocalypse, the English Puritans were intent on removing all Catholic leanings from the Church of England. But they realized they could achieve their aims only by establishing their own version of the church in a new land. "Religion stands on tiptoe in our land, / Readie to pas to the American strand," wrote one poetic minister.[13]

Other New World immigrants shared the philosophy that the wilderness was the place to assemble for the Second Coming. Perfectionists sought different modes of preparation to receive their savior. For example, the German Pietist Johannes Kelpius (1673–1708) interpreted passages in Revelation to peg the year of the big event as 1694; the place was somewhere in the rurals of the province of Pennsylvania. Together with his small cadre of followers—they called themselves the Society of the Woman in the Wilderness—Kelpius sailed across the Atlantic and set up a communal living quarter in the valley of Wissahickon Creek in Philadelphia, then home to 2,000 people. There they lived in celibacy, meditated in caves, and held meetings in a centrally located building, all the while searching the sky with their telescope for signs in heaven. Applying Joachim of Fiore's three-age millennial dispensation of history to the wilderness, the Pietists saw time unfold from the "age of the barren wilderness" to the "fruitful wilderness" to the "wilderness of the elect of God." They made it their mission to sacralize the landscape by cultivating and perfecting it, both agriculturally and spiritually.

Cotton Mather (1663–1728), a self-proclaimed adept, was among the most ardent end of time colonial visionaries. Descended from a long line of American Doomsday prophets (his father, Increase Mather [1639–1723], believed Revelation's red horse of the Apocalypse foretold King Philip's War [1675–1676] between the colonies and the Indians), Mather claimed to have witnessed a preview of coming signs in nature indicating that volcanoes would provide the source of the great conflagration. Among the earliest American prophets to co-opt the language of contemporary science, Mather described these "Subterraneous Combustions and such Amassments of Igneous Particles" as the real Eternal Fire. He concluded that, in 1709, the Lord would finally have his "Holy city in America."[14] Among the other dates Mather calculated for the Second Coming of the Lord were 1697, 1716, and 1736. Regardless of when, he was certain about *where* it would happen: New England. "Look upon [our] towns and fields, look upon [our] habitations and shops and ships, and behold [our] numerous posterity, and great increase in the blessings of land and sea," wrote an optimistic Mather, a stark contrast to his paranoia about earthly disaster (he also feared witches and wrote widely on the need to purge them out of society).[15]

Further fashioning his premillennial scientific-sounding prognostications, Mather drew on the well-established trend in the ideology of late seventeenth-century English prophets, who believed that time's end would be signaled by a series of natural disasters that would accompany a general spiritual disintegration of the world—including drought, the drawing of a veil across the face of the sun (clearly a reference to a solar eclipse), a rash of earthquakes, and volcanic eruptions that would be sufficient to cause the entire world to burst into flames. Once the periodic nature of Halley's Comet had been discerned, following its dramatic appearance in the night sky in 1682, comets could always be called upon as portents of global disaster. The close passage of one of them was thought by some to have been connected with Noah's flood.

An earthquake that rattled Boston in 1755 prompted further speculations of the end of time. One printer alleged the event had been predicted in an earlier publication, which he reissued. *The Strange and Wonderful Predictions of Mr. Christopher Love* told of wars and earthquakes that would occur in that decade, culminating in Antichrist's rise in 1761 and the end of history in 1763.[16] A rival publication issued shortly afterward reset the clock forward to 1766.

Mather was but one of a host of fiery preachers in early colonial America who spoke in strong reformist language, exhorting sinners to root out evil in and around them. He was also one of the forerunners of American "dispensationalism," the belief that God relates to humans in different ways in a series of periods, or dispensations, during which ways to salvation differ.

Historian Jonathan Butler characterizes American dispensationalism as a series of cultural awakenings that follow a formula for cultural change. It begins with a period of social unrest and the breaking of rules people regard as no longer effective. Some unpatriotically attack the establishment and arouse broader awareness, leaving the mainstream suspended in a state of stressful social limbo between the older and newer orders. This confusing state of affairs is precisely when millennial movements arise, as people search for a revitalized society. They feel a need to find a way to redeem themselves, a new way to judge themselves, a pathway toward the making of a "new man."[17] During such critical periods the prophet emerges to set the new rules. In the final phase, the rules solidify and act to shape a revitalized culture and build a new community.

Two major awakening periods make up this early history. The First Great Awakening (1730–1755), which took place in New England, served as the platform for dissenters like Cotton Mather, who helped usher it in as he sought to purify the decadent Church of England. It was initiated by a somewhat less fiery preacher, Jonathan Edwards. Speaking from his pulpit in Northampton, Massachusetts, Edwards advocated personal renewal of the spirit as the pathway toward recovery of a decadent society.

The First Great Awakening was about as far from an age of skepticism as one could imagine. The renewal process would be achieved by holding revivals in which communities would pray together to prepare for the new millennium, after which the great battle between God and Satan would take place. This was a time of intense widespread mass worship, often accompanied by emotional gestures, shaking, and weeping. Laying the groundwork for today's evangelism, it emphasized personal conversion and strict biblical authority. Revealed phenomena and signs in nature became common, shared experiences. Auguries and apparitions were thought to take place all around us, and those who could manifest and interpret them seemed ever present to offer spiritual direction to the flock.

Apocalyptic prophecy served as excellent fodder for connecting the Bible to current events. For example, during the French and Indian War (1754–1763), the French Catholic colonizers became ideal Antichrist candidates in the eyes of the Protestant colonists who lived south of them. As the desire for independence swelled, the British rulers acquired that sinister label. As proof, one biblical decoder noted that the letters comprising the words "Royal Supremacy in Great Britain," translated into either Greek or Hebrew and numerologically interpreted, yielded 666.[18]

Speechmakers at college graduation ceremonies on the eve of the Revolutionary War began to evoke a different kind of millennialism, a secular postmillennialism, the belief that the millennial kingdom would constitute a "golden age" achievable through victory by the church and the Gospel. Only after the culture had been won over by Jesus's teachings for 1,000 years would he then return to claim his kingdom. The American nation, predicted one of them, would become "the principal seat of that glorious kingdom, which Christ shall erect upon the Earth in latter Days."[19] Wrote another, "That remarkable Jewish tradition" of a millennium of "peace, purity, and felicity" would be fulfilled in America. "Arise, shine, for the light is come."[20]

To summarize briefly, there is a stark conflict between these views that existed side by side during the First Great Awakening. The bleak and violent premillennial scenario, exemplified by Cotton Mather's early rhetoric, regards the Second Coming as happening only after a dark period of war, famine, and wickedness, accompanied by the wrath of God's punishment in the form of natural disaster. In contrast, the postmillennial attitude, more prevalent especially during the latter part of the Awakening, offers a much more hopeful progressive, participatory eschatology: yes, there will be suffering and setbacks, but ultimately good will prevail. *We* will make it happen. For example, the British surrender that ended the American Revolution was compared by more than one preacher to God's giving Palestine to the Jews as result of his divine plan, thus characterizing the fulfillment of prophecies relative to the millennial state.

Regardless of millennial outlook and the form it took, prophesying was central to the thinking of early American intellectual leaders of all stripes. Historians of Christianity note the odd coincidence that the renewed vigor in religious activism during the First Great Awakening happened around the same time as the birth of secular humanism,[21] what historian Peter Gay characterizes as a kind of skepticism and disenchantment toward religious beliefs that developed out of a "recovery of nerve" that the scientific understanding of things could lead to a better world.[22] Here, Gay believes, began the still-ongoing war between science and religion, whose battles in regard to end of the world ideologies we will explore in coming chapters.

Thus the fires of the First Great Awakening would be dampened by a reconsideration of the relationship of God to man occasioned by the widespread circulation of scientific ideas and discoveries of the Enlightenment. New questions were posed. What does the end of the world mean if the world is, in fact, but one of a retinue of planets that circle the sun? And if planet Earth is not the center of the universe, then what becomes the meaning of the time-worn phrase "man is the measure of all things"? Where are heaven and hell? How does God intervene in motion subject to Newton's laws? How can the sound of a trumpet change the course of an atom?

The problem of the reconciliation of apocalyptic religion with reasoned science thus began to force itself onto the agenda of human salvation. How do natural phenomena reveal God "insinuating Himself into nature"? to borrow the words of Perry Miller.[23] Thus, in his 1681 *The Sacred Theory of the Earth*, Thomas Burnet attempted to reconcile the deluge with science. He calculated that a minimum of eight oceans would be necessary to cover the world. Unable to account for such a source in all the clouds and existing rivers and oceans combined, he applied scientific reasoning to the task, concluding that the original chaos was due to a mass of swirling atoms, the heaviest of which sank to the center of the Earth, while lighter liquid ones floated to the top, solidified, and formed the Earth's crust. (To this point Burnet's account isn't a bad rendition of the process of early planet formation in the solar system as we understand it today!) Then the sun baked the crust, causing it to crack. Water gushed up from below. It was time to build an ark.

As we already discovered, even Cotton Mather was not unaware of the need to reconcile his predictions about catastrophe with the growing body of scientific knowledge. God's intention in smiting the army of Sennacherib is clear—even if these horrible people might have been killed by lightning, he conjectured. Yes, the causes behind comets and eclipses have to do with gravity, but they can *still* be evil portents: "The admirable Sir Isaac Newton will rule henceforth as the 'Perpetual Dictator of the Learned World,'" for he had so expounded physics that men must forever confess "that Philosophy is no enemy but a mighty and wondrous 'Incentive to Religion.'"[24]

As American revolutionary ardor took center stage, apocalyptic expectations expounded in sermons by Mather and others began to wane. While there were some who believed that America's war for independence heralded Christ's return to earth, with King George III now playing the role of Antichrist, others, like deist Thomas Paine, thought they were creating a new age with their actions. "We have it in our power to begin the world over again," he wrote in *Common Sense*.[25]

Interrupted by the revolution, the spark of reform-minded American religious passion flamed back to life again in the 1790s; the fires burned brightly, reaching maximum luminosity during the 1830s and 1840s, until 1860—essentially the period between the Federalist era and the Civil War. This period historians have named the Second Great Awakening. It spawned a host of alternative religions and conversion movements, including Millerism. Utopian religions built around a variety of communal living arrangements appeared about the same time as Miller's version of Adventism. Most of them involved human action and were concerned with perfecting society as a way of preparing for heaven on Earth. Unlike Millerism, utopianism was broader in scope, often addressing how property and labor were to be distributed, what were the proper roles of men and women, how the family was to be structured, and the role of sex in society. Abolitionism, feminism, temperance—even dietary reform—were among these religions' social concerns.

Religious tolerance promoted by the US Constitution, together with a liberal immigration policy, had resulted in a variety of European-derived sects that began to flourish during the early decades of the nineteenth century. Operating outside mainstream Protestantism (Presbyterian, Baptist, Methodist, Lutheran, Episcopal, and Congregational), more radical sects like the Amish, the Shakers, and the Rappites sought isolation from a contemporary world they viewed as corrupt. The Dutch- and German-derived Amish, especially, eschewed technology, service in the military, and paying taxes. They denied themselves all forms of personal vanity, such as wearing buttons on their clothes. Thanks to their strong social bonding, more than 200,000 of them thrive today in the northeastern United States. Originally from France and England, the Shakers, noted for the spasmlike movements they made and the strange tongues they spoke during church services, practiced celibacy and communal living; they were among the earliest Americans to pursue gender equality. Ardent millennialists, they firmly believed that their practices constituted the best way for humanity to survive as they prepared for the end of the world.

The disgruntled German Rappites, named after their Lutheran founder George Rapp, established the utopian communities of Harmony in western Pennsylvania and New Harmony in Indiana. As the name implies, these "Harmonists" conceived of a heaven on Earth made up of celibate couples who would live together like brothers and sisters, and who would hold all the property they farmed in common. This would be the embryo of kingdom come. All the radical perfectionist groups shared in their appetite for hard work, which contributed to building the strong post–War of 1812 economy. The Shakers made—and still make—furniture. The apple corer, rotary barrow, circular saw, and the clothespin are all Shaker inventions. Rappites fashioned hats and shoes and, despite their policy against consuming alcohol themselves, they brewed beer, distilled whiskey, and made wine for outside sales.

Many of these millennialist separatist groups were headed by inspired leaders who saw themselves as appointed Advent messengers or even actually divine. Ann Lee, the Shaker prophetess, for example, claimed that, as a result of a revelation she experienced, she was the female half of a dual creator, a father-mother god. Members the Amana colonies, consisting of a number of communities in eastern Iowa, held that Jesus's spirit had already reentered the world here below and lived in the bodies of the chosen few who would serve as his instruments. These people, successors of the German Pietist movement, were also known as the Community of True Inspiration.

A vociferous critic of Pastor William Miller, John Humphrey Noyes cultivated a brand of utopianism that was based on the belief that the first step in the Second Coming had already occurred long ago, when Jesus appeared in spirit before his apostles at the time the Temple of Jerusalem was destroyed in 70 CE. Believing that he himself was perfect already, Noyes advocated that we should strive to live a life of perfection here on Earth. In 1848 Noyes established a communal group in Oneida, New York, most notable for practicing free sex. Noyes interpreted the New Testament, especially the statement in Mathew 22:30 that in God's kingdom people "neither marry nor are given in marriage, but are like angels in heaven," to mean that restricting sexual intercourse to one companion was a sign of imperfection. He responded by disallowing two-person marriages in his perfected community.

The Fourierist communities, named after their original leader, the Frenchman Charles Fourier, were a more loosely formed set of "phalanxes of Associationists," as they called themselves, consisting of deists and an assortment of liberal Christians, who also honed to the doctrine of perfectionism. Fourier, a philosopher, viewed poverty as the cause of social disorder and communal work as the secret of social success. Remains of his utopian communities still exist in Texas, New Jersey, Massachusetts, and New York. His phalanxes—actually grand hotels—were four-level structures housing workers, the wealthiest at the top.

Some separatist utopian groups were led by more extreme preachers. For example, Jacob Osgood, a New Hampshire Congregational outcast, declared he could heal the infirm by the laying on of hands. Osgood also claimed that he could control the weather and the behavior of insects. Even more ambitious was Jacob Cochran, also from New Hampshire. He believed himself to be the Holy Ghost. Convinced he was blessed with the healing power and the capacity to bring the dead back to life, he told his 2,000-member Society of Free Brethren that he would be in control of the United States within a year and of the whole world not much later. The highly charismatic Cochran would violently jerk and twist parishioners upon whom he administered his own form of baptism, all the while yelling out cries of damnation. Converts were often required to lick the ground on which he stood. In the midst of a service, Cochran would routinely pick out a young female worshipper, take her into an adjoining room, have sex with her, then return with her to the group and ask her how she now saw the world. He lived with a dozen wives in a mansion in southern Maine. Eventually Cochran was brought to trial and charged with lewdness, lascivious behavior, and adultery; he was sentenced to four years in prison. He was reportedly unrepentant.

Vermont prophet Isaac Bullard sought to resurrect his own form of pure primitive religion. He and his followers never bathed or changed their clothing, which consisted of bearskins. They fasted at length, but when they did dine they ate with their hands, and sucked milk and other liquids out of communal bowls through straws made of quills. Penances consisted of standing still for several days and praying facedown in the dirt.

What unites all of the utopian ideologies described above, regardless of how they are practiced, is their conviction that they offer a means of bringing the millennium closer. Adherents would act as if it were already at hand, or at least that it could be achieved in some form in the present life. Many of these outcast groups also followed a common trend of moving westward, farther and farther out of range of the growing industrialized East Coast. Though less radical than some, the Mormons hold the record for distance traveled, the seed bearing their religious principles having been carried from Vermont to central New York, where Joseph Smith received the Golden Tablets, to Ohio to southern Illinois and finally to Salt Lake City.

To conclude, Millerism was not an isolated mid-nineteenth-century phenomenon. In the first half of the nineteenth century, "America the religious" was primed for end of the world social movements like Millerism. In the necessarily brief historical accounts of the past two chapters, I have tried to show that the strain of apocalyptic prophecy so dramatically displayed on American soil during the Millerite crisis of the 1840s rests firmly on a deep tradition that goes all the way back to the biblical Middle East. Durable and adaptable, the message inherent in the monomyth has waxed and waned throughout history. It has been interpreted and reinterpreted subject to current events and critical social developments. And it has been politicized: for example, in the rebellion leading up to the American Revolution, when disenfranchised colonists stood in for the persecuted Israelites of the Old Testament. Antichrists of Revelation have been identified from an array of establishment individuals ranging from popes to kings. The venue for the great confrontation anticipated at time's end has ranged from the hills of Scotland to the woodlands of New England.

Jonathan Butler credits historian John Higham with labeling the post-Millerite decade of the 1850s as the time when a sudden and swift transition of rule changing, from boundlessness to consolidation, took place, when "radical hopes and reacting fears" subsided, to be replaced by stability and less ideological venturing. "Americans passed from freedom to control, from movement to stability, from diversity to uniformity, from diffusion to concentration, from spontaneity to order."[26]

During the late nineteenth century, a period we take up in the next two chapters, secular prophets would live side by side with their religious brethren, as scientific terminology began to supplant biblical quotations. But all the while the theme of the prophesied history of the world, if somewhat toned down, would remain remarkably durable. Surprisingly little has changed in the narrative flow of the story of time's end since it was writ millennia ago in the ancient Middle East. But the next wave of alternative beliefs about the future of the world would seek its truths in secret knowledge derived from even more remote sources than the Old and New Testaments.

4

Fin de Siècle Secular Perfectionism

It loved Jesus and Buddha, Tolstoi and Nietzsche, liberalism and socialism and anarchism, Unitarianism and Ethical Culture and the wisdom of the east, free love and monogamy, wealth and ascetic virtue. It was scientific and poetic and adored nature and exalted man. It was pacifist and admired successful brutality. It was precious and went in for simplicity. It was soft.

—*Writer and cultural critic Gilbert Seldes*

With the Great Disappointment of 1844 behind them, those in the conservative wing of Protestant America, despite having been burned by attempting to set precise Advent dates, continued to advocate prepping for time's end. They remained charged with the Holy Spirit in the firm belief that the prophetic message about America's manifest destiny written on the back of their dollar bill would come to pass in the new century. Early hints of a countdown began in the 1880s with the charge that if millions of Protestants were mobilized worldwide, the Gospel could reach every living soul on the planet. Such a call for action made clear that America was ready to emerge as the focal point of apocalyptic religion. Though it would later be regarded as a bit too optimistic, the outburst of spirit would create the Pentecostal movement (a faith based on the infallibility of Scripture and direct personal experience with the Holy Spirit) that would peak during the next century in Protestant evangelism in America and abroad.

For the first time in history the call to human action in the face of encroaching materialism and deterministic science sought spiritual energy for social and personal renewal *outside* mainstream American religion. This late nineteenth-century renewal came in part out of what historians of religion formally call dispensationalism.[1] Like the prophecies of Joachim of Fiore referred to in chapter 2, premillennialist thinking, as we learned, holds that God's plan for humanity is arranged according to a series of stages, or dispensations. As interpreted by the influential nineteenth-century British preacher John Nelson Darby (1800–1882), who extensively toured America in the mid-nineteenth century, the cycle that ended with the Crucifixion was followed by the church age, in which we live today in anticipation of the Second Coming. Darby named the next cycle the Rapture (a term that seems to have stuck), literally a "carrying off"; this is the time when Christ will come down from heaven and reunite with his flock—but not before the seven-year rule of Antichrist known as the Tribulation, described in the New Testament book of Matthew.[2] We are all familiar with the basic outline of the rest of the story since the time of Zoroaster: in the battle of Armageddon that ends the Tribulation, Christ, accompanied by his saintly army, will defeat Antichrist and his demonic forces. Next follows the Millennium in which Christ will reign. After a final, failed effort by Satan's armies, the dead will rise up and we all will face the final event—the Last Judgment.

As we have also seen, dispensational prophecy writing appealed especially to American society in the nineteenth century, when the growing evangelical revitalist movement known as the Second Great Awakening had begun to challenge more liberal orthodox theological interpretations of Scripture. For evangelicals the wisdom written in the Bible was believed to have been divinely inspired. Add to this the growing public opinion that imagined ancient ways of thinking were being eroded by a decaying culture characterized by an increase in crime, corporate corruption and greed, and a general decline in the efficacy of its social institutions—just the sort of wickedness that would foreshadow the Second Coming. One dispensational preacher compared New York City—then, as now, the financial capital of the United States—to the Babylon described in Revelation: a place of congested wealth and excess, a wanton metropolis marked for destruction.[3] Wrote another, "I don't find any place where God says the world is to grow better and better . . . I find that the earth is to grow worse and worse . . . The general tendency is for man to degenerate."[4] At the same time there existed, alongside this general attitude of downsliding world history shared by most dispensationalists, another way of thinking and behaving that would also play a role in shaping contemporary thought. Redemption would take on decidedly more secular aspects, especially when it came to human action.

We learned in chapter 2 that millennialism—the parsing out of the road to apocalypse in 1,000-year segments—claimed roots in biblical Scripture. Though mere mileposts along the way, century markers were also thought to synchronize with nature's cataclysms. The popular French phrase for century's end that titles the present chapter can be traced back to 1885.[5] During the 1890s its adjectivized form describing literature, statesmanship, and morality in general pointed the way forward to a public weary of the misery the nineteenth century had wrought. It was as if it were an automatic process: just wipe the slate clean and start a new centennial count.

The recognition of century's end as a moment heralding cultural rebirth began in earnest at the overturn of the thirteenth, according to historian Hillel Schwartz.[6] The idea was fostered by a combination of cultural coincidences: the development and widespread popular usage of a AD/BC standard calendar, the notion of an arithmetical sense of time, the idea of depicting history in terms of periods and looking for conjunctions of events at the interfaces between them, the conservative philosophy of the decay of social institutions and moral behavior—and finally prophecy, which played a major role in setting up the arrival of a new age at the big turnover of time's odometer.

"Suddenly, absolutely, the Woman with a Past disappeared from the stage. It is remarkable. We called her fin-de-siècle. The century finished and she no longer exists."[7] So heralded a popular turn-of-the-century magazine editorial.

By the end of the nineteenth century, America had fought two wars of independence and the Civil War and was living through an economic depression. Between 1850 and 1890, as noted in the previous chapter, millennialism subsided. What remained of it during this quiescent, rule-bound period was mainly secular. Radical Millerism had become mainstream Seventh-day Adventism. Clock-setting apocalyptic anxieties had given way to perfectionist pursuits in the realm of economic and political thought. Many popular writers regarded the Gay Nineties as a hedonistic decade filled with decadent art, a loss of religious faith, and the decline of family life, characterized, as one of them put it, by a feeling of "imminent perdition and extinction."[8] But the pessimists were more than counterbalanced by the social reformers, who exuded an underlying optimism that, with the help of human action, was sure to blossom in the coming twentieth century. A host of books began to appear with the word *New* in the title. These works praised the technological and scientific advances and the general pace of progress in a nation now beginning to establish itself on an international level.

"They were all seekers of salvation, from the ecstatic Puritan to the vague yearners after New Thought," wrote Gilbert Seldes in 1927.[9] Today's version of secular perfectionism takes the form of self-help movements, such as the low-carb diet, colonics, yoga, extreme exercise, and vitamin therapy. But the New Thought movement is its unmistakable ancestor—a metaphysical mind-cure philosophy originating out of a Yankee can-do attitude spawned in the 1890s and peaking in popularity early in the twentieth century.

The idea of harnessing nature's hidden forces to improve the self was first popularized in mid-eighteenth-century Europe, when the scientific community began to conduct experiments attesting to the power of magnets. Franz Anton Mesmer, a Swiss-German physician, used *magnetisme animal* (animal magnetism), a magnetic fluid he believed permeated all living things, as a means of curing diseases. The logic was a simple spin-off of the rational, physical justification for belief in astrology: if the moon can raise tides in the ocean, could it not govern tides in the affairs of people? Likewise, why couldn't the pull of an iron magnet, which attracts certain physical elements, also affect one's bodily fluids? To experiment to that effect, Mesmer built a contraption consisting of several water-filled jars, with magnets immersed within and connected together via a metal band. He placed them in a water-filled tub and sprinkled in a coarse iron powder. Into this *baquet* he immersed his patients (very often attractive young women) in the midst of the jars, carefully placing magnets on the pained parts of their bodies. In the course of one of his therapies involving bleeding, Mesmer happened to notice an acceleration in blood flow when he approached a patient, accompanied by a lessening when he retreated. Was he, himself, a magnet? he wondered. Eventually, Mesmer would discard the ponderous bathtub and use his own animal magnetism to cure his patients. He became convinced that he could recharge himself by placing magnets in his shirt pockets, pants, and underwear. By these methods Mesmer claimed he could cure blindness, headache, backache, sexual inhibition—even boredom. His hands-on therapy necessitated prolonged kneading of bodily parts, especially thighs and breasts.

Under investigation by the Morality Police of Vienna, Mesmer fled to Paris, where he opened an even more popular and successful practice in a perfumed séance parlor decorated with mirrors, crystals, and fancy clocks. To strains of classical music, the charismatic healer would enter the parlor clad in a flowing robe, a wand in hand. In episodes akin to scenes accompanying a televangelist's sermon, members of the audience with whom he made contact would go into convulsions, ranting, raving, and writhing on the floor as their maladies seemingly fled their bodies. The commission of scientific investigators who tracked Mesmer down in Paris conducted experiments of their own. They concluded that what happened had nothing to do with magnetic forces, but rather was the result of the imagination, which diffused "tranquility over the senses [thus calling into play] the genial influences of hope."[10] But Mesmer's theory of animal magnetism, which would later give rise to the medical practice of hypnotism, remained attractive because it resonated with the newly popular idea that all phenomena could be explained by science—at least to a general, if not soundly scientifically informed, audience.

Physicians and Harvard professors alike investigated the potential of animal magnetism and its uses. Could it be employed to purify and perfect oneself, in the same way as taking a mineral bath? Perhaps, thought the new breed of secular perfectionists, a decaying lifeless society could be recharged by concentrated contact with the universal fluid that flows through it.

A nineteenth-century clockmaker from Maine by the name of Phineas P. Quimby (1802–1866) picked up on Mesmer's ideas. An avid student of mesmerism, Quimby had become fixed on the notion that magnetism possessed curative properties. Like Mesmer, Quimby experimented on those who came to him with complaints of various ailments by transferring the magnetic current he believed ran through his body to that of a patient with whom he remained in direct contact. For example, his cure for bellyache involved placing one hand on the abdomen of his patient, while rubbing the top of the patient's head with the other. Quimby also noticed that symptoms related to his own afflictions (he was tubercular) abated when he took to the fresh air in the countryside. As he began to explore what it was about the relationship between himself and nature that affected various maladies, he came to the conclusion that magnetic energy itself was not as important as the power of the mind. The message was simple: if you change what you *believe* about what ails you, then you can get better. In other words, both the cause and the cure reside in the willpower of the mind. If you can discipline yourself to bring forth your subconscious powers, then you can affect how nature influences you. You can mentally heal yourself. As Quimby put it: "I give no medicine and make no outward applications, but simply sit by the patient, tell him what he thinks is his disease, and my explanation is the cure . . . If I succeed in correcting his errors, I change the fluids of his system, and establish the truth of health. The truth is the cure."[11]

Quimby may have been one of America's earliest self-help gurus, but let's not overlook the spiritual aspects of his notion of self-perfection: first, he believed that his gifts for healing were God given, and second, he insisted that his patients surrender their will to the all-powerful God who had appointed Quimby his intermediary; for God, being perfect and all good, never brought illness nor any other form of evil into the world. Here was a novel way to deal with evil that possessed a decided advantage over the way orthodox Christianity handled it: you simply will it out of existence. Furthermore, if you can be redeemed from the imagined evils of disease, then you might also have within you the power to avert the biggest illusion and the worst of all evils—death. No wonder the dead respond to us via séances and automatic writing. They aren't dead at all, reasoned Quimby. They are just a part of the supernatural ether that pervades the entire universe.

In the hands of Mary Baker Eddy, a Quimby disciple, Christian Science, which built a perfectionist-oriented church around his philosophy, would go a step further. Unhappiness doesn't really exist. It is only a symptom of our imperfections as a human race. In the course of human evolution, which Christian Scientists viewed as a transcendentally guided, progressive development, it will go away, for the souls of men are promised better things. "Man's body is his holy temple," read Eddy's credo, and every cell of it is controlled by the mind: "We affirm that the kingdom of Heaven is within us . . . and that we should be perfect even as our Father in Heaven is perfect . . . We affirm Heaven here and now, the life everlasting that becomes conscious immortality, the communion of mind with mind throughout the universe of thought, the nothingness of all error and negation, including death . . . and the quickened realization of the indwelling God in each soul that is making a new heaven and a new earth."[12]

The power, then, is in our hands. The more we aid in the evolutionary process by practicing self-discipline, the sooner will the ultimate good of heaven on Earth come about through the hidden forces of nature.

To acquire a firmer scientific bent to his theories of healing, Quimby became attracted to the writings of a less well known but highly influential student of theology named Warren Felt Evans (1817–1889). He was responsible for codifying the concept of mental healing via six books he wrote on the subject. Evans added a tone of millennial progression to his cure by predicting the coming of a "New Age" of the Holy Spirit that would soon dawn upon the world. If we are a direct emanation from God, wrote Evans, then the human spirit must also possess godly powers. Becoming conscious of the "I am" within us is a part of the exercise that we must all get involved in if we are to pursue the universal community of new thinkers that awaits us here on earth. Evans's multivolume work would spawn a generation of mental healers, lesson givers, and public lecturers who would popularize the New Thought ideology and ultimately carry it to the mainstream.

Evans seized the findings of contemporary science to articulate his spiritualist doctrine. The existence of the *luminiferous ether*, a "light-bearing," massless substance that pervaded all space and was believed to be responsible for the propagation of light, had been gaining wide acceptance by experimental physicists in the last quarter of the nineteenth century. Few doubted the possibility that energy could be transported across pure vacuum in the vast interstellar realm. But could the ether possess metaphysical properties unknown to conventional science? Evans wondered. Thinking along the lines of Mesmer, he speculated that this "astral light," as he termed it, might be controlled by human thought and used to free the body from its present form. Could astral light be the missing link between humanity's material and spiritual essence? Indeed, might it be the very light of Christ revealed in the New Testament?

Think of the advantages of being able to harness the power of God within us to cure ourselves of disease, Evans went on. But how to get at it? He recommended practicing deep breathing in total silence as a way to evoke good thoughts that would lead to sound healing. In the generation that followed, a community of mental healers promoting lectures, seminars, and workshops coalesced around the "mental science" books in which Evans expounded his theories; for example, those who recited the pledge of allegiance of the Psychic Club of America vowed to radiate thoughts of encouragement, love, and success to their brethren. If the telegraph and telephone had made it possible to transmit words over long distances, why could not the human mind do the same via the luminiferous ether?

At a more secular level, some of the roots of New Thought are sympathetic to what historians call New England transcendentalism, especially as conveyed in the writing of Ralph Waldo Emerson (1803–1892). Emerson wrote a romantic essay entitled *Nature.*[13] His form of primitivism encouraged readers to reclaim a lost legacy from their ancient ancestors. Far from merely appreciating the sheer beauty of the natural world and all that it offers to nurture us, we need to discipline ourselves, train ourselves to tune in to nature's spiritual side. By immersing the self in nature, he believed, one experiences a deeper reality—a deeper truth. We can refashion, re-create reality. Spirit isn't just something to be believed in or not, Emerson argued—it exists throughout nature; and since we are connected to nature, it resides within us. We need to explore the connection beyond the senses and make what was once unconscious truth a part of new knowledge gained by living it—by seeing it up close in nature's manifold creations.

Emerson, who started as a Unitarian minister, practiced what he preached. Joined by members of the Transcendental Club, consisting mostly of scholarly elites from the circum-Harvard community (Henry Wadsworth Longfellow, Henry David Thoreau, James Russell Lowell, Amos B. Alcott, Louis Agassiz (a prominent Harvard paleontologist and critic of Darwinism), and painter-writer William James Stillman), he participated in lengthy encampments in the remote wilderness of the Adirondack Mountains of upstate New York. On one occasion, ten club members camped out in the woods at the edge of a lake. They fished for trout; they hiked, climbed mountains, hunted deer, and foraged berries (ably assisted by experienced guides), for weeks not once sighting any other members of their species. Stillman, the trip organizer, grasps the transcendent imagination of his friend in his diary and in a famous painting (figure 4.1); he tells us that Emerson was essentially primitive and that his first contact with the woods was a mystical experience: "He seemed to be a living question, perpetually integrating his impressions of all that there was to be seen. The rest of us were always at the surface of things . . . but Emerson in the forest, or looking at the sunset from the lake, seemed to be looking through the phenomena, studying them by their reflects on an inner speculum."[14]

FIGURE 4.1. Philosophers' Camp was located in the remote wilderness of the Adirondack Mountains in upstate New York. There nineteenth-century New England transcendentalists, including Ralph Waldo Emerson, sought to escape the corrupt modern world by reconnecting with a pristine primitive landscape. (Courtesy Concord Free Public Library.)

Emerson's lengthy poem, *The Adirondacs* (1858), which he dedicated to his fellow travelers, conveys a sense of longing to immerse oneself in the mysteries of nature:

> And presently the sky is changed; O world!
> What pictures and what harmonies are thine!
> The clouds are rich and dark, the air serene
> So like the soul of me, what if 't were me?
> A melancholy better than all mirth.
> Comes the sweet sadness at the retrospect,
> Or at the foresight of obscure years?
> Like you slow-sailing cloudy promontory
> Whereon the purple iris dwells in beauty
> Superior to all its gaudy skirts.
> And, that no day of life may lack romance,

The spiritual stars rise nightly, shedding down
A private beam into each severed heart.
Daily the bending skies solicit man,
The seasons chariot him from this exile,
The rainbow hours bedeck his glowing chair,
The storm-winds urge the heavy weeks along,
Suns haste to set, that so remoter lights
Beckon the wanderer to his vaster home.

By the turn of the century, New Thought—decidedly secular and ethnically mostly middle-class white—had turned into a social movement. It became tied to political progressivism, anticapitalism, and government care for the homeless. The movement included an interest in women's suffrage and feminism, not to mention socialism in general. Can-do advocates spun out titles such as *The Science of Right Thinking, Think and Grow Rich, Power That Wins,* and *The Science of Being Great.* Evans's flame of optimistic passion about thinking positively and being proactive would be rekindled half a century later during the postwar optimistic 1950s, in best-selling popular works by Norman Vincent Peale (*The Power of Positive Thinking*) and Dale Carnegie (*How to Win Friends and Influence People*).

The proactive philosophy of New Thought empowerment at the fin de siècle seemed a long way from the sin- and fear-strewn road to perfection trod by middle-class America at the beginning of the nineteenth century. Parodying it in this chapter's epigraph, Gilbert Seldes attributed much of the shift to a society that became weary of its interminable anxiety concerning the problems of sin, evil, and predestination regarding the afterlife, accompanied by a general attraction toward exploring the limitless possibilities for man in the work of philosophers, scientists, and engineers that developed late in that century. Revivalists like Quimby and Evans had quelled the fever of millennialism. They had seized the day by daring to advocate a sinless life on Earth capable of catapulting man to the highest order of nature.

As one might anticipate, America promoted New Thought by doing business with it. Along came the opportunistic entrepreneurs with their air-purifying machines, smokeless cigars (the electronic cigarette is today's counterpart), Sylvester Graham's crackers, John Kellogg's cornflakes, and bookstores stacked high with volumes on how to get rich by praying,

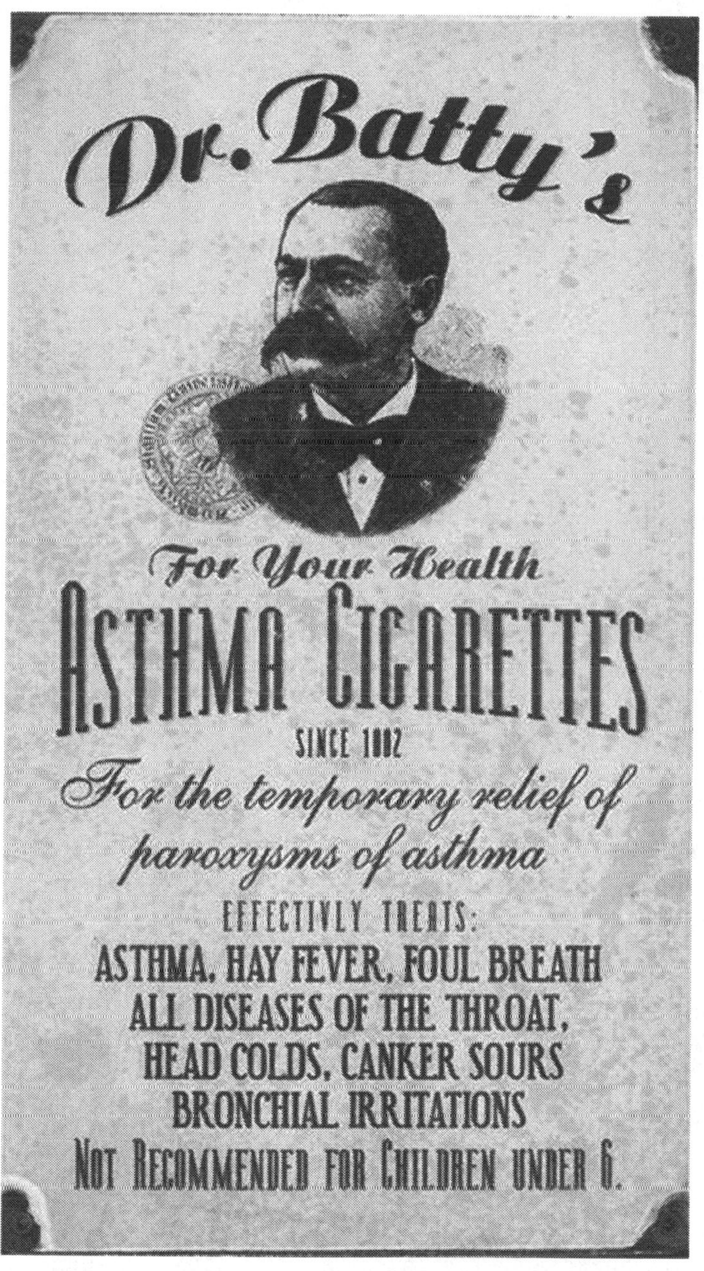

FIGURE 4.2. Ads for "asthma cigarettes," health foods, and self-help books were staples of the late nineteenth-century New Thought perfectionist movement.

developing a success-oriented mind set, and embracing a philosophy that *you can if you believe you can* (figure 4.2).

Kellogg, for example, focused his efforts on saving the lower end of the digestive tract. He recommended frequent enemas. He also set out to devise a supremely bland product to induce regularity. A devout Seventh-day Adventist, Kellogg believed the best way to purify yourself for entry into the next world was to avoid all spicy substances—which have a tendency to arouse the emotions. You should also eat plain foods to curb that terrible impulse to masturbate. Kellogg never imagined his cornflakes would become a national breakfast icon (thought not exactly for the reasons he suggested). Kellogg was influenced by Sylvester Graham (1794–1851), whom we met earlier, a devotee of the early temperance movement. His principal pathway to purification lay in vegetarianism—his recommended cure for addiction to alcohol and sexual excess. For Graham, a meat-based diet was unhealthy because it stimulated sexual desire, thereby irritating the body and leading to disease. His namesake contribution to the American diet started out as an additive-free "whole wheat" bread darker in color than the bleached product the baking industry thought more cosmetically appealing. Still, both Graham's and Kellogg's semisecular pathways to purification and self-improvement seem a long way from the alternatives that would be put forth in the New Age movement to follow.

The introduction of works on Yoga, first translated into English in the 1890s, became a part of the perfectionist jumble. There were 195 rules on how to sit, how to hold your head, how to empty your mind, how to breathe, and how to behave in general. The proper way to chew your food was especially critical. One instructional text inquired: Do you know that mastication liberates *prana* (pure energy, the active principle of life)? It separates everything you put in your mouth into minute bits. Physics and chemistry are involved, too. The more you chew the better you help liberate "electrons of food-Prana."[15] Then comes the chemical action of the saliva, which propels the food-Prana to your flesh and bone and to every part of your body, where it furnishes vitality to the cells. But if you don't pack good thoughts in your head while you're filling your mouth, nothing will come of the process. One proponent confidently tells skeptical readers that even though food-Prana electrons have yet to be detected in the lab, "future investigators will scientifically prove their existence."[16]

Meanwhile, the social turmoil that followed the fin de siècle fanned the embers of the old dispensational premillennialist fires fueled by theories about fulfillment via biblical prophecy. World Wars I and II and the Russian Revolution were all excellent candidates that fit the description of events associated with the Tribulation. Lenin, Stalin, Mussolini, and Hitler all took their turns embodying middle-class America's version of Antichrist. The ticking time clock of nuclear holocaust appeared on the scene not long after the A-bomb was dropped on Hiroshima. Many dispensationalists were ecstatic when the Jews were returned to Palestine under the provisions of the 1917 Balfour Declaration. The reestablishment of a Jewish homeland was a clear sign of the beginning of time's end. They believed the Jews had disobeyed God when they rejected Jesus as his son. But God would deal with them at the beginning of the next age, by which time they would have returned to their homeland. There they would undergo great suffering; but God would give them a chance to be saved at the Second Coming. Added to all of these seminal world events in the first half of the twentieth century were the Great Depression of the 1930s and a drastic change in population demographics, with immigrants entering the United States from all parts of Europe, bringing with them a variety of religions, most of them non-Protestant.

When you sense that prophecy is being fulfilled by events happening in the world, you are all the more driven to believe in it. In the minds of a growing cadre of evangelicals keenly tuned to the fundamentalist notion that the course of world affairs had already been writ in the Scriptures, events following the two world wars provided grist for the mill of biblical prophecy and frontloaded the machinery that would grind out New Age prognostication, the subject of part III (chapters 6–9). Of significance in these ideologies is the shared notion that deeper truth and universal wisdom can be acquired *from afar*—from the strange, the foreign, the exotic—an idea that, as we shall see after we briefly trace the fascinating history of nineteenth-century spiritualism and its relation to New Age history in the next chapter, continues to percolate through contemporary versions of New Age philosophy.

Catherine Albanese aptly characterizes American culture's continuing religious mentality as *metaphysical*, that is, highly preoccupied with questions about what lies beyond the world of the physical. That mentality is centered around four basic themes, which to this point we can see unfolding—especially in this chapter. First, there is a preoccupation with the powers of the mind and its capacity to attain altered states of consciousness, enabling it to "see" a world that lies beyond the physical plane; second, there is strong emphasis placed on the idea that a correspondence exists between these two worlds, such that what happens in one can be made to affect the other. Albanese's third metaphysical attitude is a kind of proactive notion in which energy and movement are the principal means of affectation; in other words, if there are discoverable, connectable sympathies and likenesses between the two worlds, we need only to perceive how the energies and movements in our everyday world can be controlled to affect the world beyond the ordinary senses—things that might need to be corrected, righted, overturned, and so on. Fourth and finally, America's metaphysical take intensifies during times when people yearn for salvation, feel the need of therapy, and search for ways of healing.[17] All of these attitudes involve magical thinking and magical practice, not so much in the usual way we think of magic, such as using natural means to control the transcendent, but what Albanese calls "mental magic." Here the imagination joins the body in order to attain mastery in the search for a state of contentment. You are in control. Succinctly put, "American magic comes down to salvation, and salvation means healing and therapy."[18]

5

Spiritualism and the Veiled Synthesis of Science and Religion

[The theosophical movement is] the mother of the occult and the single most important avenue of Eastern Teaching to the West.

—*Religious scholars James Lewis and Gordon Melton*

As we learned in chapter 1, the first wave of nineteenth-century spiritualism began in the Burned-over District as a consequence of the flowering of a number of alternative religions that claimed knowledge derived from secret sources. By century's end it had gone mainstream and become decidedly secular, though it still retained the philosophy of perfecting oneself handed down to it from the Second Great Awakening. Despite the sense of being overwhelmed by rampant materialism and its attendant machinery, late nineteenth-century Gilded Age reformers tended to view the world optimistically, applying a can-do attitude toward solving the world's problems: No matter how predetermined you might think the state of the world seems, you can use the untapped power of your mind to improve your situation. Cure baldness by rubbing your head and thinking good thoughts. Chew your food well to aid digestion. Smoke nicotineless cigars. Hypnotism, astrology, palmistry, and clairvoyance reached peaks of popularity in what would later come to be known as the New Thought movement. Of this all-encompassing, participatory, secular cosmology, journalist/author Gilbert Seldes mockingly remarked that it was dissatisfied with both out-of-touch Christianity and arrogant science's attempts to discredit it—yet it offered no real solutions of its own (Gilbert Seldes, epigraph to previous chapter).

Turn-of-the-century New Thought was more an avertive than a catastrophic sort of millennialism in that it held we can avoid the end by disciplining ourselves. The religious face of New Thought took on strong eastward leanings, which took root in the theosophical, or "divine wisdom" movement.[1] It was established in New York City in the 1870s and enjoys a resurgence in popularity today. (The society's headquarters is still housed on East 48th St. in New York.)

The organization sought to demonstrate to Protestant and Catholic alike that their most cherished ideals were based on the wisdom of the ancient magi; so too was all scientific knowledge and discovery. At least this was the rather ambitious mission laid out by cofounder Henry Steel Olcott in his 1875 inaugural address to the newly formed Theosophical Society, a club dedicated to exploring the secret laws of nature believed to have once been familiar to Chaldeans and Egyptians but unknown to the world of modern science.

The bible of theosophy, at least in its earliest stages of development, was mystic Helena Blavatsky's massive two-volume tome, *Isis Unveiled*, a rambling discourse on the spiritually dominated world we live in.[2] In his treatment of nineteenth-century theosophy, historian of esotericism Joscelyn Godwin lists among the major themes in *Isis Unveiled* the superiority of Eastern and Egyptian wisdom compared to modern science, the existence of a secret tradition handed down through history by adepts, the validity of all the world's religions, the evolution of the human soul, and the significance of spiritualism to human destiny.[3] *Isis* discloses Blavatsky's account of events that had transpired all around the world of antiquity, which proved that powerful forces lie hidden within all of us just waiting to be tapped. If we can harness these forces, she argued, we will be capable of propelling our ascent up a ladder of spiritual evolution that will lead to transcendent knowledge. We can do this not by contemplating the Bible but instead by getting in touch with the great Masters, or Mahatmas—wise men who reside in the distant Himalayas. As she put it: "There are, scattered throughout the world, a handful of thoughtful and solitary students, who pass their lives in obscurity, far from the rumors of the world, studying the great problems of the physical and spiritual universes. They have their secret records in which are preserved the fruits of the scholastic labors of the long line of recluses whose successors they are."[4] Here was one of the first attempts to seek truth via wisdom from sources far removed from the Western tradition—a theme that would become a staple of New Ageism in America.

Helena Petrovna Blavatsky (1831–1891), aka Madam Blavatsky, a onetime circus equestrienne and ballet dancer, claimed descent from a family of Russian aristocrats. She also identified herself as an adept, that is, one with the special capacity to access wisdom by direct psychic transfer. There was no doubt in her mind that the sources of wisdom forging the bond between man and God lay in the East. Blavatsky had traveled extensively among and acquired intimacy with Indian people. She became convinced that, by following the instructions of the sages of the East and observing their supernatural feats, such as levitations, charming snakes, and taming wild animals with magical incantations, she had rendered herself capable of comprehending a meaningful synthesis of the approaches of science and religion to the apprehension of universal truths.

Does the reader imagine that any prestidigitator could produce the same manifestation? an assured Blavatsky inquired of her audience, which consisted generally of people bewildered by the seeming inconsistencies between science and religion—the one denying the reality of psychic phenomena without even some preliminary investigation, proffering only a theory of physical evolution deprived of any recognition of the evolution of the spirit, and the other offering only blind and passive acceptance of an unresponsive deity who does his will as he sees fit. Charismatic and articulate, Helena Blavatsky navigated the rarefied middle ground between two irreconcilable ideologies. At the heart of Blavatsky's explorations of ancient wisdom lay the belief that the symbols of all the world's mythologies possess a singular scientific foundation and substance. "Who can study the ancient myths without seeing that their similarity in conception, form, and spirit, is not the result of mere coincidence, but rather a concurrent design?"[5]

In coming chapters we will see these themes of the unification of wisdom and the superiority of primitive knowledge being given credence in the scholarly world. They would blossom, for example, in the 1920s in Sir James Frazer's *The Golden Bough* into the notion that there is a common origin to all myth, with deeper universal truths rooted in the distant past.[6] This version of the monomyth would be further elaborated in celebrated author Aldous

Huxley's *Perennial* Philosophy, historian of religion Mircea Eliade's *Myth of the Eternal Return* and, later, in historians of science Giorgio de Santillana and Hertha von Dechend's *Hamlet's Mill*, a text that would become the bible of late twentieth-century New Agers and 2012 end-date prophets.[7]

Madam Blavatsky contended that the ancients knew even more about certain sciences than their modern counterparts. This is because such knowledge, in the form of "secret doctrines" (after the title of her later multivolume work) was confined to the temples, veiled from the public, and exposed only to elite priests.[8] But, she assured, the secrets long kept would soon be revealed. In the new era, promised Blavatsky, we will eventually come to understand that "ancient religion" was in total harmony with nature and "ancient science embraced all that can be known."[9]

Why the faraway East? The Russian mystic may have acquired some of her revelations directly from the work of an obscure British historian, Godfrey Higgins, who wrote a two-volume, 1,536-page work (published posthumously in 1833) with the suggestive title *Anacalypsis: An Attempt to Draw Aside the Veil of the Saitic Isis into the Origin of Languages, Nations, and Religions*.[10] Higgins claimed to reveal the existence of an ancient universal religion (he called it Pandeism), out of which all religious doctrines originated—a religion that yet survives as a secret, fragmented sect that carries its ancient messages in parts of Greece, the Middle East, and India, with its origins in the last. "[My message] will be perfectly understood by my Masonic friends," wrote Higgins.[11]

Higgins's account of world ages, which he claims to have acquired via long-held secrets of gnostic Freemasonry, is based on the theory that there was a time when the earth's axis of rotation was not inclined to the pole of its orbit. At this time, when the north polar regions were warm, God directly infused life into matter, creating the first race and imbuing it with a single religion, based on "the One." This was a golden age—war free, weapon free, money free. Vestiges of it remain in Eastern Buddhism. But disruption, including floods and an encounter with a comet, brought an end to this perfect primordial world. These disruptions created the astronomical phenomenon of the precession of the equinoxes (to be discussed in greater detail in chapter 6) and produced multiple cycles of destruction and renewal, the most recent having destroyed the great pyramids. These cycles, Higgins claims, were known to the Chaldeans, who commemorated them in their secret writings by encoding them in names and phrases wherein letters possess numerical equivalents. He tells us that cyclic changes are accompanied by wars, political divisions, and messianic expectations; thus the arrival of Jesus, Muhammad, and the Crusades all occurred at conjunction points of cosmic cycles. Higgins's purpose in writing *Anacalypsis* was to realize the secret doctrine of the ancients in order that one might cultivate one's virtue in order to be reabsorbed into the One.[12]

Historian Isaac Lubelsky traces the introduction of Oriental imagery as the root source of higher knowledge further back, to British romantic Sir William Jones. Jones was a lawyer and an authority on Oriental languages—he wrote a book on Persian grammar. Beginning in 1783 he began extensive travel in India in search of what he called the "mother-lode of human civilization."[13] With Charles Wilkins, a worker for the East India Company and translator of the *Bhagavad-Gita* creation story, he founded the Asiatic Society of Bengal, which dedicated itself to examining the East as the ancient homeland of European wisdom, specifically "the study of man and nature, science and art," advocating that "the most efficient tool . . . was the study of ancient languages."[14] Jones's idea attained scholarly credibility a century later when the influential Sanskrit linguist Friedrich Max Müller, who had become familiar with Jones's work, delivered a series of lectures in 1882, "India: What Can It Teach Us?"

For Müller, the study of language was the key to answering the question of how India, a country so backward and primitive, could ever have given rise to the intellectual glories of the West: "We all come from the East—all that we value most has come to us from the East, and in going to the East, not only those who have received a special Oriental training, but everybody who had enjoyed the advantages of a liberal, that is, of a truly historical education, ought to feel that he is going to his 'old home,' full of memories, *if only he can read them* [my italics]."[15] Lubelsky traces the blossoming of the Aryan myth that the common source of all religions—especially Christianity—lay in the Vedas, the ancient Sanskrit texts believed to be the oldest writings of Hinduism. Employing the methodology of philological research, and given his scholarly renown—not to mention his connections, especially in the English-speaking world, with scholars as well as cultural, political, and scientific figures of note—Max Müller would found the new discipline of comparative religion.

Müller believed there was a common origin to all religions that arose out of spiritual needs all humans possess—the sui generis theory of the origin of religion discussed in chapter 2. Oriental expressions of faith were closer to that universal truth than those espoused in the West. His assertions led to Darwinist attacks on his ideas and his ultimate banishment from academic circles.

Helena Blavatsky admired Müller; she fancied herself an expert on his writing. Originally, the German linguist was quite taken with this "Polish prophetess" and her theosophical ally Henry Steel Olcott; but he soon realized that there was little scholarly depth to her "wild ideas about the Veda."[16] Ultimately he pronounced Blavatsky both ignorant and egocentric. "Like many people in our time," he wrote, "she was, I believe, in search of a religion which she could honestly embrace . . . she seems to have discovered through the dark mists of imperfect translations some of the brilliant rays of truth which issue from the Upanishads and the ancient Vedanta philosophy of India . . . Unfortunately, she took it in her head that it was incumbent on every founder of religion to perform miracles . . . her ambition was to found a religion."[17]

Regardless of the most immediate sources of her claimed religious wisdom, a critical look at the ancient scientific aspects of Helena Blavatsky's ideas exemplified in *Isis Unveiled* also betrays a poor understanding of the workings of the science of her times, coupled with a naive and uncritical acceptance of randomly selected contemporary scientific reportage. For example, coincident with Alexander Graham Bell's invention of the telephone, Blavatsky tells the story of one of the Cleopatras having sent "news by a wire."[18] Likewise, she portrays Nordic Thor, handling his thunderbolt with iron gauntlets and wearing a magical belt, as having been thoroughly acquainted with the fundamental properties of electricity: Thor's belt, she tells readers, is really a closed electrical circuit; his gauntlets are electrical conductors; and his thunderbolt is actually a lightning rod. Blavatsky also discloses that the ancient Inca of Peru had inscribed sacred hieroglyphs telling of an underground tunnel that ran from Cusco, the Inca capital, to Lima and beyond—knowledge she had acquired from an accurate plan of the tunnel given her by a Peruvian wise man. This is a common trait among prophets and futurist visionaries: co-opting contemporary science by borrowing both its theories and its language. We encountered an early example of it in

Cotton Mather's writings and we will find many more in the formulations of 2012 prophets.

Darwin's 1859 publication of *On the Origin of Species* had stirred controversy in ongoing debates, dating back at least to the eighteenth-century French Enlightenment, related to the problem of understanding the natural world and humanity's place in it. The unfolding of Darwin's version of history is based on the successful adaptation of various mutated forms of life to contingent environmental conditions. A well-known example emanates from the study of the finches of the Galápagos Islands. Each bird is equipped with its own form of beak to pick up the seeds of a particular size scattered over its home island. But when the vagaries of weather and climate produce a long-term deficiency of one seed population in favor of another, things change. For example, suppose prolonged winds blow a hardier seed from one neighboring island to the next. Then the capacity of the particular finches on that island to acquire their diet is hindered. If the new replacement seed is too large to fit the open beak of these finches they will not survive. On the other hand, birds that happen by accident to be born with slightly oversized beaks will thrive; consequently they will propagate their own strain of large-beaked finches. Thus Darwin's developmental notion of change is based on chance and contingency; there is no design, no progress, no destiny. This makes his theory difficult to reconcile with an unfolding history guided by divine plan, the idea common not only to the apocalyptically minded but also to those who follow most traditional norms of religion.

Blavatsky concocted a morally based antidote to Darwin's evolutionary scheme. Adapted largely from warmed-over East Indian sacred lore, her version of evolution consisted of a reworking of many of the Christian themes evident in the book of Revelation. Creation is conceived out of an egg floating on the waters of the cosmos. The creator Brahma enters the egg to create three worlds: earth, air, and heaven. He preserves his creations for a long time before destroying them in flames. The day (one day of Brahma is 4,320,000 years long), also called one breath of Brahma, is subdivided into intervals that grow progressively shorter and during which the world becomes more corrupt. Then he re-creates the world. So begins another breath, except this time the evolutionary process reverses itself and becomes more progressive.

There will be tribulations along the way, warned clairvoyant Blavatsky. An interval black with horror lies only nine years ahead of us (1897), for then humans will stand "at the very close of the cycle of 5,000 years of the present Aryan Kaliyuga [a 1,800-year subcycle]."[19] Then, in an apocalyptic twist, Blavatsky predicts that a tear in the Veil of Nature will occur, and the enemy—materialistic science—will be dealt a deathblow.

I view the *Isis* narrative as a form of dispensationalism, in the sense that the history of the world is—past and future—predetermined or guided by stages. It makes use of the rebirthing process at each stage in human evolution via a series of "rounds" of existence characterized by rest periods punctuated by action episodes in which life's energy is suddenly redistributed. We live in one of these anticipatory stages (as in the Christian form of dispensationalism, there would be seven all together).

The races that lived in those earlier eras, including Atlantis, fell by the wayside because they destroyed themselves through greed and misuse of their resources. But we retain the potential to become godlike, the "animal Monad," the "higher self," as Blavatsky termed it, provided we use our thought to harness this magical power—thus unveiling Isis. The minds of every living being will suddenly be awakened and all our thoughts will become crystal clear. Then we shall give birth to a new race of humanity that will follow the laws of the age of purity, finally reclaiming the unified age of mind and spirit that existed before the flood.

Received wisdom about the root races in Blavatsky's theory of world ages is further articulated in the *The Secret Doctrine*. This work is worth dissecting a bit, since elements of the massive tome, especially the idea of apocalyptic—in the sense of sudden—transformations in the evolution of humanity, are central to the contemporary esoteric philosophy we'll explore later.

The theory of World Ages is expounded in *The Secret Doctrine* in a lengthy narrative that offers a morally centered Darwinesque narrative. It begins with a first generation of superhumans who inhabited an "Imperishable Sacred Land." These ethereal beings lived in a timeless, nonmaterial world. They melted away and "exhaled" a second humanity with slightly more human characteristics. The third root race produced the separation of sexes and, in at least part of its population, ego, willpower, and the ability to acquire knowledge. Such was the origin of the adepts of the future. But one segment of this population delayed its total conversion to the material state. Consequently, when these beings were ready to mate, only those of inferior degree remained to accommodate them. These would become the ancestors of the ordinary human race. Finally, the segment that further deferred its incarnation suffered the misfortune of having mated with females of an ape-like race, from which all contemporary simians descended. Thus Blavatsky cleverly counters the most contentious and degrading element perceived in Darwin's version of evolution by natural selection, both then and now, by popular culture: that humans are the descendants of apes.

The fourth race, which Blavatsky identifies with Atlantis, became adept in science and technology. It was composed of giant-sized humans, natural-born mediums capable of flying in the air. They understood the power of the stars and precious stones and metals. But they did themselves in when their leaders came under the influence of one of their sorcerers who practiced bad magic. Except for the case of the first root race, which continues its godlike existence, transformations happened cataclysmically. There were great deluges; new lands appeared as old ones subsided; and the earth's axis shifted—all inexplicably perpetrated by undesirable human action, a kind of *karmic* energy. But the divine wisdom, born of the first generation, survived. It was passed on to the fifth root race via a secret fraternity sworn to keep it safe and secure, even as the unfit ones were swept off the face of the Earth. This is Madam Blavatsky's morally centered version of the "survival of the fittest" evolutionary principle.

Though Blavatsky's dating scheme appeared even then grossly out of joint with the geological record (she placed the fall of Atlantis 850,000 years in the past), it offered the palliative of human descent from a superhuman entity and gave Homo sapiens temporal primacy since our ancestors appeared on Earth before other animals—a small price to pay in the eyes of believers. Nature itself was capable of producing the lower orders, but it took a specific power to produce man's "spiritual, independent, and intellectual power(s)."[20] We can think of this transformation of races, then, as a continued state of becoming, or awakening, in which a kind of essence (a Monad) passes through a series of forms, becoming "Man" when the "Divine Ones" project and make alive in us the "Light of the Logos."

The trauma in this history prompts us to wonder whether there might once have been a golden age, but the question arises: What happened to it and how can we get it back? The Old Testament answer is clear: our progenitors misbehaved in the Garden of Eden. The sins of Adam and Eve are responsible for the vastly degraded world bequeathed us. The New Testament adds that only the son of God can be the vehicle for human atonement at a cosmic level. Those of us who renounce all sin can reap the benefits of his sacrifice on Judgment Day.

But even if there was an element of human sacrifice in the sinning and self-destructive behavior of Blavatsky's successive races, her theory offered an appealing kind of *participatory* cosmology—it satisfied. Look at what material science along with its newly acquired Darwinism handed us instead—the gloomy prospect of the finality of death. All humans are animals who acquired their existence by pure chance. We are assured no destiny of a future beyond our mortal existence. If the human personality does not survive death, how can there be a moral code of ethical principles around which to center our lives?

The revelation of a long-forgotten history that bore the promise of received wisdom and continuity from the root of descent of all mankind seemed especially attractive to the Anglo cultures of the 1880s and 1890s. Advances in technology had led many to believe that even death could be conquered. Psychical researchers in England and America were busily engaged in experiments in automatic writing, Ouija boards, and communication with the dead by rapping out a kind of Morse code (invented in the early 1840s) to experience a taste of what life after death was like in an afterworld where souls thrived in a strife-free, progressive society. These automatist-adepts saw themselves as the vital link in a plan to use Scriptures as a kind of historical intervention that held the potential to deliver all humanity from the threat of unrestrained, amoral chaos. Such a plan allowed them to understand contemporary events as acts in a drama that would end in redemption. Thus *human* consciousness becomes wedded to *cosmic* consciousness.

It is worth noting that the idea that humanity has passed through a number of states in its development is traceable, at least in the Western tradition, all the way back to Hesiod's *Works and Days*. The ninth-century BCE Greek poet laments the downward ladder of human history via a series of ages, whose characteristics are symbolized by the value of the metals from which they receive their names: Gold, Silver, Bronze, and Iron. The central theme is that the future of the world is closely tied to the natural world, and it is determined through ritual political acts.[21]

The golden race of mortals, Hesiod tells us, lived like ageless gods, with whom they mingled in a paradise of perpetual abundance, never needing to work a day to feed themselves. They died painless deaths simply by falling asleep. Then, for inexplicable reasons, the gods destroyed their creation and fashioned a silver race of childlike beings, who nursed under their mothers' care for 100 years only to live a short time as adults. Their lives were filled with self-induced torment for, despite being watched over by the spirits of the previous age, who roamed the atmosphere, they nonetheless "committed acts of ruinous hybris [arrogance prompted by pride] against one another and refused to worship the gods."[22] When they perished for disobeying the gods, they became the spirits of the underworld.

Hesiod's third race was devoted to warfare: "Bronze was the metal their weapons were made of, of bronze were their houses, bronze were the tools they used."[23] Done in by their unceasing militarism, the people of the age of bronze were forced to remove themselves to the cold house of Hades.

The antiprogressive trend in Hesiod's version of the history of the races is reversed, however, with the creation of the fourth race, members of the heroic age. Though they lived in abundance, like those who dwelled in the age of gold, they were drawn to war like their bronze age ancestors. These were the quasi-historical heroes who fought for Helen of Troy and in the war against Thebes. Many of them were rewarded with eternal afterlife on the Islands of the Blessed.

Finally came the awful present. Laments the poet: "Would that I now were no longer alive in the fifth age of men, but had died earlier or been born at a later time. For we live in the age of the iron race, when men shall never cease from labor and woe by day, and never be free from anguish at night, for hard are the cares that the gods will be giving."[24] Our toil will be unceasing, our benefits few. Our manners will be entirely lost; brother will fight brother, sons and daughters will care no longer for their aging parents (the gods will punish them fittingly by causing their babies to be born with gray hair). "Might will be justice, and one will destroy the other's city." All that will be left for mortals is "anguishing pains, but no defense against evil."[25] As Nicholas Campion explains, this is precisely the version of history written 500 years later by the prophet Daniel in the Old Testament, copied, at least in part, from Hesiod.[26]

In sum, Hesiod's is the epitome of the going-to-hell-in-a-handbasket view of the history of the world. Life consists of a state of initial blessedness that degenerates, its barometer meting out increased impiety, injustice, and hubris. It helps us to know that Hesiod's pessimistic outlook on the course of human history was conditioned by his own experiences. He was a hard-bitten, middling farmer and by nature a grumbler, who says he needed all the luck he could acquire in his efforts to tame the gods of his hometown of Askra, which he describes as "a miserable village near Helikon which is a bad place in winter, a hard one in summer, good never."[27]

The Hindu tradition, of which Blavatsky was well aware, offers a similar account of history as a succession of ages, labeled Yugas. These are the Krita (fortunate), Dwapara (second), Trefá (third), and Kali Yuga, the age of conflict. Their lengths are, respectively, 4,000, 3,000, 2,000, and 1,000 divine years, a divine year being 1,000 human years, each 360 days long. The Greek ages, which were likely imported from the Middle East, may have had an earlier connection with the Hindu. One difference, however, is that the Hindu Yugas recur in endless cycles of 4,320,000 years total duration.[28]

Details about timing are relevant here because, as we'll learn in chapter 10, the related number 432,000 figures prominently in later elaborations of the theory of the monomyth. But before we make too much of the independent invention of world ages (recall chapter 2), it should be noted that the Hindu theory of Yugas was likely a spinoff of the 360-day-based Babylonian calendar. Historian of astronomy John North believes it developed in the third century BCE.[29]

To summarize, in both the Greek and Hindu world age theories, time is an essence perceived discontinuously as a series of pulses characterized by long periods of constancy, wherein races live in a state of perfection endowed them by the gods, followed by rapidly occurring intervals of chaos, or decay, often triggered by catastrophic events—comets, earthquakes, floods, and other "signs of the times," in which divine principles become lost. In the development of Christianity this stage of the process would come to correspond to the Fall of Man, which may have been behind the gods' destruction of the golden age in Hesiod's cosmology. But something of the good is retained when, with renewed impetus provided by the spirit, a new creation takes place.

It is in the foregoing historical context that Blavatsky's theosophical wisdom needs to be placed in order for its impact on New Age ideas to be understood. She believed not only that waves of creation and destruction were guided and patterned, but also that in these creations there existed great sages who had either deciphered the mathematics of the patterning or had acquired it via direct contact with divine forces. They then passed their writings on to other guided prophets who could make use of the ancient wisdom to predict how the future would unfold. These are Helena Blavatsky's "secret doctrines."

In the highly materialist-driven world of the late nineteenth century, when Darwin's evolutionary notions threatened the idea of human progress, world age theories patterned after Blavatsky's offered a very comforting philosophy regarding the human condition: her democratic-sounding scenario cradles the possibility of redemption, of atoning for the errors of the past; moreover, it guarantees guidance by higher authority in a time of impending chaos.

At a deeper ideological level, Blavatsky's extraordinarily complicated account of prehistory, which attempted to pull together the torn pieces of the fabric of science and religion, comforted those who could not bear the burden of the randomized existence offered by Darwin's novel, frightening theory of natural and human history. Ordinary people needed evolution with hope, with a purpose—a history over which human will and action offered a measure of control. And all of it was encompassed by Blavatsky's theory of a singular age-old truth: "So far as human intellect can go in the ideal interpretation of the spiritual universe, its laws and powers, the last word was pronounced ages since . . . Let human beings submit themselves to torture for thousands of years to come; let theology perplex faith and maim it with the enforcing of incomprehensible dogmas in metaphysics; let science strengthen skepticism, by pulling down the tottering remains of spiritual intuition in mankind with her demonstrations of its fallibility, eternal truth can never be destroyed."[30]

In hindsight Joscelyn Godwin believes that Blavatsky's three most radical claims were:

a. man lived on earth prior not only to other mammals but also the dinosaurs.

b. periodic ice ages and floods separating the ages were caused by a karmic disturbance of the world's axis; and

c. man was born of a Superior Being and that consequently the seeds of all wisdom along with the secret of immortality had already been acquired long ago.[31]

Of these claims, the last one in particular conflicts with orthodox religion. It posits that all ancient religions are based on the same received wisdom, practiced by special initiates who knew of its existence and were aware of its power. The first two are more at odds with the findings of science.

Though the foundations of scientific dating systems were admittedly in their infancy in the 1880s, the techniques and empirical results, today clearly established, yet go ignored by many New Age prophets. To cite a contemporary example, consider the theories of John Anthony West, an independent researcher and TV producer who, in 1990, managed to persuade an American geologist employed at a legitimate university to look into weathering patterns affecting the Egyptian Sphinx. (West had read a statement in the literature suggesting that the sphinx had been subject to water erosion.) The results suggested that the rock out of which the monument was carved had indeed been exposed to lengthy periods of heavy rain, suggesting a date of origin well prior to the time of the Egyptian dynasties (7500–5000 BCE), early enough to support the theory of the lost continent of Atlantis. But both these findings are drastically out of line with the 2500 BCE date established by vastly more precise, convergent archaeological methods. Significantly, the geological findings were never presented to a body of peers for review. Instead, they were included in a piece in an edited book and publicly displayed via a sensational 1993 TV documentary entitled *The Mystery of the Sphinx*. (Today West advertises "Magical Egypt" trips for enthusiastic travelers.)

The West incident is worth mentioning at this point for two reasons that we shall take up in further detail shortly. First, even though the study purports to be scientific, it reveals blatant disregard of scientific evidence in the promotion of attention-getting theories, motivated largely out of ideologically based self-interest; West is an avowed Atlantean and a proponent of astrological prediction. Second, it is an excellent example of how one unorthodox theory leads to further unorthodoxies. Take, for example, Graham Hancock's monomythical *Fingerprints of the Gods*, which posits a worldwide culture that created Stonehenge, the pyramids of Egypt, and other great stone monuments around the world before it was destroyed by flood at the end of the Ice Age; and Robert Bauval and Adrian Gilbert's *Orion Mystery*, which dates the pyramids, via alignment with the stars of Orion's Belt, to 10,500 BCE.[32]

New Age historian Gordon Melton calls the theosophical movement the "mother of the occult" in contemporary America and "the single most important avenue of Eastern teaching to the West."[33] The March 1970 issue of *McCall's* magazine heralded Helena Petrovna Blavatsky as "The Founding Mother of the Occult in America." The timely rebirth of the popular movement she founded would give rise to a host of books about her profound influence on the occult side of the twentieth-century American psyche.[34]

In closing, clarification of the oft-misused word *occult* is worth giving here. James Webb defines the term as knowledge rejected based on its relationship to the dominant institutions associated with Christianity, rather than with establishment science, which validates acceptable knowledge on the basis of its capacity to be falsified via empirical test.[35] Systems of belief attached to occult knowledge are suppressed in the interests of achieving religious hegemony, with the result that worldviews based on rejected knowledge develop in direct opposition to those that prevail—what Michael Barkun calls "the cultural dumping ground of the heretical, the unfashionable, and the dangerous."[36] He cites nineteenth-century spiritualism, theosophy, fringe Christian sects, and the increased role of the pseudosciences, with which we will deal in the next chapter. Webb and Barkun agree that occult ideas often lay claims to having been derived from ancient wisdom or to being "the alleged recovery of a body of knowledge more recently acquired."[37]

Barkun uses the term "stigmatized knowledge" to define truth regarded by believers as "verified despite the marginalization of those claims by the institutions that conventionally distinguish between knowledge and error," for example, universities and the scientific community in general.[38] Occult groups react to their rejection by developing hostility to the church and/or university. They seek their own ideological communal environment, thus creating a kind of shadow history, advocating that *any* widely accepted belief must be false. This leads to Barkun's term "culture of conspiracy."[39] One of the subcategories of Barkun's definition is "suppressed knowledge"—suppressed by the establishment because its institutions are either afraid of the consequences of the knowledge being accepted or, worse, because the establishment possesses an evil motive for keeping society at large from the truth.[40]

In sum, theosophy was an optimistic, progressive philosophy that promoted a secular attitude of self-empowerment about how to deal with the supernatural. And it fit in well with the times. Nicholas Campion notes that such ideas proliferated at a period when, in the American South, racist theories were employed to suppress recently emancipated slaves, and when women and the working class were protesting denial of their rights.[41] Its spiritualistic tools—speaking with the dead, experiencing trance states as a medium of transcendental contact, practicing the rigid self-discipline necessary to become adept—would lead a few generations later to the practices of channeling, clairvoyance, and crystal gazing. Being adept would become practically a birthright during the optimistic New Age that was to come.

PART III

New Age Religion and Science

6
The Age of Aquarius

I was drawn to the symbolic power of the pervasive dream in our popular culture: that after a dark, violent age, the Piscean, we are entering a millennium of love and light.

—*Author Marilyn Ferguson*

The goal in the the next four chapters will be to understand how millennial thinking influenced the development of the various segments of New Age philosophy out of which nativist movements such as Mayanism, an avertive form of apocalypticism, developed.

Historian Wouter Hanegraaff has detailed the prominent role of theosophy and late nineteenth-century spiritualism in shaping the postmillenarian character of the Second Coming.[1] In the strictest sense, believers hold that a New Age will come about via an evolutionary process powered by superhuman agency. Rather than via a literal personal appearance of a savior, the transition to utopia on Earth will be more spiritual in nature. It will not result from an apocalypse, such as a catastrophe wiping out the old imperfect society and totally replacing it. Borrowing scientific concepts, proponents explain transcendent phenomena in terms of "energy" or "new principles." Astrologically interpreted lines of demarcation in very large astronomical cycles, for example, the "age of Aquarius," are a part of the evolutionary scheme as well. In its broader sense, revealed New Age knowledge, according to Hanegraaff, consists of a complex social movement involving a host of loosely organized cross-cultural manifestations and techniques, such as channeling and healing mechanisms, encompassed in a magical worldview. Some of these incorporate millennial beliefs while others do not.

Anthropologist John Hoopes traces the term *New Age* back to the eighteenth-century futurist prophet Emmanuel Swedenborg, who foresaw it as a time of metaphysical enlightenment.[2] The term also appeared in a later poem written by William Blake, himself a Swedenborgian. There it refers to a time when the value of the Bible will supersede the pagan writings of the classical world.

Emmanuel Swedenborg (1688–1772) began as a well-grounded Swedish scientist (he studied metallurgy, math, geology, and astronomy), and a good skeptic. Swedenborg spoke several languages; he invented an air-powered gun and a type of submarine, and served as the assessor of the Royal College of Mines. But his midlife was suddenly interrupted by a series of vivid dreams in which, he recounts, he held conversations with Jesus, Plato, Aristotle, and God. He claims to have visited both heaven and hell. All these contacts portended the Apocalypse and convinced him that he must become the messenger to convey to the world here below the seminal messages from above. Ever precise, Swedenborg wrote out a manifesto with secular overtones, a detailed exposition dictated by angels and acquired via trance-channeling from famous dead spirits, detailing what awaited us in the afterlife. The main theme of these missives was that we all possess two simultaneous existences: the outer, tangible, natural one, and the inner spiritual one. Over time, however, we lose contact with the inner side of our existence. But after we die, wrote Swedenborg, the inner existence keeps its memory bank, so that everything that ever took place in our lives is there for eternity. (We will encounter this idea of the loss of contact through time with the deep meaning of life when we deal with the perennial philosophy and the influential ideas of historian of religion Mircea Eliade in chapter 11.)

Swedenborg is one of the proponents of the "heaven and hell" concept as we have come to know it: once we die we pass through a process of self-evaluation; those we know on Earth are present to help us through the transition. In the makeover process we get to choose our own heaven and hell. For example, if I'm a materialist, I can go to hell and continue being one as long as the sins I commit don't exceed those I performed in my earthly life.

My fellow souls will see to it that I toe the line by punishing me if I step off. On the other hand, if I choose to go to heaven and permanently dedicate myself to the communal life and its requisite self-perfection, I must be considerate of my neighbors. Swedenborg claimed to have acquired much of his insight via out-of-body space travel, during which he communicated with spirits who lived on nearby planets including Mercury, Venus, Mars, and Jupiter. He tells us that Jovians, for example, are a tall and majestic people, a spiritual race that knows no sin. Professor of communication James Herrick has dubbed Swedenborg the father of the "Myth of the Extraterrestrial" (a subject we'll deal with in the next chapter).[3] The good news spin to the spiritual message of Swedenborg's scientific mythology led to the creation of several sects built around his philosophy.

The words "New Age" were first popularized in England, being used in 1914 in the titles of both a London newspaper and a Freemasonry journal; each offered advice on psychological and spiritual issues. The term was reinvented in America in the late 1960s due in no small measure to the Broadway rock musical *Hair*, which spawned the celebrated tune "The Age of Aquarius." Like its New Thought predecessor, New Age philosophy was optimistic and timely. In the wake of all the misery suffered through two world wars and a third ongoing in Southeast Asia, a shift to good times must surely lie ahead—it is written in the stars! New Age rhetoric stressed a desire for wholeness; it promoted living in a world that would open itself to the presence of God, a world of love and possibility in the midst of ordinariness.[4]

New Age philosophy was also laden with bio-activism: our planet is sacred; it's a living organism and we're all an active part of it. We need to band together "to create a world in which humanity, nature, and the domain of spirit work together in ways that are mutually empowering and co-creative."[5] A skeptical *Time* magazine derided the movement as a combination of spirituality and superstition: "The underlying faith is a lack of faith in the orthodoxies of rationalism, high technology, routine living, spiritual law-and-order . . . New Agers believe there must be some secret and mysterious shortcut or alternative path to happiness and health. And nobody ever really dies."[6]

What segment of American culture did New Age philosophy attract? Historian Catherine Albanese summarizes: They were "mostly white, more often female, often middle-aged . . . frequently urban dwellers."[7] Socially, they came from the middle class; they were better educated than average and, surprisingly, most of them were not terribly alienated from society. Religiously, they derived from mainstream Christianity, but there were a significant number of Jews. Perhaps as much as 25 percent of the US population identified with basic features of the movement by the late 1980s.[8] Editor-writer Mitch Horowitz's summary of the movement's shared beliefs shows they resonated strongly with its ancestral New Thought philosophy:

1. Spiritual thought has therapeutic value.
2. The mind-body connection plays a role in your health.
3. Human consciousness is undergoing an evolution toward higher stages.
4. Thought, to some degree, determines what is real.
5. Spirituality is attainable outside any reference to a specific religious doctrine.[9]

The millenarian component of the New Age of the 1960s focused on an end-time for planetary and human salvation centered on personal change. The implication of the constellation of Aquarius in New Age transformation lingo comes from what I would term the "precession myth" which, by odd coincidence, finds connections with early Christian millenarian chronology. The science is simple enough: we know that the gravitational pull of the sun and the moon on the bulge at the Earth's equator (due to our planet's rapid rotation) causes its axis to gyrate slowly like a spinning top. The direction of the wobble of the polar axis etches out a wide circle on the sky, pointing to different polestars as it moves through time. The polar circuit is completed in a little less than 26,000 years—25,770, to be precise. Another consequence of precession is that the place of the sun on a given date among the twelve constellations of the zodiac also shifts slowly through the ages; for example, today the sun on the vernal equinox, or first day of spring, resides in the constellation of Pisces; but before the birth of Christ the equinox sun was situated next door in Aries; prior to that time, in the days when the pharaohs ruled Egypt, it was positioned in Taurus. (Precession of the equinoxes should not be confused with the annual motion of the sun. The sun moves all the way around the zodiac, passing through every constellation over the course of a year. Precession alters the position of the sun in the zodiac *on a given date*. So over long time periods your zodiacal birth sign will change. The choice of the vernal equinox, March 20 or 21, as the starting point was motivated by the fact that it commenced the growing season in ancient agricultural systems of the Middle East.)

The link to millenarianism in the arithmetic of precession is pretty simple. If it takes 25,770 years for the position of the sun on any given date of the year to complete a circuit through all twelve constellations of the zodiac, then the approximate time for the sun to pass through one of its zodiacal signs is 2,147.5 years, a period fairly close to two millennia. This convenient cosmic computation implies that one "world age," that is, the time the sun on any given date spends in a single zodiacal sign, is just about double the old Augustinian millennium-long creation era discussed earlier. Could human destiny be fixed in the stars? Without a doubt, responded many New Agers.

One interpretation of the world age theory of the evolution of human history posits that the present age opened with the reign of Christ when, on the first day of spring, which represented the start of the seasonal year in the calendar of the Roman Empire, the sun entered the constellation of Pisces. Indeed, Christ is symbolized by the Pisces fish symbol in the old Roman Catholic Church.

The age of Aries, which preceded the Piscean age, is said to have begun with Moses's arrival on Mt. Sinai, which coincided with the entry of the vernal equinox sun into the realm of the sign of the Ram. In the age preceding it, people worshiped the golden calf, Taurus the Bull, because that sign of the zodiac then housed the slowly shifting vernal equinox sun. Marching forward in time from the present, at the precessional rate of about one degree every 70 years (if you divide the precessional cycle of 25,770 years by 360 degrees, you get 71.58 years), you'll find that the vernal equinox sun actually will not reach the Aquarian boundary until about 2700 CE; so the 1969 tuneful anticipation of the age shift was about seven centuries too early. This slight offsetting of the zodiacal clock seems to have had little effect on prophecy regarding the imminent nature of solar movement on cosmically induced change; many believers simply conflated the arrival of the age of Aquarius with the millennium, then less than half a century away.

John Hoopes's detective work traces the earliest modern Piscean-Aquarian transition reference to a pamphlet put out by the Theosophical Society in 1899, an apparent revival of a concept laid down by a Baghdad astrologer 1,000 years earlier. Early twentieth-century psychic Edgar Cayce popularized his prognostications on the destined Aquarian spiritual enlightenment, which, he prophesied, would be prefaced by catastrophic global change. But it was a best seller written by an obscure journalist that would seize upon the Aquarian myth and transform the hippie form of eclectic New Ageism into a mainstream self-help industry.

This is, in the words of the popular song "The Age of Aquarius," "the time of the mind's true liberation," wrote reporter Marilyn Ferguson after the quotation in this chapter's epigraph.[10] Thus she explained the title of her influential 1980 book, *The Aquarian Conspiracy: Personal and Social Transformation in Our Time*. For Ferguson, human potential was boundless—the whole world a borderless country with room for both outsiders and traditionalists. One of modern America's first self-help books, Ferguson's tome became every New Ager's bible. Its chapters on self-healing, transcendentalism, and the transformation of fear (fear of failure, fear of giving up the material life, fear of sickness, and so on) into positive action were filled to the brim with the sweet taste of Helena Blavatsky's prophecy in a Quimbian New Thought vessel: America is the social matrix, the place where positive change is destined to happen (recall the words on the back of the US dollar bill). And *we* can make it happen.

Ferguson believed that the social activism of the late 1960s and the revolution of consciousness centered on cultivating the powers of the mind to acquire a sense of higher awareness of reality were the beginning of a great convergence. She wrote convincingly of countless incidents in which healing, problem solving, and the recovery of buried memories would all conspire—"breathe together"—to change social institutions. (This was the meaning of *conspiracy* she meant to evoke in the title of her book.) Members of her leaderless "conspiracy" broke with the key elements of Western thought—intellect and logic as well as belief in the continuity of history—in favor of appealing strongly to insight derived from the earliest recorded thought. Ferguson claimed that the spirit, the soul, was an instrument capable of acquiring knowledge and deeper meaning via "direct communion with ultimate reality."[11] Only those who actually experienced it would know that it happened. You arrive at a different reality that makes things that were scientifically inexplicable, such as paranormal events and synchronicities, clear and absolute—*and you know it to be so for sure*. But, Ferguson continues, only the mind cultivated to apprehend it can enter the enlightened domain of Unitary knowing—a domain of absolute certainty of knowledge. Above all, wrote Ferguson, cosmically induced change, now desperately needed, is at our doorstep. For the first time in human history "we have come upon the control pattern of change," the change of change, as she called it. "Now is the time in which we can intentionally align ourselves with nature for rapid remaking of ourselves and our collapsing institutions."[12]

Ferguson's belief in the convergence of the Piscean age with a true liberation of the mind as a natural consequence of human evolution draws heavily on the dispensational ideas of the Jesuit philosopher and paleontologist Pierre Teilhard de Chardin (1881–1955). Teilhard believed the universe possesses its own evolutionary history, and the development of an increased cosmic consciousness is a major component of it. The complexification of evolutionary processes culminates in the "Omega Point," at which time human consciousness acquires total unity. Teilhard called this collective domain of the future union of the physical and psychic the *noosphere*, a term that remains popular today. Like Blavatsky before him, Teilhard drew on Darwinian concepts; he regarded the noosphere, the sphere of human thought, as the last stage in human evolution, following the geosphere (the development of inanimate matter) and the biosphere (that of living things). Teilhard's driving noospheric spirit is the "cosmic Christ," who is oriented to the creative process of motivating humankind toward making the great transition rather than to mere redemption. The noosphere found appeal because the acquisition of the psychic energy to assist the evolutionary process along the climb to higher stages of "hominization" became the goal of a partnership between people and their creator. In other words, believers get to participate in their collective cosmogenesis.

Getting to Ferguson's true liberation (or Teilhard's Omega Point) necessitated hard work—experiencing the perfection of concentration, focus, and training. One way was meditation and here, once again, the Far East exerted its influence. Maharishi Mahesh Yogi's popular method of Transcendental Meditation, or TM, involved the lengthy recitation of mantras. A trained instructor gives you a secret word. The student gets in a comfortable position and repeats it over and over again mentally. This clears the mind of distracting thoughts—puts it into a passive attitude and thus makes it open to higher revelations. Do this three times a day. In the early 1980s many companies in Britain and America adopted TM for training their employees.

Kundalini, a more scientific-sounding method, is among a number of contemplative New Age therapies that involves a bit more effort along the road to self-perfection. Among dozens of so-called body work practices for attaining higher states of consciousness, this revamped ancient Indian method requires the student to visualize a "fiery serpent," the *kundalini*, said to be located at the base of the spine. Normally dormant, once activated through stepwise meditation, a serpentine force passes upward through an imaginary channel parallel to the spine. The *prana* it transmits can stimulate successively higher *chakras* (invisible ganglia that radiate throughout the body). Though one may experience sounds resembling cricket chirps, buzzing bees, and bells, the unmistakable boom and roar of a distant ocean is the key that one has arrived at the Resplendent Void, the rarely attained highest state of noospheric bliss. In that condition normal thought processes are put on hold, the ego vanishes, and all things become unity. Only then is the self absorbed into the infinite, the ultimate transcendent—a part of the universal consciousness of which Ferguson speaks.

Psychedelic, literally making your soul manifest, is an experience in which you engage altered states of consciousness. You can trigger this mind-altering state by ingesting psychoactive substances such as cannabis, cocaine, heroin, mescaline, certain fungi, and a host of other (mostly) plant-derived substances that have found human usage dating back to the time of Zoroaster. Maya priests licked hallucinogenic toads; Huichol Indians munched on peyote; and keepers of Greek oracles got high on fumes issuing from terrestrial fissures—all in the pursuit of higher truths.

As characterized by the neuroscientific community, psychedelic states of mind can lead to *psychosis* (a loss of contact with what is going on in the real world), delusional behavior, and confusion; but they can often induce in the user a mind-opening feeling, the experience of acquiring revealed truth, enlightenment, and access to knowledge never before encountered. Among the most famous twentieth-century users in the realm of alternative spirituality were Timothy Leary, Allen Ginsberg, and William S. Burroughs—all leaders of the New Age "Joyous Revelation," and, from earlier in that century, Sigmund Freud and Aldous Huxley (whom we will meet in chapter 11).

Seventy years before the psychedelic 1960s, philosopher William James, one of the founders of the discipline of psychology, wrote that, to those who experience them, mystical states offer "insight into depths of truth . . . illuminations, revelations, full of significance and importance." They can't be sustained for very long, but when they occur one acquires a feeling of "continuous development in what is felt as inner richness and importance."[13] James, whose father was a Swedenborgian, had held a lifelong interest in metaphysics. Inadvertently, James also kindled the psychedelic movement in America when he wrote in detail about his "anaesthetic revelations," which he claims to have acquired by experimenting with nitrous oxide, the so-called laughing gas once used in dental offices.

James's simple experiment consisted of gently heating a test tube containing ammonium nitrate crystals. This released nitrous oxide, which he collected in a bag. By inserting a rubber tube into the bag he could draw the intoxicating gas into his lungs in the manner of smoking a waterpipe. In *The Varieties of Religious Experience* James reports the results: "One conclusion was forced upon my mind at that time, and my impression of its truth has ever since remained unshaken. It is that our normal waking consciousness, rational consciousness as we call it, is but one special type of consciousness, whilst all about it, parted from it by the flimsiest of screens, there lie potential forms of consciousness entirely different."[14] Stuggling to remain scientifically objective about the deep reality of his experience, James continues:

> We may go through life without suspecting their existence; but apply the requisite stimulus, and at a touch they are there in all their completeness, definite types of mentality which probably somewhere have their field of application and adaptations. No account of the universe in its totality can be final which leaves these other forms of consciousness quite disregarded. How to regard them is the question—for they are so discontinuous with ordinary consciousness. Yet they may determine attitudes though they cannot furnish formulas, and open a region though they fail to give a map. At any rate, they forbid a premature closing of our accounts with reality. Looking back on my own experiences, they all converge towards a kind of insight to which I cannot help ascribing some metaphysical significance.[15]

It is especially noteworthy that James did not necessarily adopt the beliefs that might result from such experiences. He admits only that what happened was real: "I feel as if it must mean something, something like what the Hegelian philosophy means, if one could only lay hold of it more clearly. Those who have ears to hear, let them hear; to me the living sense of its reality only comes in the artificial mystic state of mind."[16]

In the early 1970s, mescaline and LSD were the most common trance-inducing choices aiding the pursuit of self-revelation. Among the testimonials Ferguson cites: "After many years in intellectual, left brain pursuit of 'reality', I learned from LSD about alternative realities—and suddenly, all bibles made sense."[17] Claimed the promoters of mescaline: psychedelics amplify mental processes; they give access to a domain in which past, present, and future are juxtaposed; space seems limitless and matter becomes patterns of energy. One directly experiences microcosm, macrocosm, vibrating molecules, spinning galaxies, archetypes, and deities, "even what seems to be their own birth or uterine existence," notes Ferguson.[18] She suggests that if any of these states offer a valid source of information about the real universe, then maybe we ought to think about abandoning our derogatory term "altered states of consciousness" to describe them.

Clinical studies conducted in the late 1950s and 1960s claimed to verify that psychedelic drugs can induce religious experience, in the sense of a perception of the supernatural. Documented effects included the slowing down of time, an awareness of an interdependence of things hitherto seen as unrelated, and an awareness of eternal energy, usually characterized by intense light.[19]

In the 2010s *ayahuasca*, a hallucinogenic drink from the Amazon, has become the recreational drug via which young affluent urbanites acquire insights into inner growth.[20] Users describe feelings of emotional intelligence and enhanced empathy. Part of the contemporary purification movement, therapeutic sessions are often preceded by abstinence from alcohol, red meat, spicy foods, and sex. The more wealthy set may travel to a retreat in Brazil or Peru to participate in ceremonies conducted by an authentic shaman who knows how to administer the brew and monitor its side effects. Legally the US government categorizes ayahuasca as a tea for religious purposes, "an instrument to help us get in touch with our own spiritual nature," according to Jeffrey Bronfman, who heads a group that distributes ayahuasca.[21]

America in the 1970s seemed ripe for seekers of new ways to change the world, and if the psychedelic experience could open doorways, all the better. It was a time of civil rights activism, the Vietnam War, and the rise of the feminist movement—all accompanied by serious doubt and dissatisfaction with traditional churchgoing. Significant numbers of people were seeking new forms of spirituality. Ferguson's *Age of Aquarius* struck a nerve. At the time she wrote it, polls indicated that 80 percent of respondents surveyed nationally expressed strong interest in the "inner search for meaning"; 40 percent had undergone an actual mystical experience, 53 percent believed psychic phenomena were real, and more than one in ten were involved in a mystic discipline.[22] Meanwhile, 10 million Americans were actively engaged in exploring some aspect of Eastern religion and about the same number indulged in various forms of spiritual healing. The most devout practitioners tended to be members of the high-income class, but a substantial segment of the engaged population was middle class. Seeking transcendence and spiritual questing, especially finding the God-in-Man, were about as mainstream as they would get in century number twenty.

With its focus on personal development and the quest for greater awareness of nature, Ferguson's version of a paradigm shift seemed particularly welcome to those dissatisfied with status quo politics. Why not shift attention in the medical world from questions of expense and technology to contemplating the nature of wellness? Why not focus attention in education more on the nature of learning itself instead of expending so much energy (and money) creating new curricula? (From my own experience as an educator I detect a certain naiveté in Ferguson's recommendations. Deep discussions about what constitutes learning were being actively engaged in the academy well before she wrote her book. Maybe Ferguson was out of touch because such efforts weren't making headlines in the popular media.)

Despite its popular appeal, Ferguson's best seller failed to catapult the New Age movement into a major ideological force. Historian of religion Damian Thompson thinks the reason the alliance between self-help science and sociology espoused in *The Aquarian Conspiracy* didn't happen is because of the "millennial undertow" that continued to remain a part of New Age thinking.[23] As rational sounding as Ferguson's message might appear, beneath it lay a too-spiritual/supernatural component. "The 'intuitive leap' which will give birth to the paradigm shift is essentially a leap of faith: faith in mankind's ability to transcend physical and psychological limitations which orthodox science regards as intrinsic to the human species."[24]

I agree with Thompson (who wrote in 1996) that since the 1980s, Ferguson's conspiracy metaphor has not penetrated the domain of the sciences and social sciences; nor has it developed into the foundation of a new world religion. On the other hand, Ferguson's philosophy has become the refuge of occult practices, which tend to view the paradigm as an apocalyptic idea rife with end of the world scenarios, practices such as crystal gazing, astral projection and, especially lately, UFOlogy, which lies just ahead on our agenda.

Having lived through it, I found the New Age movement difficult to apprehend, mainly because the beliefs that allegedly held it together seemed to undergo continual shifts. The intense focus on channeling switched to pyramidology. Native American wisdom superseded Buddhism. Tarot and astrology ruled, then crop circles, then aroma therapy, then iridology, then colonics. As Thompson has suggested, there's a flavor-of-the-month quality to it all. What unites this leaderless movement—if it can be called a movement at all—is the anticipated shift of consciousness and its long-familiar earmarks: prophecy, the resolution of the perceived notion of good and evil being highly polarized and, because it is all just around the corner, we will be here not only to witness it but to actually make the shift happen.

Inexplicably, a general calm—call it a relaxation in interest—set in as the millennium, Y2K, approached. Gordon Melton, who coedited of *The New Age Encyclopedia*, attributes the lull to a general tiring of New Age ideology beginning in the early 1990s.[25] He cites persistent ridicule of channeling and crystals by outside critics, along with public attention to adepts who charged excessive fees for their services. Meanwhile, skeptics from the scientific community had mounted a successful campaign at the level of popular culture by attacking the claimed scientific properties of crystals.[26] Add to these developments the damaging critiques leveled by respected theoreticians within the New Age movement itself; for example, New Age author and proponent David Spangler who, like William Miller a century before him, admitted that sudden global transformation in our lifetime was perhaps a bit naive.

But let us not toss New Age religion into the dustbin of metaphysical history quite yet, warned Melton. Whole Earth conventions were still attracting hefty crowds at century's turn. Personal trainers, life coaches, alternative healing therapies, clubs promoting weight loss, quitting smoking, and detoxification were all beginning to become part of a communal mainstream effort to perfect the self. Secular New Thought revisited might better be termed "body thought" this time around.

Finally, on the spiritual side at the turn of the millennium, the New Age of the 1970s and 1980s was being displaced by what Catherine Albanese calls an *exoteric* America—a post–New Age American spirituality or metaphysical religiosity. Found already in its proto-form among the mix of people in North America in the early seventeenth century, this kind of spirituality remained as "resilient" and "chameleon-like" as ever.[27] The mind had acquired a body and that "mind-body self" refused to become categorized. The new spirituality operated across all religions and political affiliations and its capacity for mass marketing only grew with the techno-computer revolution.

7

Techno-Angels of the Alien Advent

When a view denounced by scientists as false is, nevertheless, popular with the general public, the mere fact of that popularity is evidence in favor of its worthlessness.

—*Author and biochemist Isaac Asimov*

This is how sci-fi writer Isaac Asimov summarized one of the common characteristics of the "heretic writer"—one whose claims run against the grain of scientific orthodoxy. They are of two kinds, he contended: those who arise from within their professional disciplines, the "endoheretics," and those who come from without, or "exoheretics." Endoheretics include Galileo and Darwin. Their ideas are dealt with in the context of science's self-questioning, self-correcting structure, even though public opinion often has a tendency to run against the grain of the scientific establishment. Exoheretics basically write to appeal to the public and, as we have seen, they tend to employ impressive disciplinary jargon to bolster their claims to knowledge. According to Asimov, this offers them the reward of convincing themselves that their position is related to the value of their views. For example, Bauval defended the validity of his pyramid alignment theory on the basis of its wide public reception. Moreover, favored public opinion can be lucrative. And once it draws out negative comments from members of the establishment, they open themselves up to being characterized as an arrogant, close-minded clique. In turn, the heretic becomes a martyr.

The most well-known example of Asimov's characterization of an exoheretic is Immanuel Velikovsky, a Russian-born psychiatrist whose 1950 book, *Worlds in Collision*, sought to demonstrate the literal *scientific* truth in the Bible.[1] Rather than holding a key to the future, Velikovsky's reading of Scripture sought to open the doorway to our apocalyptic past. He was convinced that the Old Testament account of the flight of the Israelites from Egypt contained an accurate record of natural disasters that arose from the Earth's encounters with the planet Venus, which originally had been ejected from the bowels of the planet Jupiter (recall Godfrey Higgins's account of celestial billiards published a century earlier [chapter 5]). Despite overwhelmingly negative reviews from astronomers, archaeologists, and biblical historians, the Doubleday Publishing Company, over the protest of academic critics, reprinted the book.[2] It became a best seller.

When his ideas were popularized anew in the early 1970s, in the wake of the resurgence of interest in world ages, Velikovsky became an antiestablishment hero to a new generation of New Agers. Here was a man who worked all his life on a grand idea only to be persecuted by the scientific power establishment. A group of young American students established a journal, called *Pensée*, which published ten issues during the period 1972–1974 championing Velikovsky's ideas. Today Velikovskianism has receded into the background of the history of exoheretical scientific controversy, but apocalyptic postmillennialism, which has drawn on it, still enlivens the body of current popular literature generated by certain groups that prophesy time's end. To Asimov's negative assessment quoted in this chapter's epigraph, I would add: blame the poor state of science education.

Signs in the sky have long been interpreted to be a reflection of moral behavior. Eclipses, comets, meteors, lightning, and thunder were regarded as religious prophesies of things to come. Wheeled chariots, dragons, and galloping horses—scenes straight out of Revelation—were often witnessed in the sky. In 1651, for example, two women claimed to have watched two armies battling in the sky, followed by owl-faced angels blue in color.[3] And, at the time of England's Black Plague in 1643, an army of horsemen was seen galloping across the heavens. Interpreting unusual things we see in the heavens to presage calamity had as much to do with the embedded belief of the connectedness of humanity and nature as it did with ignorance about natural causes. Enter the domain of science.

FIGURE 7.1. Discoveries allegedly made in 1835 by astronomer John Herschel through his telescope revealed an ideal world far away in space. Civilized bat-winged creatures live peacefully alongside a race of Pooh Bear–like beings on the moon. (Wikimedia Commons.)

Not unlike the mid-nineteenth-century transcendental philosophers from Boston, who sought to reconnect humanity and nature via a purer life in the woods, at least a segment of UFO devotees are wedded to the notion that there's a faraway extraterrestrial world that's better than our own and we urgently need to make contact with it.

In 1835 the *New York Sun* published a series of six articles alleging that the famous astronomer John Herschel had spied, with his immense telescope at the Cape of Good Hope in South Africa, animals such as goats and bison living amid the trees and oceans of the moon alongside at least two races of advanced civilized beings—all in total harmony (figure 7.1).[4] Bat-winged humanoids and teddy bear–like creatures inhabited houses made of straw. The bat people were vividly portrayed: they were about four feet tall and covered with short, copper-colored, curly hair. They had yellow faces and their wings, joined to their bodies from the shoulder all the way down to the leg, were made of semitransparent membranous tissue. They worshipped at a temple constructed out of sapphire with a golden roof.

The articles, authored by *New York Sun* reporter Richard Locke, turned out to be part of a hoax. Locke probably wrote his pieces to increase sales of the penny newspaper (the price soared by 30 percent before the hoax was confessed three weeks later); but he also may have intended the series as a satire on earlier reports of the discovery of the existence of large buildings on the lunar surface by an otherwise reputable German astronomer, and on calculations attributed to one Rev. Thomas Dick, who wrote a popular book suggesting that there were more than 4 billion lunar inhabitants. Emerson was among Dick's admirers.

An interesting science-laden spin on the ancient sources of transcendent wisdom finds high-tech extraterrestrial masters replacing Blavatsky's Christ and the wise men of the East. Flying saucers, the twentieth-century version of salvation from on high, are a phenomenon of the nuclear era. Contact prophet George Adamski would popularize UFOs in two best sellers, *Pioneers of Space* (1949) and *The Flying Saucers Have Landed* (1953).[5] Adamski claimed to have sighted an immense cigar-shaped spacecraft hovering over his home-made observatory in 1946. Approaching the vehicle, he says he encountered a handsome male blond Venusian. Via telepathic communication the alien told Adamski that he had come on a peace mission. His race was concerned that the nuclear weapons being developed by earthlings might pose a threat to the inhabitants of neighboring planets. In a third book, *Inside the Spaceships* (1956), Adamski expressed a particular fascination with the technological capabilities of alien flying machines—magical shiny saucers equipped with antigravity capabilities.[6] A transcendent, scientifically educated prophet had come from far away, descending to warn a chosen member of the human family of the consequences of our evil actions and to appoint him to tell the world about it—a theme that would take on millenarian aspects among later contact groups.

Readers were deeply touched by wisdom come from other planetary races. To judge from Amazon reviews half a century later, Adamski's story retains its mass appeal. To many readers, the alien advice is well worth heeding: "We must get beyond ignorance, war, material goods, the ego"; "Beings on other planets don't experience the troubles, strife, and violence so common on earth"; "I could feel the love and goodness of these other people"; "They have compassion for us."[7] Many found Adamski a believable good guy who was being ridiculed by the cynical scientists he worked for at NASA in a job they believed he used to credentialize himself.

Adamski's experience in the California desert followed on the heels of the dropping of the atom bomb on Hiroshima. No surprise then that his testimony expressed concern on the part of his alien contactees over radioactive fallout from terrestrial atomic and nuclear clouds that might endanger their planet. Along with the message of concern, Adamski believed, would come "great secrets of life" that we on Earth today have either forgotten or never known, and "a great deal of wisdom being handed down to us."[8] The film *The Day the Earth Stood Still*, which debuted the year before Adamski's contact tale, reflects many of his concerns. Klaatu, a kind of secular Christ-alien who descends from a flying saucer that lands on the White House lawn, warns of the horrible consequences to all galactic inhabitants from atomic weapons—a warning that goes unheeded.

George Hunt Williamson, a friend of Adamski, was influenced by Velikovsky. He was also well read in the theosophical works of Madame Blavatsky and became absorbed in references to Eastern wisdom having been originally brought to earth by superhuman Venusians. Williamson produced a series of books detailing the secret ancient history of humanity. Most well known among them is *Secret Places of the Lion*, written in 1958.[9] It tells of radiant beings from heaven, possessors of universal wisdom, self-sacrificing guardians of the human race who became incarnated as terrestrials in order to help earthlings prepare for the New Age. Indeed, it was they who also aided in the founding of both the Jewish and Christian religions.

"The mistake lies not with *history* but with the historians," Williamson wrote, adding a moral spin to Velikovsky's dating of physical catastrophes in Exodus and Egyptian papyri.[10] *Real* history is not what we have been taught. Rather, Velikovsky's "ages in chaos" refers to a time when souls not belonging to planet Earth came here to assist us in our struggle from beasthood to manhood. According to Williamson's interpretations, the Star of Bethlehem was the same spacecraft that had led the children of Israel out of Egypt. The angel who appeared to Mary and the light of the Lord both came from the same craft—and the Resurrection was accomplished via the vibrational frequency in a beam from it.

The first widely disseminated UFO sighting occurred early in the summer of 1947, when a pilot flying over Washington's Cascade Mountains on a search mission for a lost Marine transport plane spotted a chain of nine fast-moving shiny objects. "They flew like a saucer would if you skipped it across the water," the aviator told the press.[11] Thereafter sightings increased, as did reports from literal-minded history buffs about the inexplicable aerial phenomena referred to in ancient sources going all the way back to the Bible. Conspiracy theorists claimed that the US government was well aware of the existence of the aliens who piloted the UFOs and were keeping their findings secret, perhaps to avoid alarming the public. When the Condon Report, a government-funded study published in mass paperback form and discrediting forty-five case studies among hundreds of sightings that had been reported since 1950, was issued in 1969, critics branded it a cover-up—the same public response accorded the scientific establishment when it tried to debunk nineteenth-century claims of contact with dead spirits.[12]

Following the social scenario embracing stigmatized knowledge articulated by Webb and Barkun (chapter 5), contact proponents, many with an impressive cadre of followers, began to achieve popularity, especially when the storyteller was judged to be sincere and in possession of some degree of charisma. Take the Raëlian movement, a UFO cult whose high-tech foundation myth connects with the Bible, including both Eve's apple and Noah's ark. It began in 1973 when French racecar driver and pop musician Claude Vorilhon claimed to have witnessed an alien craft descend to the top of an extinct volcano. His story from that point reads like a space age version of Genesis: A green-skinned, bearded alien the size of a child emerged and invited Vorilhon on a six-day journey—they would return on the seventh.

During his travels Vorilhon says he was instructed in the true, scientifically based meaning of the Bible: life is the creation of extraterrestrial scientists who had conducted DNA experiments in a lab on their home planet 22,000 years ago. They intended to bring the fruits of their research here to Earth, where they would develop a new race out of their own genetic material. That's where Adam and Eve came from, explained Vorilhon, who changed his name to Raël (Hebrew for "messenger"). Drawing on the Old Testament myth, Raël regarded Adam and Eve's expulsion as the result of a disagreement over whether the experimenters ought to give the first humans knowledge of their extraterrestrial origin. The opposition political party was opposed to creating humans in the first place, out of fear that they would rival their creator. Members of the transgressor group that decided to teach science to the race they created were left here on Earth as punishment. They proceeded to mate with Earth women. This offered proof of humanity's negative ways. So the creator-experimenters destroyed them in a nuclear holocaust, which was followed by a flood—but not before the earthbound aliens saved a handful of homegrown specimens to send back home. They were later reimplanted on Earth and given a second chance—just like Adam, Eve, and Cain in Genesis. Incidentally, there's a bio-tech spin to Raëlian immortality. It's achieved through cloning, which cult members perceive as a fulfillment of divine will. Thus, if the first humans were created in an alien laboratory from the experimenter's own DNA, the idea of cloning would be deemed a godlike act, and consequently an attempt by humans to become godlike.

The Raëlian myth comes with a warning and a deadline: if we spread the word and unite in world peace, the aliens promise to return to Earth in their starships and share the secrets of their advanced technology. If not, they will disappear, leaving us behind to destroy the world in the next nuclear holocaust, toward which we are clearly headed. The choice of whether to walk the path toward salvation is left up to each of us.

The charismatic aspect of the Raëlian cult is due entirely to its leader. Raël fancies himself a shaman, aware of senses and abilities above and beyond those of mere mortals—except that, as sociologist Susan Palmer, who has made a thorough study of the Raëlian phenomenon, puts it, "Where ancient shamans' mythic ancestors possessed the superior senses of creatures with scales, fur, or feathers, who spoke animal languages before the fall, . . . the contemporary urban shaman does not bother with the animal kingdom, whose species humankind has conquered and debased. Raël's mythic ancestor was not a beaver or a raven, but a superscientist from another planet who arrived in a spaceship."[13]

With the exception of presenting himself as the only authority when it comes to superior knowledge, like William Miller, Claude Vorilhon is otherwise described by followers as quite ordinary. He tells jokes to his audience; he sings and dances. He draws his acolytes to him with his democratic, free will–based ideology. Like George Adamski, he comes across as the chosen everyman, neither wealthy nor attractive—and not even all that scintillating a speaker, say some witnesses.[14] Notwithstanding, also like that of Miller, Raël's image is carefully managed; one witness likens his stage presence to

FIGURE 7.2. The Heaven's Gate cult, which looked to Comet Hale-Bopp (1997) as a means of transcendental transport, was one among a number of late New Age UFO religious groups. (Courtesy of the Telah Foundation.)

that of a rock star. Recounts another: to an opening theme from *Carmina Burana*, "Raël bounded on to the stage wearing his customary white padded suit and samurai top knot and stood beaming while his Raëlians gave him a standing ovation . . . as we waited for his signal he began to bump his hips in rhythm, so the clapping became a beat and the Raëlians swayed their hips in sympathy."[15]

Palmer contrasts Raëlianism with a number of other minisects in the history of UFOlogy that developed in the latter decades of the twentieth century, among them Heaven's Gate (figure 7.2). In this instance Comet Hale-Bopp (1997) would play the role of nature's portent on the eve of the third millennium's most well-publicized UFO-related preview of biblical Armageddon. Heaven's Gate was headed by Marshall Applewhite and Bonnie Lou Nettles. They viewed themselves as "the two" who witnessed, together with the apostle John, the preservation of the temple of God in Revelation: "And I will grant any two witnesses power to prophecy."[16] Combining Christian salvation with evolution, Applewhite and Nettles attracted a small but dedicated following (in 2007 they numbered 2,300) as they traveled about the United States in the 1980s and 1990s lecturing on the theme of an Earth about to be recycled—a world that could be reinhabited only by those prepared to give up not only their material possessions but even their mortal flesh before the planet would be wiped out. Thus they would become the children of the Next Level, where human suffering and deprecation cease to exist.

Conveniently, the sign in the heavens that destruction was imminent came just four years before the turn of the millennium. Applewhite believed Hale-Bopp was being trailed by a space vehicle inhabited by descendants of ancient astronauts, who had planted the human race on Earth. Now they were returning to reap the harvest, which consisted of those who had sacrificed themselves to get to the next step in the universal course of galactic civilization. Accordingly, between March 24 and 26, 1997, thirty-nine members of the cult donned identical shirts, sweatpants, and Nike shoes, and downed a phenobarbital-laced concoction to prepare for their cosmic pickup. A few days later they were found in a rented mansion in San Diego lying dead in their bunk beds covered in purple cloths and with plastic bags over their heads.

The eagerly awaited aliens have been described as "technological angels," a term depth psychologist Carl Jung once used to characterize UFOs.[17] These space age saviors parallel Advent prophecy from earlier times, one significant difference being that, in tune with New Age secularism, UFO cults attempt to integrate science and religion. Imagined inhabitants of the cigar- and saucer-shaped crafts of old that people witnessed whizzing across the sky had become the transcendent beings of the post–World War II era. Now the god who delivers the message of salvation is replaced by the alien. What else might one anticipate in an age dominated by science and technology?

As late as 1992, and starkly reminiscent of what George Adamski wrote half a century earlier, noted astronomer and head of the Search for Extra Terrestrial Intelligence organization (via radiowave contact) Frank Drake, responding to a question about what he thought alien contact would bring, wrote: "I fully expect an alien civilization to bequeath us vast libraries of useful information to do with as we wish. The 'Encyclopedia Galactica' will create the potential for improvements in our lives we cannot predict."[18]

Claims of UFO sightings—even direct contacts—burgeoned in the late twentieth century. The poll numbers over the years are fairly consistent. In 1966, 46 percent of Americans believed UFOs were real. By 1978 that number reached an all-time high of 57 percent. During the 1990s it held in the mid-40s, with as many as 17 percent believing in alien abduction. A 1992 Roper survey indicated that 2 percent of Americans, or 3.7 million people, believed themselves to have been abducted. In a 1996 Gallup poll 71 percent of subjects responded affirmatively when asked whether the government knows more about UFOs than it is telling us.[19] A 2012 National Geographic poll concluded that 36 percent of Americans (80 million) believe in UFOs.[20]

Unlike how most alien encounters were imagined during the Cold War, during which I grew up watching gory sci-fi movies, these cosmic visitors were here not to dine on us, but more often to warn us to straighten up and fly right. Adepts claimed to be able to "channel"—to use the then-common TV nomenclature—the extraterrestrial message. But despite pushing the philosophy of self-empowerment, most New Agers, including those who tuned in to the heavens, were actually tuned out when it came to being self-motivated, constructive participants in changing the world: they needed help from above.

Often at odds with mainstream society, prophet-contactees transmitted messages to their followers about aliens who would intervene in human affairs in order to set us on the proper course to the end of history, even as the government establishment threatened to create its own military-industrial Armageddon.

The gifted "channelers" (the modern term for trance mediumship) of the television age who communicated with extraterrestrials replaced the mediumistic contactees of nineteenth-century spiritualism—the ones who sat in trance states to acquire the message of salvation from the Eastern wise men, via ESP, or by tapping out Morse Code to the dead.[21] The word channeled from heaven included predictions of a global cataclysm, the total collapse of all governmental structure, terrestrial pollution and desertification, and the warning that remnants of humanity could be saved only by giving up their worldly possessions and following their leader to a wilderness camp, where they would be met by extraterrestrial saviors and teleported to a superhuman nirvana—another scenario that resonates with Pastor Miller's setting for the Second Coming.

Peru and the Pleiades are about as far away from middle America as one can imagine, but there were secrets channeled to Earth from far away in the high Andes, according to *Out on a Limb*, the 1983 autobiography of actress Shirley MacLaine.[22] Later made into a TV film, MacLaine's book did a lot to propagate the view that the wisdom of the masters resides up above and far away in aliens who serve as our advisers, offering us strategies and directions for perfecting ourselves as much as the state of the world. Her book would become one of the best-selling texts of the 1980s. Encouraged by trance channelers, MacLaine told readers that she had traveled to a remote location in the Andes where locals had reported frequent sightings of UFOs. There, she says, she began to receive messages from a young woman from the Pleiades star group. MacLaine was not the first to become convinced that she had been singled out to deliver the simple truth emanating from the extraterrestrials, the only beings in the universe who fully understood the meaning of life's spiritual dimension.

In a series of best-selling books that would follow, celebrity MacLaine explained how she was able, through the deep meditation techniques learned from extraterrestrial missives, to free up the "Higher Self" that lay dormant within her. Meditating, chanting, and seating herself in the correct position for cosmic alignment helped her to become "attuned to harmonious love and light energy."[23] According to MacLaine, the ancient Egyptians, North American Indians, African tribes, Incas, and the ancient Greeks all knew that our bodies are merely an outward manifestation of all the godlike energies that underlie it and convey who we were meant to be. MacLaine's philosophy of becoming the God-self had carryover potential, for example, into the domain of paranormal phenomena such as ESP and psychic surgery. Like Marilyn Ferguson, she advised, "'Trust the loving and well-ordered magic" of who you're meant to be and anything is possible.[24]

Michael Barkun recognizes two stages of development of UFO conspiracy theories.[25] In the first, the late 1970s, there existed a wide range of themes, from abductee implants to cattle mutilations to Nazi involvement. The second phase, during the mid-1980s, intensified the scope of conspiracy and became more commensurate with political ideas about conspiracy emanating from the extreme Right. Barkun specifically cites literature alluding to the notion of a secret "government within a government." By the 1990s UFO conspiracy theories had merged with ideas about the New World Order from the subculture of Christian patriot-militia. As Barkun sees it, belief in UFOs is stigmatized only by science, the universities, and government, but its themes have remained adaptable enough to steer it comfortably within the stream of popular culture.

Psychologist Carl Jung once described UFOism as an "opportunity of seeing how a legend is formed, and how in a difficult and dark time for humanity a miraculous tale grows out of an attempted intervention by extra-terrestrial, 'heavenly' powers."[26] What Jung characterized as a myth of escapism in the face of nuclear annihilation in the Cold War 1950s would, by the end of the century, turn into one ingredient in a catchall mélange of overlapping beliefs and techniques that conflated ancestral American spiritualism, transcendentalism, and New Thought to form the loose mainstream version of a post–New Age in which apocalyptic prophecy in the new millennium would thrive.

Folklorist Daniel Wojcik sees UFO phenomena as a major contributor to religious components of New Age belief systems that derive from earlier supernatural traditions, including revelation through personal encounter.[27] Their noninstitutionally based, grassroots quality has exerted enormous appeal in popular culture. Some UFO cults connect the Christian Advent directly with the saucers. Members of the GAI (Guardian Action International) group claimed that channeled messages they received indicated that when Jesus returns he will be escorted by angels in golden spaceships with enough seating to whisk some 200,000 believers off to the galactic hereafter. The chosen ones will then return to populate the home planet after the dust clears. The channeler of choice, assigned especially to our solar system, is one named Ashtar. He has been transmitting the word to terrestrial adepts since the 1970s. Ashtar foretold the disasters, both nuclear and natural, that signal the countdown to Armageddon and the Great Exodus—the year 2000.

The Aetherius Society, which has been around since the 1950s, bases its "Prayer Power" motto on founder-contactee George King's intelligence channeled via "cosmic masters" from Mars and Jupiter—and from Jesus himself. Concentrated prayer timed to avert disaster, whether via earthquake or nuclear bomb, holds the key. The ultimate challenge resides in a cosmic war between the masters and evil forces, for example, from the dying planet of Garouche (the scientists are singled out). We can help, provided we are committed members of the team who share in the goal of preventing the annihilation of our sector of the universe and saving fellow believers. Only then can we transform planetary consciousness.

Writer Michael Grosso places this sort of UFOism in a millenarian context by drawing on the similarity between the idea of being abducted by UFOs from on high, literally "raptured away by humanoids," and the biblical prophecy of the Rapture, in which we "shall be caught up together with (the dead) in the clouds to meet the Lord in the air."[28] Likewise Robert Flaherty, who has surveyed the UFO cult concept of the arrival of aliens on Earth inaugurating a new era of scientific achievement coupled with spiritual transformation, regards the phenomenon as a form of avertive apocalypticism, a rationalization of the dispensational biblical myth of Rapture and Apocalypse that developed as a response to the threat of nuclear holocaust.[29]

Astrologer Dane Rudhyar, a 1970s disciple of theosophy and mentor to José Argüelles, who would emerge as a key prophet of the 2012 phenomenon (see chapter 12), believed contacts with UFOs—even mere sightings—could cause a dramatic change in human consciousness. This would often result in physical healing by, as he put it in his typically pirated scientific lingo, radiating "waves causing the witnesses to become temporarily attuned, or to resonate in their consciousness and even cellular-atomic rhythms to the higher galactic vibrations exactly the way a Hindu guru can arouse psychic vision."[30] These vibrations, he continues, "induce a slow gradual yet basic mutation in the matter of the earth and therefore of our bodies and perhaps more specifically of man's capacity to consciously respond to higher galactic forces."[31] Like the great adepts and masters, they operate within us. You don't need to go to heaven, wrote Rudhyar. You can reach galactic space by transforming not physically but rather spiritually, provided you're open to the vibrations that promote a transfer of consciousness.

Finally, UFOs emerge as demonic forces in the writings of a number of Christian dispensationalist New Age philosophers. Perhaps the most famous is tugboat captain turned evangelical minister Hal Lindsey, with whom we will deal in the next chapter on the resurgence of the religious aspects of time's end in the popular media. Commenting on the terrors and great signs from heaven in 2012, Lindsey shocked many of his Christian radio listeners when he characterized UFO inhabitants as fallen aliens, demons who possess great intelligence and power. These demons, who are constantly at war with God, will land on Earth. He warns that they will claim to come from a benevolent culture in another galaxy, here to check on the progress of the human race they planted here long ago—but beware, for these false prophets will deceive us.

8

Resurgent Christian Dispensationalism and the End of Time in Popular Media

The planet's just in a foul mood, and the meds don't seem to be working.
—*Writer Terrence Rafferty*

It was scary growing up in the early post–World War II era. I remember being frightened by the middle school classroom drills, when we were all instructed to dive beneath our desks to protect ourselves from mock A-bomb blasts. Some of our neighbors stocked their cellars with canned goods, while others dug fallout shelters in their backyards. Amid a widespread climate of fear with each atomic test and Cold War confrontation, we all watched the official "Doomsday Clock" on our black-and-white TV sets tick off the number of minutes to time's end.

The symbolic clock face first appeared on the cover of the June 1947 issue of the *Bulletin of Atomic Scientists*, when it was arbitrarily set to 11:53 p.m., and it has appeared in varied settings on the cover of every issue since. The minute hand's proximity to midnight was originally intended to express the opinion of the board that published the journal regarding how close the world actually was to global nuclear disaster. Since 2007, climate-changing technologies and other scientific developments seen as threats to life on the planet have been added as criteria. Resets in response to near catastrophes occurred during the post–Korean War period (1953–1960), when the clock read 11:58, the Cuban missile crisis of 1961 (11:53), and the 1984 escalation of US-Soviet tensions (11:57). In the wake of increased nuclear stockpiling by rogue nations, the clock in June 2014 was set at 11:55. Its face has never looked back at us with a reading earlier than seventeen minutes to midnight, which it achieved during the Strategic Arms Reduction Treaty of 1991.

What scared me too were the pessimistic portrayals of the outcome of the creations of technoscience in popular films, which replaced the big tents and handbills of the nineteenth century as the foremost media delivering the end-time missive. A large segment of the public was assailed by black-and-white evil-laden sci-fi movies like *It Came from Outer Space* (1953), *War of the Worlds* (1953), *Invasion of the Body Snatchers* (1956), *The Brain from Planet Arous* (1957), *Saucer Man* (1957), and *I Married a Monster from Outer Space* (1958). All held to the theory that if the aliens were not here to devour us, they certainly were up to no good.

I remember being particularly troubled when, at the age of nine, I watched MGM's *The Beginning or the End* (1947), a film about the secret development of the A-bomb. I recall especially the movie poster, a montage of frightened faces accompanied by the words: "Behind a forbidden door is a terrifying secret." Nevil Shute's *On the Beach* (1959), which appeared half a generation later, offered a dismal account of what takes place in the aftermath of a nuclear war, as the Earth's rotation gradually propels a radioactive dust cloud southward toward the last survivors on Australia's beaches, who seek comfort from one another as they wait for inevitable death.

Blockbuster movies of a later generation, such as *ET* (1982) and *Close Encounters of the Third Kind* (1980), helped rekindle the increasing public appetite for the possibility of spiritual awakening from the great beyond, provided we do the right thing. Today viral epidemics and disasters induced by global climate change, usually connected in one way or another with humanity gone wrong and in dire need of redemption, have replaced the space invaders of the Cold War era I grew up in, with science often playing both villain and hero. For example, in *12 Monkeys* (1995), an evil scientist introduces a supervirus into the medical community. But a good scientist from the future, faced with the threat of annihilation, sends a convicted criminal back to the present to stop its release. The outcome is left in doubt.

In *28 Days Later* (2002), scientists experimenting on chimps lose control of a rage-inducing virus that turns human victims into bloodthirsty zombies. The resulting viral apocalypse destroys most of the population of England before our postapocalyptic heroes, a pair of accidental survivors who become romantically linked, emerge. In the tradition of *Invasion of the Body Snatchers* (remade in 1978), viewers don't really know who the enemy is. In one scene an infected priest attacks the male hero. The two survivors manage to fire-bomb most of the hard-to-identify transgressors. The plot thickens (as does the blood), with the outcome once again left uncertain.[1]

Another avertive apocalyptic film, Mel Gibson's *Apocalypto* (2006), explores the consequences of brutality that humanity can inflict on itself, especially when societies grow too large and lose contact with nature. The setting is the Maya jungle of Yucatán just prior to Hispanic contact. Savage warriors from one Maya city carry out a raid on a neighboring city, killing many of its warriors and cruelly enslaving the women, including the pregnant wife and the son of the tribal leader. Gibson revealed in interviews that his intention was to depict the corrupt moral qualities accompanying a civilization in decline, one aspect being the senseless attack of one nation upon another (the United States and the Iraq War are explicit references). Other deplorable offenses graphically depicted in the film include savage gladiatorial combat, wanton prostitution, and the squalid condition of the poor. Scenes of blood sacrifice show hearts being snatched alive out of the bodies of victims, while royalty, perched on thrones, delight in the spectacle, the result of efforts to appease false gods in a culture gone horribly wrong. Here Gibson, a devout Roman Catholic, seems to be making a comparison with the true meaning of sacrifice upheld in his own religion. In the midst of a series of riveting action scenes, the leader of the assaulted city finally emerges as the hero. He avenges the cruel deeds of the leader of the opposition by slaying him, then rescues his wife and son. As the film closes, Spanish ships alight on the shores of Yucatán, and viewers are left to wonder: is this the start of yet another cruel invasion or will the Christian missionaries offer a new kind of hope?

A secular tone still permeates many of these apocalyptically oriented movies. In her analysis, which includes the last three films discussed above, American studies professor Lee Quinby sees in such cautionary tales of human self-destruction an "assertion of the value of human agony" inconsistent with the element of predestination that colors premillennial views depicted in films such as *On the Beach* and the black comedy *Dr. Strangelove* (1964).[2] This shift of viewpoint to a desacralized Apocalypse, she believes, harkens back to the civil religion historians believe underlies American civilization.

Film historians argue that, in contrast to those of the Cold War era, in many contemporary films the cause of the Apocalypse lies within the natural world; however, humans can act to prevent it.[3] In most cases the human messiah is the heroic male. The most popular current trend in the swinging thematic pendulum of sci-fi Apocalypse films, such as *4:44 Last Day on Earth* (2011), *Melancholia* (2012), *Seeking a Friend for the End of the World* (2012), and *Take Shelter* (2011), seems to be the *pre*-Apocalypse, focusing not on the disaster itself—nor even on the science-minded heroes who desperately work 24/7 to try to avert it—but rather what happens in the lives of people already resigned to their fate. *Seeking*, for example, features two strangers forming an unlikely connection in the face of disaster, while in *4:44* and *Melancholia*, the protagonists are plagued with depression. They want only to die with peace of mind and they need neither institutions nor solidarity with the human race to acquire it. The cause of the Apocalypse is scarcely addressed. Viewers of *Take Shelter* aren't really sure whether the main character is a bona fide schizophrenic or a person with the extraordinary mental capacity to detect signs of the destruction of the world.

I think the numbing resignation evident in these recent films stems from apocalyptic overload during the decade between 9/11 and the Maya 2012 end of the world phenomenon (Google hits on Maya 2012 grew from 250,000 in 2009 to a billion on the eve of the 2012 winter solstice). In contrast to the days of *On the Beach*, today's brand of dread, argues film reviewer Terrence Rafferty, "is a good deal more amorphous, a gathering cloud of unease about shaky economics, dysfunctional institutions, climate change"; the skies are thick with ill omen.[4] As the epigraph to this chapter suggests, so many things have gone wrong and there doesn't seem to be much we can do about it.

Alongside secular avertive apocalypticism, Christian premillennial dispensationalism remains alive and well, with more than 40 million adherents in the United States.[5] Its prophets, we recall, guarantee time's end in a foreseeable, if not precisely datable, future. Today's media of choice for dispensing the message are the Internet, film, and still, the paperback book. Contemporary Rapture films portray the wrath of God as the supernatural destructive force;

they tend to play to a more select audience. Straight out of Revelation, *Left Behind: The Movie* (2000), based on a series of novels, deals with what happens to those abandoned at the time of the Tribulation. Laden with conspiracy theory, *Tribulation* (2000) and *World at War* (2005) take place during the reign of Antichrist, head of the United Nations, who tries to establish a post-Rapture worldwide religion. The "Tribulation Force" (composed of Christians) opposes him. *Right at Your Door* (2006) tells of the bombing of Los Angeles by terrorists, while *Flood* (2007) conjures up a Noachian event that decimates London. In *End of Days* (1999) a man (aptly named Jericho Cane) emerges as the true action hero only after he regains the faith in God he lost after his family was murdered. At the cost of his own life (he is about to kill himself just as the devil begins to possess his body), he overcomes Satan and foils his plan to rule the world.

Most of these films were inspired by the Left Behind series of sixteen novels written by Christian Right activist Tim LaHaye and writer Jerry Jenkins between 1995 and 2007. Centered on the Rapture, the novels tell of a world in global chaos as the beginning of the end unfolds. Antichrist emerges in the form of a charismatic, seemingly compassionate leader, who hoodwinks his way to the head of a totalitarian world government. The underdog opposition forces are the evangelicals. Divinely inspired, they confront and attempt to overcome the Satanic forces. Plagues, floods, and earthquakes—Gods punishment for the wicked—comprise a large portion of the narrative. Despite harsh critical reaction from reviewers—for example, the British *Daily Telegraph* wrote that the plot "sounds completely bananas" even to good Christians—the Left Behind series has netted over 65 million dollars in sales and the later entries in particular have each reached number one on the *New York Times* and *USA Today* best-seller lists.[6] One in nine Americans has read at least one of them. The novels owe much of their success to a brilliant marketing strategy that sells not only to bookstores but to Costco and Walmart. Historian Glenn Shuck notes the appeal of the characters in the narrative to mainstream evangelicals seeking to define who they are as a community.[7] Though they attract readers of thrillers and romance novels, the Left Behind books are unabashedly right-wing conspiratorial, anti–big government, and anti-cultural pluralism.

Behind Left Behind resides a 1970 work by Hal Lindsey entitled *The Late Great Planet Earth*, which sold 30 million copies in the first twenty years of printing. Delivered via mass paperback, Lindsey's message, like that of Pastor William Miller more than a century before him, is based on social pessimism and the need for reform.[8] According to USC communications and journalism professor Stephen O'Leary, Lindsey's rhetoric became flexible enough to lay an ideological foundation for the mainstream New Christian Right activism that has flourished since the 1980s.[9] O'Leary thinks the rise of active Christian dispensationalism was aided by a number of circumstances, including the growth of Christian broadcasting and computer-generated direct mailings, which tapped an increased source of revenue from a wealthy sector of the economy. Lindsey's message evidently got through. According to a 1994 survey, one-third of all Americans were convinced that Rapture lay just around time's corner.[10]

Lindsey's reading of Revelation interpreted locusts with scorpion tails as helicopters that spray nerve gas out of their tails. The ten-horned beast stood for the (then) ten nations of the predecessor of the European Common Union (ECU)—the contemporary equivalent of the Roman Empire. Israel played a key role in Lindsey's version of Armageddon. The return of the Jews to their homeland is his "Fuse of Armageddon." It sets off a zany timetable that begins with the ten-horned one protecting the Jews, led by an unnamed false Christ who, though he unites the Middle East, also exacts strong economic loyalty from his subjects even as he prosecutes them. He orders the Muslim quarter of Jerusalem destroyed and the Temple of Solomon reconstructed in its place. This sets the climactic scene for time's end, the biblical text providing narrative details. Enter the Soviets, who invade Jerusalem. A nuclear war follows, with the ten nations emerging victorious. Next comes an attempted takeover by an army of 200,000 Red Chinese. But in the heat of the battle that intervenes, Christ emerges, defeats the Satanic forces, and Armageddon turns to Rapture as Christ protects the faithful. The Jews, whose destruction was foretold, constitute the sacrifice necessary to bring about the Second Coming. But there's good news for them: some are converted to Christianity and manage to be saved and returned to Earth for life eternal after the dust clears. Some of Lindsey's evangelical followers believe that supporting the Israeli military complex will accelerate the pace of the inevitable historical sequence of events that will ultimately lead to the Advent.

Hal Lindsey has emerged as the single person most responsible for prophesying, in the popular media during the second half of the twentieth century and beyond, biblical apocalypse based on his interpretation of contemporary events. From the 1970s through the 1990s three best sellers and several other books have earned him the title of "the father of the modern prophecy movement."[11]

Critics wonder how Lindsey's pessimistic fundamentalism, which portrays the decline of the world willed by God, squares with the optimism that usually goes with political activism, in this case antigay and antiabortion crusading, and conservative military and economic policies. O'Leary finds that a paradox viewed from the outside.[12] As we learned in our discussion of Millerism, to insiders the fulfillment of religious doctrine is perfectly rational. But viewed from the periphery, the pessimism of the secular Left deploring nuclear escalation and global warming, for example, seems just as out of place alongside the anticipated dawning of the age of Aquarius and the elevation of human consciousness that attends it. The blow up or bliss out alternatives to the future of our world, which we will revisit when we turn to 2012 end of the world prophecy, developed in parallel chronological frameworks; for example, the highly influential intellectually oriented text *Hamlet's Mill* (to be examined in detail in the next chapter), which would guide the New Age ideology, appeared at just about the same time as Lindsey's prophetic work on the Bible's message.

Sociologists continue to grapple with the widespread popularity and commercial success of Lindsey's book and the LaHaye and Jenkins novels, despite the blatant religious nature of the message they deliver. Normally, subcultures that make it into the mainstream do so because they become sanitized via treatment in the media, and thus purged of their radical claims, such that yesterday's lunacy becomes today's hot consumer item.

But this theory of cultural incorporation doesn't seem to apply to Doomsday media fiction, a large segment of which remains boldly uncompromising in its Christian dispensational leanings.[13] Good marketing and the proliferation of spin-off products—movies, computer games and related downloads—help, as does the style copied by authors from the successful romance/detective story and action thriller genre. So does the timing. The Left Behind novels were created in the midst of world events that engendered apocalyptic thinking; for example, sales increased by 70 percent in the two months that followed 9/11.[14] You don't have to be an evangelical Christian to become absorbed in this sort of fiction. Whether you buy into the Lindsey and LaHaye and Jenkins version of Doomsday or not, its anti-institutional, anti-intellectual message still resonates decades later in American pop culture.

Apocalyptic video games are a more recently deployed medium for Christian dispensational ideas. One of the most popular depictions of apocalyptically oriented virtual realities appears in the Halo Series, which follows the theme in Wolfgang Peterson's film *The Never Ending Story* (1984): an elite solider (the gamer), armed with the latest high-tech weapons, confronts a series of feats requiring agility, strength, and acuity of wit. The threat lies in an alien Antichrist cult known as "The Covenant," which seeks to rule the cosmos. In a newly released post-Apocalyptic version of the game, "Halo Reach," the protagonist plays to restore order. Anthropology student and ardent gamer Grant Stauffer says that playing the game gives him a sense of participation in efforts to save the universe: "Just as the Maya practiced dramatic rituals in accordance with their myths, millions of gamers routinely participate in contests in online communities and contribute to [the hero's] attempt to rescue the earth from destruction at the hands of the Covenant."[15]

Contemporary Doomsday preppers act out the pre-Apocalypse condition by creating entire micro-worlds of their own to inhabit when the big day dawns. They are abetted by a whole genre of "how-to" publications and websites. How shall we prepare? One 2012 survival manual offers this advice: develop your coherence by breathing exercises; cleanse your colon with Bentonite clay, the better to facilitate reception of the pranic energy; work on modifying your difficult feelings and rigid attitudes; choose someone you appreciate and "radiate" a feeling of appreciation in turn; next do the same for the planet; and, on a more practical level, lay in a good supply of food and water, a first-aid kit, and a gas stove; and archive all your important dates on your memory stick.[16]

National Geographic TV produced a popular series of programs entitled Doomsday Preppers (2012), which depicted survivalists staked out in remote areas, digging shelters and practicing Marine Corps–type survival skills. Atop the underground supply cellars stocked with nonperishable edibles and fresh water—some good for a two-year stay—were heavily armed defense posts. The prepper population was comprised largely of heavily tattooed Caucasians. If you're too lazy to build your own you can purchase an easy-to-assemble version via a host of Internet sites. One sells for $5,500 and is guaranteed to withstand the rigors of most Doomsday event scenarios. If you can afford to opt for the luxury model, one outfit put together a 137,000-square-foot underground timeshare bunker capable of housing 900 people. It includes a Laundromat and fine wine cellar. Down payments start at $150,000.

Contemporary Christian dispensational apocalypticism is not without political implications. Today's Antichrist has been garbed in the fashion of the times by extreme evangelicals. Because of his internationalist tendencies and commitments to expand the role of government, Barack Obama is among the most recent to don the mantle.[17] Like Franklin Roosevelt, his predecessor during the years of the Depression and World War II, he held the office in hard times that fueled fears of fascism and the anticipation of the creation of a dictatorial superstate.[18] At the time of Obama's campaign for gun control legislation in the aftermath of the horrible mass murder of Newtown, Connecticut, schoolchildren in December 2012, Wayne LaPierre, head of the evangelist-supported National Rifle Association, mounted a pro-gun effort in the US Congress. He warned: "The American people clearly see the daunting forces we will undoubtedly face: terrorists, crime, drug gangs, the possibility of Euro-style debt riots, civil unrest and natural disaster."[19]

Accepting what one believes to be inevitable and turning attention to how to deal with its consequences by setting the mind to thinking about resources, self-defense, emergency medicine, and disaster management in general relieves anxiety. Like advocates of the right to bear arms, the survivalists, applying the old Puritan do-it-yourself hard-work ethic, find themselves well prepared for a post-Apocalyptic future that lies just around time's corner.

9
Astronomical World Age Theories Resurrected

[*Hamlet's Mill*] is likely to remain . . . a lion in everybody's path for years.
—*Cover endorsement for the book* Hamlet's Mill

Every once in a while a provocative new book comes along with a message that radically alters our way of thinking about things. In 1962 Rachel Carson's *Silent Spring* awakened the world to the perils of pesticides and the possibility that human activity can have drastic effects on the environment. Desmond Morris's *The Naked Ape* (1967) brought the behavior of humans and their immediate ancestral species much closer—some say too close—together.

In 1969, premillennial prophesying acquired a huge bump in legitimacy, especially among intellectual circles, when a pair of science historians, Giorgio de Santillana of MIT and Hertha von Dechend from Frankfurt, published a controversial book entitled *Hamlet's Mill: An Essay Investigating the Origins of Human Knowledge and Its Transmission through Myth*. I vividly recall my more avid students begging me to discuss its implications with them. These were significant: this thick, scholarly tome challenged the conventional meaning of the word *myth* by positing the idea that all the great myths from around the world derive from a common astronomical origin. De Santillana and von Dechend's spin on the theory of the monomyth argued that the gods and mythic places that populate ancient and contemporary tales are really stand-ins for universally recognized celestial phenomena that harken back to a golden age (circa 5000 BCE) when the calendar was invented. Breathing new life into the theory of world ages, the authors also contended that major changes in pan-global civilizations were conditioned by responses to cosmic shifts, specifically to the passage of the vernal equinox point from one constellation of the zodiac to another—the precession of the equinoxes. Drawing on an old millenarian theme we encountered earlier, they alleged that ancient people would have regarded the travails of their times—invasions, prolonged wars, natural disasters, and so on—as inevitable preludes to a new condition related to the tilt of the Earth's axis, a condition that, in the minds of careful skywatchers, would precipitate a new world age. Put simply, the fate of humanity is written in the stars. Recognition of the crucial times of the passage of the equinox sun from one constellation of the zodiac to another opened the gateway to social change.

The Milky Way, which would play a major role in Maya 2012 end of the world theorizing (to be discussed in chapter 12) was also highlighted in *Hamlet's Mill*. De Santillana and von Dechend proposed that ancient astronomers would have recognized this luminous, circum-celestial band as stable and crisis resistant because it is not subject to the precession of the equinoxes. Unlike the crossing point of the celestial equator and the plane of the ecliptic (the zodiac), which marks the equinoxes, the place where the plane of the zodiac crosses that of the Milky Way remains unchanged (in fact, it does not, though the change is much slower and more difficult to detect—about one-fortieth the normal rate of precession).

Not surprisingly, a number of New Age prophets picked up on de Santillana and von Dechend's brand of cosmic determinism; for example, blending the ideas in *Hamlet's Mill* and the language of modern astrophysics, astrologer Dane Rudhyar contended that changes in the polar axis would result in "galactic forces . . . enter[ing] the electromagnetic field of our planet's organism." Applying principles of the popular Kundalini and Yoga techniques of the 1970s, he explained that "the orientation of the polar axis brings the spinal column of our globe in line with a succession of polestars, and thus with a specific region of the galaxy—which, for man, represents at least symbolically the Spiritual World, the world of divine Hierarchies."[1] Rudhyar set the year 2060 as the end of the current segment of the precession cycle.

Hamlet's Mill drew inspiration from the work of early twentieth-century classical scholar Sir James Frazer, whose popular text *The Golden Bough* expanded on a professional study of fertility cults and religious practices in the Aegean to include cultures well out of contact with the Mediterranean world.[2] Critics thought Frazer took unwarranted leaps to find superficial connections and common ground among these cultures, for example, the recognition of seasonal deities and human sacrifice as a consequence of fertility ritual. Taking the same universalist approach, de Santillana and von Dechend viewed the stars as the "essence of being . . . the kingly power, silent and unmoving. They stand for the laws that rule the world."[3] The planets are the gods, the hidden powers, each with its own aspect. They represent the forces, the will, that operate within the law. In this cosmic framework *Hamlet's Mill* analyzed myths as diverse as Nordic, Maya, and Japanese in search of common sky objects worshipped in similar ways by diverse cultures; for example, one conclusion was that the polestar, pivot of all sky motion, evoked the idea of falling down from heaven.

Let me take one of the examples from this set to illustrate: the Lapps say that the nearby star Arcturus, an archer, shoots down the world's pivot, Polaris, with his bow and arrow, causing the heavens to crash down to earth. By contrast, Siberian tribes view the stars that connect Polaris with the bowl of the Little Dipper as a rope fastened to the two end stars in the bowl, which represent horses. A wolf lurks nearby and, though protected by the seven watchmen (the stars of the Big Dipper), it is inevitable that the time will come when the wolf will kill the horses. Then the sky will fall. In yet another culture, Ursa Minor is a dog tied to the pole. He continually gnaws at the rope that binds him. Eventually he will succeed in severing the cord. Then the end of the world will come. De Santillana and von Dechend believed that stories like these underlie a very ancient, forgotten history—a human history that unifies all cultures.

After interpreting myriad mythological examples grounded in celestial references, de Santillana and von Dechend pose the question: Can it be coincidence that these stories—of the polestar, the Pleiades, the Milky Way, and other sky objects—are so alike? Surely they must have descended from a common origin in a celestially based cosmology, the "synapse" through which cultural transmission took place. In many of these myths the cosmic machine that represents the sky turning about the Earth is conceived as a mill, a drill, or a churn, hence the "mill" of the book's title. The mill is Hamlet's because that tormented and self-questioning literary character typifies—like the authors—the dissatisfied intellectual.

At first I found *Hamlet's Mill* to be an imaginative, erudite, and highly provocative exercise in comparative mythology, both in the content and the variety of cultural myths the authors used to support their case. While fascinated lay readers and a number of academics warmed to it and uncritically accepted its premises, some scholars detected a number of flaws in the interpretation of myths specific to their own areas of cultural expertise. For example, folklorist Hilda Ellis Davidson called the work "amateurish in the worst sense, jumping to wild conclusions without any knowledge of the historical value of the sources or of previous work done."[4] She cited, in particular, the authors' ignorance of progress made in her own field of Norse mythology; for example, she pointed out that the idea that Finno-Ugaric peoples were cut off from the Scandinavians until recently is pure nonsense, adding, "and one might continue on these lines [of misinformation] endlessly."[5]

Yes, it all *could* be coincidence, responded other reviewers. My own view, as an astronomer, is that if you think about the visible cosmic imagery, there may be only a limited number of ways to relate sky and Earth via the movement of the stars around a fixed pole: why did the emperors of ancient Beijing and the pharaohs of Egypt liken their dynasties to the pivot of all celestial motion, the so-called nail of the sky? Maybe independent invention offers a better explanation than the monomyth: because the ruler in the terrestrial is like the pole in the celestial realm. Both are destined to remain fixed. Is it so far out of the realm of reason to imagine that diverse cultures, remote and well out of contact from one another on the globe, might independently devise similar celestial metaphors?

On the contrary, there are many astronomies that apply different cultural constructs to the same sky phenomena. This was one of the criticisms lodged against the astral monomyth by Harvard astronomer Cecelia Payne-Gaposchkin. She regarded *Hamlet's Mill* an exercise in textual cherry picking.[6] While Payne-Gaposchkin acknowledged that one could read the individual chapters of *Hamlet's Mill* with great delight, thus acquiring a sense of kinship with our remote ancestors, she thought that, taken as a whole, the argument that ancient myth finds its origin in a pattern dependent on a knowledge of the precession of the equinoxes was too loosely knit. True, our ancestors may have been *capable* of perceiving precession, but "to use the myths as evidence that they *did*, and to use this conclusion to interpret the myths, smacks of a circular argument."[7] Furthermore, she added, setting Time Zero all the way back to 5000 BCE, as the authors do, seems wildly improbable and totally unjustified.

The prize for the most vituperatively negative criticism of *Hamlet's Mill* surely must go to British anthropologist Edmund Leach. In the opening sentence of a *New York Review* piece sarcastically titled "Bedtime Story," he openly admits, "My reaction to this book is hostile."[8] Leach's abhorrence for *Hamlet's Mill* stems not so much from the mistakes, omissions, misinterpretations, and failure to cite evidence—all of which he takes considerable trouble to point out—but rather from the influence of the ideas of Leo Frobenius on one of the authors (von Dechend was his student). In 1897 this German ethnologist established the concept of *Kulturkreis*, an argument about revealed truth that uses the geographic distribution of cultural elements to historically reconstruct hypothetical civilizations of the past. At the root of Frobenius's philosophy lies the idea that *Ergriffenheit*, or *emotional* involvement, was the crucial development that would lead to the emergence of a culture, such that "Once man is gripped by the world about him, the particular nature of the things in his world and the existential order within which he lives are revealed to him."[9]

Leach observed that both Kulturkreis and Ergriffenheit seemed to serve as templates for the narrative structure of *Hamlet's Mill*, especially the idea that the dramatic awareness of the precession of the equinoxes was responsible for elevating early civilization in the Middle East to a sophisticated understanding of the relationship between time and the cosmos. Encoded in the language of mythology, this profound scientific discovery, say de Santillana and von Dechend, reappeared in fragmented form in later cultures in the classical world, Scandinavia, and even the Caribbean and Polynesia, as the authors' close attention to relics, fragments, and allusions is intended to demonstrate. In other words, a single archaic system for understanding and expressing the role of cosmology in human culture, now largely lost but partially rediscovered by the authors, had prevailed on a global scale during the first four millennia BCE.

The year 1971 also saw the publication of *The Roots of Civilization*, another influential book that would have the effect of bolstering theories about the advanced scientific knowledge known to our forbearers.[10] Authored by science writer Alexander Marshack, *Roots* offered evidence for the existence of a form of prehistoric scientific notation related to celestial phenomena. Marshack analyzed marks he regarded as patterns gouged into an 8,500-year-old piece of carved bone. He interpreted them, and similar artifacts, as constituting nothing less than a calendar designed to follow the phases of the moon. Largely accepted by establishment archaeologists and astronomers, Marshack's discovery rolled back the clock of advanced human cognitive development by millennia. If you think about it, recording changes in the aspects of the moon long before the invention of writing makes practical sense. Precise knowledge of periodic nocturnal light and dark periods would have been useful to hunter-gatherers. Marshack's bone had the effect of motivating scholars to think about the possibility that other precise information about the relationship between nature and culture might lie buried in the past, awaiting discovery.

New Agers in late twentieth-century America were profoundly attracted to the inclusive, unifying message, not only across world cultures but also between present and past, inherent in the astral monomyth laid down in *Hamlet's Mill*. A spate of texts on cosmic renewal followed in its wake. The Egyptians, the Babylonians, the Etruscans, the Inca, and the Maya were variously portrayed as having been well aware of the effects of the Earth slowly gyrating on its axis, and, more important, of the cosmic warning signs that lay at the root of social change in each of them—and perhaps us. A few examples are worth exploring.

One intriguing tale promoting the theory of the "star-fixed ages of man," as the *Saturday Review* termed the cosmic shifts resulting from precession, is told in British science writer George Michanowsky's 1977 best-seller *The Once and Future Star*.[11] Drawing on UFO mythology, Michanowsky claimed to have deciphered a Sumerian cuneiform tablet proving that a visit from an ancient supernatural being sometime between the ninth and fourth millennium BCE had elevated human knowledge to its greatest heights. This "semi-human," as Michanowsky described him, taught the people to calculate the position of *his* polestar, which was marked by the sudden outburst of the great supernova in the southern constellation of Vela, a supernova remnant that had been receiving much attention from radio astronomers at the time. Though the ancient knowledge that came with the polar shift has vanished, the reportage on the tablet was the source of the kind of world creation mythology dealt with in *Hamlet's Mill*. Ironically, the language of death and transfiguration are often applied to the life story of a supernova, as modern astronomers typically characterize it: a dying star suddenly resurrects itself by blazing forth and creating new chemical elements out of old. Unfortunately, Michanowsky never takes his readers through the process he used to translate the mysterious Sumerian tablet containing the secret code of the polar shift that changed the early history of the Middle East. Worse still, he fails to provide an illustration of this key document in his text.

A second example of how cosmic determinism allegedly launched social change occurred when Boston University religion professor David Ulansey breathed new life into the *tauroctony*, or bull slaying ritual, often portrayed in Mithraic art and passed on to the Roman Empire, where the Persian cult thrived during the Augustan (first century CE) era. Earlier scholars had interpreted tauroctony scenes, especially those that included planetary signs, as a graphic representation of the world's horoscope. In *The Origins of the Mithraic Mysteries* (1989) Ulansey makes the case that the order of the constellations carved on a bench depicting the bull slaying in a Mithraeum, or underground temple of cultic worship, located in Ostia Antica, the port of ancient Rome, represents the sun's position in the constellation of Taurus at the spring equinox.[12]

According to Ulansey, the scene was intended to record the discovery of the precession of the equinoxes, which ancient Persians had ascribed to a cosmic deity who possessed the power to move the entire universe. When their god, Mithras, represented by the constellation of Perseus, slew the bull, he freed the equinox sun to pass into the next house of the zodiac, an action that would renew the world. In Ulansey's words, "It would be difficult to conceive of a more appropriate symbol for the precession than the symbol of the death of a bull, representing the death of the previous Age of Taurus brought about by precession."[13] The constellation of Perseus, ideally situated directly north of Taurus, offers convenient imagery suggesting Perseus as the agent of death. Thus, according to Ulansey, the hero slaying the bull symbolizes the movement of the equinox sun out of Taurus and into Aries, the next constellation of the zodiac. Here, then, is a testimony to the lost knowledge, from a very ancient past, possessed by the Mithraic cult. In Ulansey's eyes, Mithraic iconography emerges as a kind of cosmological code that symbolizes their possession of secret knowledge of a "newly discovered god so powerful that the entire cosmos was completely under his control."[14] Those assured privileged access to the fatal forces residing in the heavens and embodied in this powerful deity might also acquire salvation when they passed on via their journey to the planetary spheres.

A third, more recent, example of a popular work on cosmic determinism directly influenced by *Hamlet's Mill* is a text coauthored by Belgian engineer Robert Bauval. His cosmic axis is revealed in the orientation of Egypt's three principal pyramids which, he argues, were expressly laid out to align with the three bright stars in the belt of the constellation of Orion. Bauval calculated that the best fit of the celestial template to the pyramids would have occurred in 10,500 BCE, approximately 8,000 years before the building date of the earliest of the three structures verified by archaeological excavations. Notwithstanding, Bauval argued instead that while the pyramids were built later, their arrangement was in accord with an ancient layout derived from a lost culture. Like Rome's Mithraic cult, the Egyptians, too, had discovered precession. Careful examiners of Bauval's alignment theory will discover that the pyramids are off by 10 percent in their relative separations and 32 percent in the angle of deviation of the small pyramid from the line connecting the larger ones. Moreover, engineer Bauval never explains how the Egyptians managed to take naked-eye observations of the three stars and project them onto a terrestrial plane thousands of feet long.

After the *Orion Mystery* (1994), in which he revealed his theory, in *The Egypt Code* (2006), Bauval set out to prove that the remains in the Nile Valley hold the key to a secret geographic plan that entombed all of the cosmic principles behind the advanced civilization that preceded the pharaohs.[15] This mother culture, he contends, was run by "astronomer-priests" and headed by a sun king—and it lasted more than three millennia. Bauval finds room in *The Egypt Code* to palliate the indifference to his work among academics by pointing to the massive public and media interest accorded his lifelong project.

Nor were the Americas free of cosmic determinism. Independent researcher William Sullivan's 1996 *Secret of the Incas* attributes the birth of the Inca Empire of the South American Andes to the discovery of a cosmic shift that led to a new dawning of reality.[16] Sullivan's event of choice was a close conjunction in 650 CE of Jupiter and Saturn, which happened to coincide with the coming together of their terrestrial counterparts, identified respectively by Sullivan with the god Viracocha and the first Inca king, Manco Capac. He further claims that earlier cosmic changes affecting drastic social transformation were also steered by planetary conjunctions. He even names a few of them: the age of agriculture, the age of sacrifice, and so on.

Sullivan uses the then newly developed technology of astronomical computer software to connect his seminal 650 CE planetary conjunction with the coincident heliacal rise, or first appearance, of the Milky Way on the December solstice viewed from the Inca capital. As he boasts, his accuracy "can be checked against a modern computer program."[17] Yet a simple computation made by hand, together with a visual check via careful observation, demonstrates that the accuracy of the kind of dating Sullivan proposes cannot be achieved to a tolerance less than 300 years. It is worth noting that the tactic of deploying the latest impressive techno-advances to back up an argument favoring heretical theorizing has often proven effective, at least to the casual reader. Gerald Hawkins's bold statements about what the invention of the IBM 7090 computer did for his ability to "decode" Stonehenge in 1963 is a good example. When the brash young astronomer announced that the odds were better than a million to one that the set of lunar alignments, which he calculated using one second of machine time, were not due to coincidence, he was rewarded with extraordinary media attention. Later, archaeologist Richard Atkinson, in a scathing (though not widely circulated) review, demonstrated, using only pencil and paper, that bettors might be offered a more reasoned payoff at far lower odds.[18]

According to Sullivan, the people of the Andes had worked tirelessly for millennia to force social reality to conform to the changing patterns they saw in the sky. But in the early fifteenth century, when the Incas beat off their rivals, the Chancas, and created their highland capital of Cuzco, an architectural wonder whose trampled remains modern tourists barely glimpse today, they saw as their foremost mission the unleashing of a war against time. Why? Because the secret heavenly message attached to the next great social overturning (which Sullivan contends was also broadcast to the Aztecs of Mexico via the network of the psychic unity of mankind) portended their fatal demise. Responding to the cosmic dilemma, the Inca king sought to forestall cosmic prophecy both by moving New Year's Day to a different time and by sacrificing humans "to persuade the Powers

Above to stop Time."[19] This is the "secret of the Incas," the disclosure of which is promised in the title.

Hamlet's Mill played a profound role in each of the foregoing accounts of the secrets of the prehistoric past. Indeed, five decades after its publication, the prophetic prediction of an *Atlantic Monthly* reviewer that appeared on the original book jacket (reproduced in this chapter's epigraph), has been proven true.

But the astrally induced world age theories of Michanowsky, Ulansey, Bauval, and Sullivan share additional common ground: all contend that mythology is the mother of science. In each theory "myth" is perceived as the technical language that was designed deliberately to transmit complex lost astronomical knowledge, especially the precession of the equinoxes. In the cosmic shifts proposed by each writer, new stars or planets replace old ones, the planets and stars are the gods, and the animals that make up the zodiac and the topographic references become the metaphors for the location of the sun in the cosmos—literally a New Age recasting of Joachim of Fiore's dispensational theory of the three ages of history in an astrological mode, as historian Michael York views it.[20] World endings announced by disasters, such as floods and earthquakes, mark new creation points signposted by the close gathering of planets or the shift of the equinox or solstice sun from one zodiacal constellation to another; for example, the arrival of Noah's ark high on Mt. Ararat is thought to be an expression of the sun arriving at the summer solstice, thereby attaining its highest point in the sky.

Because of the lack of acceptance of their theories by a large segment of the scholarly establishment, many promoters of the monomyth tend to portray conventional disciplines, such as archaeology and anthropology, in a negative light—as enclaves relying too much on the idea of independent invention as opposed to the widespread diffusion of important ideas from a common prehistoric source, which they favor. As Sullivan puts it, "The technical language of myth is simply too idiosyncratic to have been reinvented over and over again."[21] This is a claim all too often made by those who do not take the trouble to study cultures and cultural history in the detail required to elicit converging factual support for their theories.

Solstice or equinox suns entering and leaving the Milky Way, bringing with them connections and disconnections with the gods, beginning and ending world ages—this is one of the common denominators of many monomythical hypotheses. In Sullivan's book, for example, the Milky Way is alleged to be a bridge that connects the people to their ancestors and to the land of the gods. It had been destroyed (that is, it became invisible), but when it was re-created the spirits of the dead were able to return to instruct the living so that, once again, they would be "ready to be born from the uterus of the great celestial mother."[22] As we'll discover in chapter 11, the Milky Way womb, replete with a solstitial alignment, would be refitted with Maya clothing a generation later in 2012 theories of world transformation.

Finally, though secular in nature, the monomythical theories analyzed in this chapter share many of the attributes of the Apocalypse-tainted Christian teleological interpretations discussed earlier. First, their views of history follow the sui generis idea of the origin of world religion which, as we recall from chapter 2, differs from the inward directed, random, and often illogical way most historians believe civilizations evolve. Monomythical happenings are highly ordered and predestined to take place. Second, each makes a claim regarding access to secret knowledge derived not from biblical sources but rather from a largely unknown antecedent civilization—knowledge acquired via revelation that elevates the status of prehistoric humanity. So our ancient ancestors seem more like us. A third common denominator of monomythical theories is that knowledge encoded in celestial phenomena, once discovered by a small segment of society, exerts a profound effect on culture—so profound that it causes societies to undergo drastic shifts in behavior. One has the sense that some transcendent power embedded in nature preordained the future course of human events. For each of the authors I singled out, not only is the future "written" in the preliterate past via the oral transmission of myth, the past *guides* the future. Global mythologies are understood to be preliterate forms of science and the time cycles embedded in each of them directly connect humanity and the world of the sacred. What especially appeals to the general reader is the message that offers hope to those among us dissatisfied—like Hamlet—with the status and direction of our own society. The monomyth appeals to the counterculture because it promises the possibility of salvation.

The cosmically controlled account of history in this chapter on ancient myth is titillating. It is uplifting. It is a kind of "easy history" crafted to appeal to readers unfamiliar with the methodological intricacies of scientific archaeology, for example. This sort of history is more titillating than the orthodox (non–best seller) interpretations of the rise and fall of the Egyptians, the

Incas, the Babylonians, the Persians, and other high civilizations, which conventional historians believe to have evolved via tightly controlled rituals, monument building, and other bureaucratically organized mechanisms alongside diverse invented mythologies, many of them astral in nature, that provided rationalizations for empire building.

At a psychological level, conventional explanations disappoint because they reveal the ordinariness of human civilization. They teach us that our ancient ancestors were every bit as honorable and corrupt as we are today. The conventional interpretation of history offers little hope for a contemporary culture desperately in need of exalted alternatives to the reality we have created for ourselves. That narrative is simply too devoid of romance.

> I met a traveler from an antique land
> Who said: "Two vast and trunkless legs of stone
> Stand in the desert. Near them on the sand,
> Half sunk, a shattered visage lies, whose frown
> And wrinkled lip and sneer of cold command
> Tell that its sculptor well those passions read
> Which yet survive, stamped on these lifeless things,
> The hand that mocked them and the heart that fed."

In these lines from his 1818 poem *Ozymandias*, Percy Bysshe Shelley reflects on the transitory nature of life inspired by walking among ancient ruins.[23] Babylon, Rome, Luxor, Machu Picchu—all symbolize an imagined greater past now fallen in decay. The contrast between grandeur and decay revealed through the eye of the romantic grabs the imagination. If only we could experience the past without the necessity of reading stacks of books and learning about the cultures and their languages, as the linguists, the archaeologists, the anthropologists, and the historians insist we must do to truly understand them. In my view romance is also what attracts the contemporary pilgrimages to antiquity we are about to confront in the remaining chapters—most especially the Maya 2012 phenomenon.

PART IV

Episode 2

December 21, 2012

10

The Fathers of Y12 Prophecy

Americans who sought to create their own reality had discovered that they needed to get directions—both on the reality and on the programmatic strategies for obtaining it—from somebody else.

—*Religious studies scholar Catherine Albanese*

America since the turn of the millennium finds itself once again in the midst of a campaign—not unlike that of the 1840s, though far more secular owing to the historical developments surveyed in previous chapters—to warn the world of the imminent end of history. Few will disagree that M3K so far has been an awful time, marked by terrible events and trends too depressingly familiar to enumerate and certainly capable of enticing even the most rational segment of the citizenry to desperately seek unorthodox pathways to the future. Still, there is nothing new under the sun in the latest, recently elapsed countdown. All the elements that informed the most attention-getting contemporary Doomsday—December 21 (the winter solstice), 2012—have long been in place. In fact, the table setting for the menus of both Doomsday 2012 and 1844 came out of the same kitchen cupboard.

Just as the fixing of the October 22, 1844, Doomsday clock arose out of developments during the Second Great Awakening, the contemporary date setting for the postmillennial cataclysm had its roots firmly implanted back in the hyperactive mid-1970s, especially after the publication of *Hamlet's Mill*.

Of seminal importance was a countercultural book authored in 1975 by a pair of intellectually minded brothers engaged in psychedelic shamanism: the McKennas, Terrence and Dennis. It was titled *The Invisible Landscape: Mind, Hallucinogens, and the I Ching.*[1] For the McKennas, the drug-induced trance state served as the conduit to revealed knowledge of the lost discoveries of the ancient past.

Terrence McKenna was a science-oriented student with a BA in art history from Berkeley who got into psychedelics in the hippie environment of San Francisco's Haight-Ashbury district. He then traveled to Tibet in search of shamanic wisdom, and later, with his younger brother Dennis, to the Amazonian rainforest. There the pair experimented in ingesting what they called "power plants." According to the McKennas, the basic theory behind power plants is that their chemicals free the mind, thus allowing deep spiritual insights to emerge from the depths of one's consciousness. Stated simply, the power to perceive the true underlying reality already lies within you, but you must be proactive to bring it to the surface. In resonance with a number of exoheretical themes familiar to us from previous chapters, the elder McKenna explained the brothers' motivation: "We were refugees from a society that we thought was poisoned by its own self hatred and inner contradictions. We had sorted through the ideological options and we had decided to put all of our chips on the psychedelic experience as the shortest path to the millennium, which our politics had inflamed us to hope for."[2]

During one of their experimental mushroom-ingesting episodes, Terrence heard his brother emit a loud, strange vocal tone. The brothers became convinced that this unorthodox emanation had accidentally put Dennis in contact with an alien dimension of reality. Experimenting with various hallucinogenic cocktails, the pair attempted to replicate the sound in hopes of opening the doorway that would allow escape from ordinary historical time, believing that this held the potential to transform reality completely, instantaneously joining mind and matter together in a higher dimension, so that human will would then—and ever after—be reflected *perfectly*. The process, which they characterized as a "teleportation at warp speed," would result in, to further quote their borrowed scientific language, "a molecular aggregate of hyperdimensional, superconducting matter that receives and sends messages transmitted by thought, that stores and retrieves information in a holographic fashion in neural DNA, and that depends on superconductive harmine as a transducer energy source and super conductive RNA as a temporal matrix."[3] Harmine (harmalol methyl ether), incidentally, is a white crystalline alkaloid ($C_{13}H_{12}N_2O$) found in harmal seeds. The harmal plant comes from India and the Levant, where its strong-scented seeds find frequent use as a stimulant.

Where does cosmic timing fit in? Once again Eastern wisdom comes into play. The McKennas based their calculations on resonances they claim to have discovered between the *I Ching* divination system and major astronomical cycles, among them the lunar year, the sunspot cycle and, again, the precession of the equinoxes. Thus, one of the major cycles that emerged out of their complex calculations, 4,294.8 years, turns out to be almost exactly double the time it takes for the vernal equinox to pass through one sign of the zodiac. The brothers pointed out that the so-called eschaton time wave, about which all the cycles resonate, was due to peak around the year 2012. They arrived at this date by adding the last subcycle of 67 years to 1945, the date they selected as the last in a series of "great novelties" in the history of the world, namely, the creation of the A-bomb. This is the first mention of 2012 in the literature as the culminating moment of history, the prefixed date when all humanity would be cosmically predestined to move into a higher dimension beyond ordinary history. The brothers McKenna believed that in their psychedelic trips they had been experiencing the initial moments of this millennial event—what they called, after Teilhard, the "Omega Point."

The McKenna prediction, like the date settings we encountered in Millerism, incorporates a highly selective process (a kind of cherry picking, to use Gaposchkin's term) of, in this case, natural and historical phenomena whose base periods can be manipulated to produce a magic number or date; for example, skeptics might inquire why the McKennas chose as one of their pivotal cycles the lunar year of thirteen months, or 384 days, instead of that of twelve months, or 354 days, and why the eleven-year sunspot cycle? The theory the McKennas lay out to justify precisely what makes these two cycles, along with the precession cycle, so important among the countless number of time loops they might have selected to mesh together is very difficult to follow.[4] As best I have been able to discern, their theory consists of a number of elements worth detailing here, if only to demonstrate the nature of their reasoning process.

This is where the *I Ching* comes into the picture. Historian of religion Olav Hammer notes that New Agers who were exploring individualized non-Christian forms of religiosity were as familiar with the *I Ching* as they were with Jungian psychology.[5] Briefly, the *I Ching*, or Book of Changes, is a Chinese divinatory system resembling geomancy, which may have descended from as early as the third millennium BCE. Oracular statements are laid out in sixty-four combinations of six-line sets known as *hexagrams*. The latter are drawings made up of solid (yang, or the creative principle) or dashed (yin, or the receptive) horizontal lines. They are perhaps most familiar to us depicted on the South Korean flag. To understand the process of change, one needs to divine the hexagrams. This involves reading the book, no easy task owing to its elliptical language, and treating it as an oracle—what students of divination call *bibliomancy*.

Now, the McKennas began by noting that if you multiply the number of hexagrams in one particular arrangement of the *I Ching*, known as the King Wen sequence, which they believed to be related to an early lunar calendar, by the number of lines contained in each hexagram, you get 383.89. Successive multiplications of this unit, they argued, generate resonant cyclic occurrences, for example, the sunspot and precession cycles. Next the McKennas took note of how many hexagram lines changed with each multiplication. They presented the result graphically; then they paired each number with its opposite in reverse sequence. This yielded a second graph—the "eschaton time wave" itself (figure 10.1). Then comes the crucial connection between the cosmos and human destiny: the McKennas claimed that this particular wave maps out historical time, its peaks and valleys signaling points of ingression and conservation of novelty, respectively, such as instances when the space-time manifold is open to drastic change. Finally, the McKennas slid their graph back and forth chronologically to lay stress on the decades of the immediate future. After all, argued the brothers, the troubling situation of the twentieth-century world signals a climax—it must be placed in time very close to a major "concrescence" of the wave keyed to the number 64. This leads to the 1945 date setting. From that date they calculated, via backward multiplication, the times of earlier concrescences:

1.3 billion years ago = the beginning of life;
1.3 billion divided by 64 = 18 million years ago = the peak of the age of mammals;
18 million divided by 64 = 275,000 years ago = the emergence of Homo sapiens;
275,000 divided by 64 = 4,300 years ago = the beginning of historical time;
4,300 divided by 64 = 67 years ago = the development of the A-bomb.

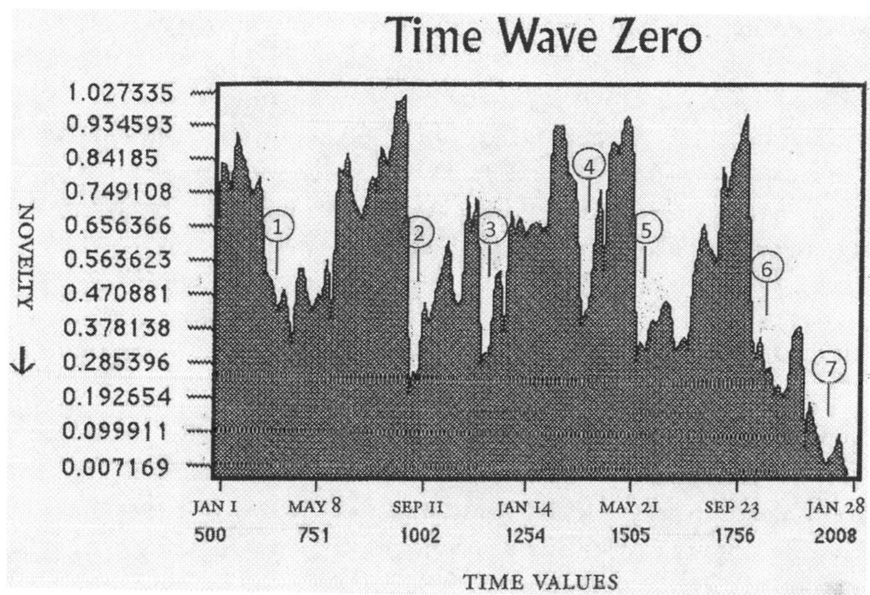

FIGURE 10.1. The McKenna brothers' eschaton time wave zero parses out world "novelties" they believed would lead up to time's end in 2012. (Figure 28: "Time Wave Zero" from *The Invisible Landscape: Mind, Hallucinogens and the I Ching* by Terence McKenna and Dennis McKenna. © 1994 by Dennis J. McKenna and Terence K. McKenna. Reprinted by permission of HarperCollins Publishers.)

The end point of these cycles (the first two are open to challenge by biologists, the third by historians), and consequently the termination point of all time, is arrived at by adding 67 years to 1945: thus 2012. It is worth noting that the McKennas never mention any connection between 2012 and Maya prophecy.

How, then, did the Maya get mixed up in this contemporary form of dispensational millenarianism? To address that question we need to inquire into what was going on in Maya studies four decades ago. The mid-1970s was a time when great advances were being made in the decipherment of Maya writing as well as in the study of ancient Maya astronomy. In 1973 a group of Maya scholars trained in a variety of disciplines retreated to a modest resort near the ruins of Palenque in the jungles of the southwest Yucatán peninsula. There they set about the task of deciphering the inscriptions on monuments that had been discovered at this classic (200–900 CE) Maya site a century earlier. Keys to the success of their work lay in the discovery that

Maya writing possessed a significant phonetic component and the realization that contemporary variants of the Maya language still spoken today matched syllabic equivalents carved in stucco at the Palenque and other ruins. Once the breakthroughs reached the scholarly community, the "Palenque Mesa Redonda," or Palenque Round Table discussions, as participants termed them, became an annual event that attracted an interdisciplinary team of linguists, anthropologists, archaeologists, and Maya aficionados from all over the world. Within a mere decade the Maya code was essentially cracked. The hieroglyphs carved in stone would reveal the detailed history of the many dynasties that governed Palenque, Copan, Tikal, and the other great ancient Maya cities during the first millennium CE.[6]

Meanwhile, the complexities of the astronomically based Maya calendar were also beginning to be understood. Studies of the codices, the few surviving ancient books, revealed that Maya astronomers had charted cycles of Venus, Mars, and eclipses of the sun and moon. They aligned special buildings—even the axes of whole cities—to be in harmony with sacred celestial phenomena occurring along the local horizon, the better to render performative aspects of the rituals of dedication of their ruler to the ancestor gods more effective.[7]

The Palenque Round Table meetings began just a few years after I had become attracted to Maya studies. Trained as an astronomer, I marveled at what I had read about the accomplishments of Maya skywatchers. The handful of published accounts of Maya astronomy portrayed these people as having acquired a capacity to track celestial phenomena with extraordinary accuracy. They possessed neither computers nor telescopes, yet their written documents made it clear that they could pinpoint the location of Venus in its cycle to an accuracy of one day in 500 years. And they computed the length of the lunar month to just seven minutes short of the value obtained by contemporary astronomers. How had they acquired such knowledge?

I was also intrigued by a number of oddly shaped and oriented Maya buildings, like the Caracol of Chichén Itzá, a round tower containing windows directed to various points along the local horizon, and the House of the Governor at Uxmal, an immense structure that faced outward—away from the central axis of the city—and was markedly misaligned with the architecture that surrounded it. Why the odd shapes and skewed alignments? Could they be Maya "observatories" built to focus on celestial phenomena seen at the local horizon? I set up a research program to map these unusual structures with the goal of determining whether architectural alignments might intersect with the cycles and timings so clearly depicted in the codices. I was not surprised to find a number of building orientations that matched the locations of Venus at key positions in its seasonal movement along the local horizon. To anyone unacquainted with precision skywatching, these accomplishments seemed virtually unattainable by ordinary low-tech civilizations. For many, the Maya were proving to be quite *extra*ordinary. The opening, in the early 1980s, of la Ruta Maya, an "easy-on, easy-off" touristic highway loop in the Yucatán peninsula, made these ancient ruined cities accessible to everyone, which led to their increased popularity.

As a teacher of science, I think the unwillingness to believe that low-tech cultures could achieve levels of knowledge we are capable of acquiring only with the aid of sophisticated techno-tools is one source of the popular tendency to fantasize about sources of scientific achievements of ancient societies. To quote popular writer Erich von Daniken: "Incredible technical achievements existed in the past. There is a mass of know-how that we have only partially rediscovered today."[8] The process of acquiring this tech know-how took place too suddenly "to have been the product of a long and tedious development."[9] Rather, contended von Daniken, intelligent civilizations from extraterrestrial worlds must have bequeathed this higher knowledge to us in the distant past. These sorts of speculation, which fuel hypotheses about lost Atlantean or galactic civilizations possessing skills the equal of our own, bypass the basic question of whether another civilization might have acquired precise knowledge about the heavens without the necessity of resorting to our contemporary scientific way of getting it.

Actually, it is easy to show that "amazing feats" can be achieved by repeated and persistent observation with the naked eye. Take the moon's phase cycle as an example. Suppose you and I observe a full moon together and we note the date. We part, but not before we agree that we will faithfully persist in noting the dates of recurrence of successive full moons as well as the intervals between them for, say, the next ten years. Now, anyone who has viewed the moon close to full phase knows that precisely timing when a full moon occurs is not an easy task. If you look carefully, you may notice a tiny, ragged edge on one side, or a slight ovalness to the shape of the disk. This is easier to recognize if you tilt your head right or left. Now, suppose you reckon the date of the next full moon 30 days after the date we first viewed together, while I observe a 29-day interval. Suppose further that we both land on 30 as the interval separating the second and third full moon, and that each of us adds 31 days to get to the fourth observation; then I list 30 for the next interval compared to your 29, and so on. Finally, armed with our lengthy list of independently recorded full moon intervals, we reunite after ten years and compare the results of our observations. When we compute the average, we will find that we have arrived at almost exactly the same result, just a few minutes away from the modern value of 29.5306 days, computed from the modern study of the elements of the moon's orbit. The same can be said about timing the cycles of Venus or Mars, eclipse cycles, or the length of the year. Realizing the power of the unaided human eye and what it can achieve when driven by a persistent will to employ it tirelessly inspires me far more than the idea that what we have come to know was acquired from a race of hypothetical ancient beings made up of cardboard cutouts of ourselves. But the antiestablishment mood of the 1970s was far more attuned to a romantic account of gleanings from the Maya written record.

The Maya first enter the world of 2012 prophecy via autobiographical novelist Frank Waters, whose 1975 book *Mexico Mystique: The Coming Sixth World of Consciousness* came out within a year of the scholarly publication of the *First Palenque Round Table* (1974).[10] Waters's book was one of a number of publications, among them Peter Tompkins's *Mysteries of the Mexican Pyramids* (1976), Luis Arochi's *Pyramid of Kukulcan* (1984), and Erich von Daniken's *Chariots of the Gods?* (1970), that extolled extraordinary Maya achievements.[11] Tompkins claims that Maya wisdom transcended even the bounds of Christian heaven: "Moving and undulant, the serpent in Mesoamerica symbolized life, power, planets, suns, solar systems, galaxies, ultragalaxies, and infinite cosmic space."[12] Oddly enough, these visionary writers, as far as I have been able to discern, appear to have had little or no direct contact with one another.

Waters laid the groundwork for his theories about Nativist world rejuvenation in an earlier (1963) popular work, *The Book of the Hopi*, in which he interpreted testimonies he collected from Hopi elders.[13] These implied that we are on the verge of a great transition between the completion of the Fourth World and the beginning of the Fifth. In each of these previous creations, humanity, for one reason or another—war, techno-abuse, and so on—had lost its connections with ancient principles once held sacred. Just as the Hopi awaited the arrival of their long-lost white brother, Pahána, to lead those who would serve him in the Fifth World, so, too, the Aztecs had held out for Quetzalcoatl and the Maya for Kukulcan (their version of the Feathered Serpent god). Waters assigned the Spanish chronicler's tale about the return of Quetzalcoatl deep significance, "an unconscious projection of an entire race's dream of brotherhood with the races of all the continents. It is the unfulfilled longing of all humanity."[14]

Waters's Hopi prophecies would prove especially attractive to 1970s New Agers, whose central goal lay in the search for universal meaning that transcended all cultures, all religions, and all political systems—what anthropologist Armin Geertz labels a kind of primitivism "which locates the best human condition in the beginnings of time and nature and that subscribes to the *sui generis* theory of the origin of religion."[15]

Waters's views, notes historian Philip Jenkins, resonated with prophetic and apocalyptic ideas that had been popular in American religious thought since colonial days, and that had regularly inspired new religious movements.[16] He characterizes Waters's New Age stereotype of the Hopi as not unlike later romanticized versions of Native American people portrayed in films such as *Dances with Wolves* (1990) and *Pocahontas* (1995). He terms Waters's consumers "dream catchers," less interested in objective reality than in scrambling for spiritual refuge in the time of Vietnam, Watergate, assassinations, urban rioting, and looming ecological catastrophes.[17]

In *Mexico Mystique*, Waters shifts the focus of his theory of the rejuvenation of lost knowledge to Mexico. There he claimed to find the embodiment of a global belief, a "widespread conviction that mankind throughout all its stages of existence has appreciated and reflected in some measure the spiritual laws governing its evolutionary progress."[18] Following in the cherry-picking tradition of Frazer and de Santillana and von Dechend, though at a more superficial level, in my reading, Waters discovers the universal imagery he's looking for; for example, he compares aspects of the Mexican worship of Venus as Quetzalcoatl with that of the Middle Eastern deity Ishtar, goddess of love. Though they are of different genders, each undertakes a voyage through the underworld. In both cases the deity mediates between light and darkness, and therefore, Waters infers, between good and evil and "with the power of transcending these opposites within man himself."[19] To support his hypothesis, Waters points out that these diverse cultures also developed the same calendar to reckon the appearance of the deity in order to conduct the appropriate rites, a 2,920-day (eight-year) cycle that counts five returns of Venus to the same place in the heavens. Clearly, these people must have possessed advanced powers that have become understood by modern science only recently.

Now, one who pays little attention to the sky might explain these similarities as the product of an archaic latent consciousness shared by Homo sapiens. But as I argued earlier, I think it far more likely they resulted from the independent realization, based on simple observation, that the third-brightest object in the heavens always remains close to the sun. Its frequent appearances and disappearances when close to the horizon become obvious candidates for metaphors of death and resurrection, or passages into and out of the underworld. Moreover, any persistent Venus watcher is well aware that there is a recognizable 5/8 beat in its cycle with that of the seasons. Put simply, wherever Venus is in the sky tonight, it will be in virtually the same place eight years from tonight. Finally, at the mythic level, Waters imposes a Western version of the Venus story on a culture that he hadn't really bothered to study in detail; for example, both "sin" and the good/evil duality he refers to are biblical concepts not at all recognized in Aztec and Maya thought. In the same monomythical vein, Waters links Mexico's pyramids and those of Egypt to a prototypical source, not only in form but even down to the fundamental units of measurement that lay at the basis of their architectural plans.

Thanks to Waters's skilled narrative style, the theory of world ages emerged as another appealing cultural universal, the common denominator being reflected in the Maya long count (to be discussed in the next chapter), replete with a projected end of time (yet another biblical derivative) in the not too distant future: "The duration of these five worlds, granting each a life-span of 5000 years, totals 26,000 years; and thus closely approximates the great 25,920 year-cycle of this precession of the equinoxes."[20] "The end of the Great Cycle and the Fifth World," he goes on, "will occur on December 24, 2011 AD, and it too will be destroyed by catastrophic earthquakes."[21]

Like other exoheretical 2012 prophets to follow, Waters harbors a feeling of discontent with the status quo that resonates throughout all of his work regardless of which culture he examines. Like the Hopi and the Maya civilizations, ours is in for it as well. Revolutions are already spreading to every corner of the globe, he tells us. Economic and social values are being discarded. Orthodox religious systems have lost their appeal. But salvation lies just over the horizon of time: "The Emergence to the future fifth world has begun. It is being made by the humble people of little nation tribes, and racial minorities. You can read this in the earth itself."[22]

That the Maya were aware of the precession of the equinoxes there is no doubt, many of the prophets of Y12 would argue. They would cite evidence in the Maya inscriptions demonstrating an indigenous knowledge of the seventy-plus year interval, the time it takes the sun on any given seasonal date to advance by one day along its precessional pathway through the zodiacal highway. Uncannily, this same period had already been employed to support arguments that Christian inscriptions in the book of Daniel had also made reference to precession.[23]

Drawing on texts such as Mayanist Eric Thompson's *Maya History and Religion* and Michael Coe's 1966 edition of *The Maya*, Waters's *Mexico Mystique* fixed readers' attention on the fact that the long count, largest of all Maya time cycles, would soon turn over.[24] Following Coe, who appears to have miscalculated the impending date as December 24, 2011, probably by neglecting the fact that there is no year zero in the old BC/AD chronology, Waters pegged that specific date for the Mesoamerican version of the Advent—the descent of the Mexican feathered serpent deity Quetzalcoatl from heaven, and the initiation of a New Age.[25] As I suggested earlier, this interpretation may have been influenced by imagery in the Central Mexican codices that depict the feathered serpent deity descending from the sky on a cotton cord (figure 10.2). Interpreted out of context, such images have provided rich fodder for cross-cultural comparisons of the Second Coming with chroniclers' descriptions of Cortez as a resurrected Christlike figure, which they themselves fantasized.

In sum, the McKenna brothers and Frank Waters were the principal table setters for the grand buffet soon to be hosted by a new wave of hungry Y12 prophets. The Maya ruins themselves, made popular by scintillating articles in *National Geographic* and accessible for easy on-off sacred tourism, along with Maya hieroglyphic workshops directed toward amateurs and hosted in major American cities, their results widely disseminated via the Internet, would serve up a rich menu for Maya romantics.

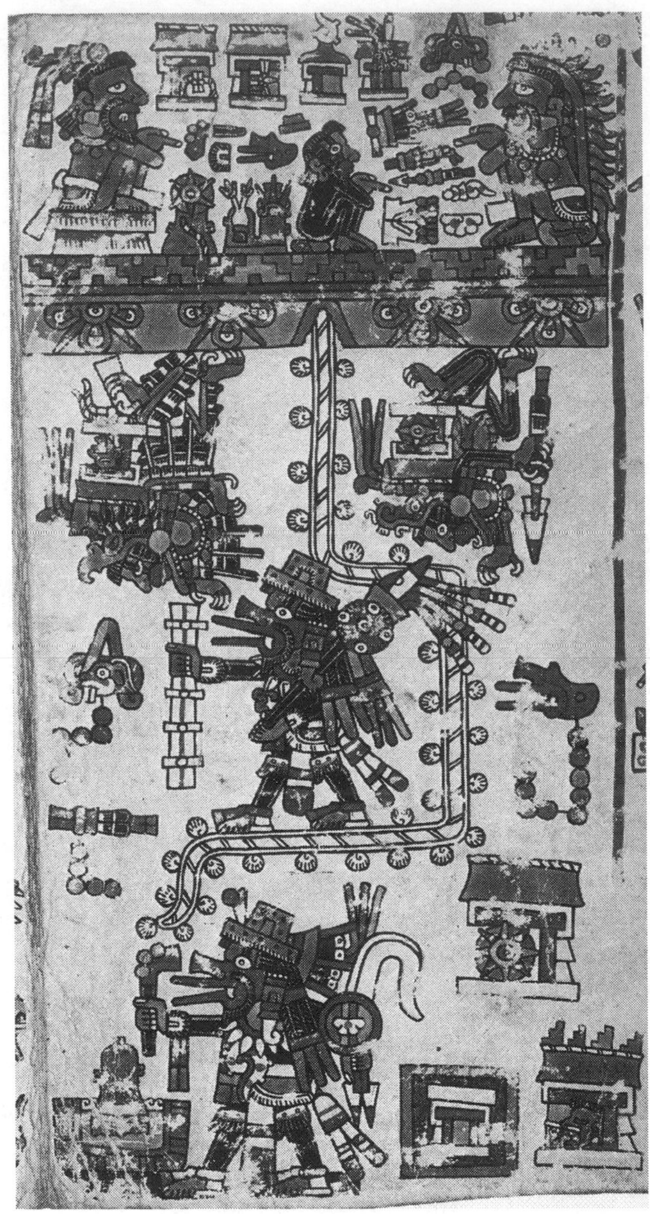

FIGURE 10.2. Quetzalcoatl, the Aztec deity, descends from the sky on a cotton cord. Some Maya 2012 prophets saw him as the god of the Advent. (From the Vienna Codex, a pre-Columbian document from highland Mexico, Akad Drück-u Verlag, Graz.)

11

2012 and the Perennial Philosophy

Philosophia Perennis . . . the psychology that finds in the soul, something similar to or even identical with, divine Reality; the ethic that places man's final end in the knowledge of the imminent and transcendent . . . [It is] immemorial and universal. Rudiments of the Perennial Philosophy may be found among the traditionary lore of primitive peoples in every region of the world, and, in its fully developed forms it has a place in every one of the higher religions.

—*Writer Aldous Huxley*

Most 2012 end of time predictions share in a longing to return to a more perfect past, a primordial tradition believed superior to the corrupt present-day world. Subscribing to the sui generis theory of the origin of religion, 2012 prophets adhere to an unshakeable faith in the veracity of the past. We found manifestations of it in Marilyn Ferguson's *Age of Aquarius*, in Native American dream catchers like Frank Waters, and in the McKenna brothers' substance-assisted search for the doorway of escape from history.

Most perennialists possess secular leanings. They have little religious training and even less grounding in the study of religious belief systems, though they claim to have acquired their revealed knowledge via faraway scriptures such as those from Egypt, India, Tibet, Mesoamerica—even Atlantis. Olav Hammer characterizes the search for singular truth in Philosophia Perennis as part of the esoteric religious tradition of attempting to incorporate a variety of competing faiths into the same grand scheme.[1] Esotericists view adherents of these gnostic faiths as not having reached the true state of understanding of the deeper unity of all religious traditions. The driving force,

Hammer believes, emanates from the need to cope with religious relativism, to solve the problem of why human faiths seem so diverse.[2] Esotericism finds its core in mysticism—and organized religion is the enemy.

We glimpsed this holistic way of thinking in nineteenth-century American spiritualism, with its ties to Eastern metaphysics and religion. Access to esoteric knowledge is often facilitated though the use of psychoactive substances, which, users say, enable the revelation of an integrated view of the cosmos. Aldous Huxley and Mircea Eliade loom as the most prominent among twentieth-century thinkers whose writings inspired the sort of New Age thinking that underlies 2012 Maya prophecy. In this summarizing chapter we trace their contributions.

The term *Philosophia Perennis* can be traced back to the seventeenth-century philosopher-mathematician Gottfried Wilhelm Leibniz. Essentially it finds divine Reality (the capital denoting the absolute nature of the truth) in the human soul, and it rests on the ethic that places our final end in a knowledge of the transcendent. Huxley believed perennialism to be embedded in every religion of the world, especially in the traditions of primitive people, where it had acquired its purest form. In his principal work on the subject, *The Perennial Philosophy* (1945), from which the epigraph to this chapter is borrowed, Huxley outlined the characteristics of the universal framework that underlies all spiritual traditions in the form of several basic principles summarized by Hammer.[3] Most important among them are:

1. The phenomena we experience are but passing, partial manifestations of an underlying divine eternal reality.
2. Though limited by their ego, human beings can experience this higher knowledge intuitively; but this requires a cultivated shift of consciousness, a shedding of one's "self-serving egoism."[4]
3. Since, in addition to the ego, all humans possess a sense of an eternal self, this higher plane of shared consciousness is accessible to all, provided these dual aspects are placed in correct relationship to one another.
4. Human potential is fully achieved when we act in deference to the unitary principle.

Joseph Campbell, Fridtjof Capra and, much earlier, Carl Jung would, to varying degrees, share in this notion of absolute truth—a truth attainable *in this lifetime*.[5]

Huxley was a frequent user of mescaline, the psychoactive component of peyote. At the time, the ingestion of mescaline by the Huichol Indians of West Mexico had been receiving popular attention in the literature. In *The Doors of Perception* (1954), Huxley detailed the highly positive benefits of his "trips" and the insights he experienced.[6] He tells us that the drug broke down his ego. Along with prayer and meditation, this allowed him to reach a higher spiritual form of enlightenment. A longtime critic of materialism and technology, Huxley had already produced his famous masterwork, *Brave New World* (1932), a futuristic sci-fi tale paralleling George Orwell's later *1984* (1949), that railed against the impending negative outcomes of supertechnology. Huxley was in the midst of struggling to reach out for alternatives to the awful prospect of humanity being led farther and farther astray from nature. Alternative psychotherapies and exotic healing techniques were also among Huxley's enduring interests—at least enduring enough to convince him that his personal perennial philosophy was shared by mystics and healers in all religions. Interestingly, Huxley's last novel, *Island*, published in 1962, describes life in a utopian community that promotes the intelligent use of drugs to create a better society. Unfortunately it results in leaving people too blissed out to confront the aggressive world outside; ultimately they are taken over and destroyed.

A more explicit treatment of these concepts appeared in Eliade's even more influential *The Sacred and the Profane*, published in 1959 after he had acquired an academic position at the University of Chicago.[7] For Eliade, all primitive religions possess the same basic symbolic structure, part of an integrated cosmic worldview. We in the modern West have demythologized it, made it meaningless. Unless we reacquire this spiritual orientation there is no hope for us. Philip Jenkins characterizes *The Sacred and the Profane* as a book that "carried an angry, antimodernist agenda," one that appealed to 1960s intellectuals who felt immersed in "the poverty of modern concepts of nature [which] had become so familiar as to be almost clichéd."[8]

Perennialist Eliade was strongly influenced by depth psychologist Carl Jung's theory of *archetypes*, or ancient imagery that derived from what Jung called the collective unconscious. Jung hypothesized that the psyche, or the totality of the human mind that organizes all of our experience, actually consists of two parts. There is the conscious mind, which is personal and based on what an individual experiences. There also exists an unconscious portion of the mind. He describes it as universal, impersonal, and basically identical in all individuals. Jung defined this collective unconscious as a group of inherited images consisting of preexisting forms, or archetypes. He linked the collective unconscious to what Freud referred to as "archaic remnants," or mental forms that cannot be accounted for by any events that happened in an individual's own life. Such forms, he believed, are aboriginal and innate; they are inherited in all human minds.

How to access this lost realm of consciousness? One of the archetypes of the cosmos cited by Eliade as universal is the sacred pole, pillar, or ladder, through which people connect the place they live to the unknown worlds above and below them—territories beyond their sphere of experience. By conducting rituals that focus on that macroscopic construct, they make their place sacred; they communicate with the gods—they actualize the initial creation of the universe by re-creating it in microcosm.

To back up his theory Eliade cited examples from diverse cultures, for example, the Kwakiutl Indians of the northwest coast of North America, the Achilpa of Central Australia, and the pre-Christian Celts. The Kwakiutl, for example, believe that a copper pole passes through three levels of the cosmos: the underworld, the earth, and the sky. The doorway where it enters the sky is visible to all as the Milky Way. It manifests itself in the Kwakuitl ceremonial house in the form of a pole made of cedar that projects upward through the roof. This pole sacralizes or cosmicizes the house; it constitutes what Eliade termed an *imago mundi*, or image of the world. Thus it acquires a cosmic structure and those who conduct rites about it sing, "I am the center of the world . . . I am the post of the world."[9]

Eliade's generalization of interpretations of the polar archetype is both dense and complex, but it is worth reconstructing in brief, especially because so many post–New Age philosophies cling to his sui generis terminology. Eliade regarded his culture-based examples as a sequence of religious conceptions and cosmological images that are inseparably connected and form a system that may be called the

> system of the world prevalent in traditional societies: (a) a sacred place constitutes a break in the homogeneity of space; (b) this break is symbolized by an opening by which passage from one cosmic region to another is made possible (from heaven to earth and vice versa; from earth to the underworld);

> (c) communication with heaven is expressed by one or another of certain images, all of which refer to the *axis mundi*: pillar (cf. the *universalis columna*), ladder (cf. Jacob's ladder), mountain, tree, vine, etc.; (d) around this cosmic axis lies the world (= our world), hence the axis is located "in the middle," at the "navel of the earth; it is the center of the world.[10]

Sacred time parallels sacred space. It happens when an individual conducts rites, which, Eliade argued, are all reenactments of an initial sacrifice revealed by a god at the time of creation. All such rites that replicate those conducted "*in illo tempore*," or in the beginning, become the "imitation of archetypes."[11] All other acts are without meaning; they take place in the realm of profane time, the time associated with duration, or what we in the West call "history": "For traditional man, the imitation of an archetypal model is a reactualization of the mythical moment when the archetype was revealed for the first time."[12]

Eliade credits his studies of shamanism for first leading him to the idea that in the primitive world all acts and objects were capable of acquiring value. The shaman is a religious specialist who acquires transcendent knowledge via trance or an altered state of consciousness, which enables access to the spirit world. In *Shamanism* (1964), Eliade noted that certain objects or acts were consciously perceived to take part in a reality that transcended them; for example, one stone among many can become sacred when it is revealed to constitute a *hierophany,* that is, when it displays some manifestation of the sacred.[13] Activities such as hunting, fishing, playing games, or having sex can be perceived to be sacred once the individual is conscious that whatever he or she participates in is a repetition of the primal form of that act. Eliade uses dance as another example. Dancing, he noted, was always conducted with the idea of a transcendent model, such as a totemic animal whose motions the dancer re-creates to access its presence—to bring the essence of the animal into the dancer's human form. Thus, the dancer spends every moment of a performance connecting with or reliving the past. For the dancer, reality becomes the imitation of an archetype. Eliade argued that we in the modern world find the distinction between sacred and profane difficult to comprehend because we have desacralized most objects and acts. But deep down in our subconscious we haven't lost the innate desire to get back to our origins.

The philosophy of Eliade sounds very appealing to those seeking an antidote to the evils of modern society. His insistence on expressing key terms in Latin (*axis mundi, imago mundi,* and so on) lends his work a timeless quality. Moreover, it also carries a heavy dose of Christian leanings in its charter: all primitive societies live in the paradise of archetypes. For them "time is recorded only biologically speaking without being allowed to become history, . . . that is without its corrosive action being able to exert itself upon consciousness by revealing the irreversibility of events—these primitive societies regenerate themselves periodically through the expulsion of 'evils' and 'confession of sins.'"[14] According to Eliade, this habit of periodic regeneration through purification was felt more profoundly in archaic civilizations than in modern society.

Central to Eliade's cosmology is the concept of Homo Religiosus. Found only within the human species is a natural impulse to break through to transcendental experience, such as to participate in revelation. In other words, every person is naturally empowered with the capacity to make the eternal return to the sacred. Furthermore, Eliade contended, the cosmological ideas associated with *all* ancient religions are the same everywhere. We can trace them by comparing ancient artifacts and analyzing ancient myths.

In retrospect, it is easy to see that Eliade was influenced by Frobenius's comparative theory of cultural development (discussed in chapter 9). Standing in the way, however, is "the terror of history"—our own Judeo-Christian account of human events—which is hinged to linear time; that is, history as we know it.[15] Along its linear course, time carries us toward that singular engagement with the immanent, the ultimate realization of an eternal heaven on earth. This is not so with archaic "traditional" man, who engaged in cyclically timed rituals characterized by reenactments of archaic archetypes of a deeper truth that resided in nature. Because ancient human beings were sensually much more proximate to land and sky than we, it is only by acquiring their knowledge that we can reconnect with these truths or, as contemporary 2012 prophets would put it, with our "true self." Eliade's philosophy was part of a quest to develop what he called a "new humanism." As he put it, "By attempting to understand the existential situations expressed by the documents he is studying, the historian of religions will inevitably attain a deeper knowledge of man. It is on the basis of such knowledge that a new humanism, on a worldwide scale could develop."[16] In other words, by returning to our origins we have the power to abolish the terror of history.

As we shall see in the next chapter, Huxley's perennialism and Eliade's spin on Jungian archetypes clearly resonate not only in José Argüelles's and others' writings but also with the idea of the monomyth articulated earlier in *Hamlet's Mill.* My own suspicion, first suggested by John Hoopes and developed via informal discussions with him, is that many of these ideas were influential as well in Schele and Freidel's *Maya Cosmos*, which would become required reading and serve as an inspiration for Maya 2012 prophets.

Take, for example, Eliade's symbolism of the center, in which houses, temples, and even entire cities become "real" via their perceived connection to the "center of the world."[17] Eliade posits that all sacred temples have their celestial prototypes; for example, when David gave Solomon the plan for the Temple of Jerusalem he told him, "All this . . . the Lord made me understand in writing by his hand upon me, even all the works of the pattern" (I Chronicles 28:19), i.e., "he had seen the celestial model."[18] The same concept is reflected in lines uttered in the Christian Lord's Prayer: "Thy Kingdom come, on earth as it is in heaven." Architecturally it all plays out via a set of archetypal symbols. The sacred cities are those where heaven and Earth meet (the center of the world). It is at this point that Eliade employs the term (whose origin neither Hoopes nor I have been unable to trace beyond Eliade himself) that resonates throughout contemporary millenarian prophesying: "The *axis mundi*, seen in the sky in the form of the Milky Way, appears in the ceremonial house in the form of a sacred pole . . . the pillar, the ladder, the center of the world."[19] In the city it becomes the temple, which is regarded as the meeting point of heaven, Earth, and hell. Curiously, Eliade is rarely cited directly in later borrowings of his ideas. It is as if most students of latter-day prophesying take it for granted that we are all hardwired to commune with the archaic transcendent via the world axis.

Eliade's notion of time and history and the underlying sui generis origin of religion have been strongly challenged by anthropologists on the grounds that Christian cosmology and cyclic time are *not* discordant, that not all ancient religions incorporated cyclic time, and that the notion that there once existed a worldwide pre-logical mentality that differed from rational thought is nothing more than a projection of Western Judeo-Christian philosophy.[20] Anthropologists in particular point out that Eliade had never lived among any of the cultures whose rites and beliefs he claimed to apprehend and furthermore that, like de Santillana and von Dechend, he overgeneralized material he had acquired from reading pure text. Critics also note that, prior to acquiring his status as a philosopher / historian of religion, Eliade had authored fantasy novels set in exotic places.

There are also political implications—what historian of religion Russell McCutcheon calls a "politics of nostalgia"—in much of Eliade's theorizing.[21] In addition, philosopher Tony Stigliano traces Eliade's motives for his new humanism not so much to an intellectual quest, but rather to a desire to reacquire purity and beauty in the decadent European society of the 1920s, an action motive that was picked up by fascist and nationalistic movements.[22] Not simply dissatisfied with the present decadent state of the world, many believers in Eliade's elevation of ancient knowledge above the present launched an all-out attack on modernity that bordered on anti-intellectualism. By locating their faith in the superiority of lost knowledge, the contemporary scientific establishment becomes the enemy. Thus, there is an acquired hostility, or at best ambivalence, on the part of the perennial thinker toward new knowledge acquired by scientific methodology, which is embedded in the historically based theory of progress.

Stigliano also explores some of the common ground with Eliade in works by Carl Jung and Joseph Campbell, which have enjoyed wide appeal among New Age thinkers. First, both saw myth as a universal way of understanding people's social, cultural and, most important, individual identities. Second, by decontextualizing myth they allowed its elements to be recombined in ways that give meaning to the present human condition. This eliminates the necessity to engage in deep study of indigenous language, ethnography, and the archaeological remains associated with the parent culture whose worldview they claim to interpret. Finally, and most dangerous of all, perennialists apply myth to the solution of contemporary world issues without recourse to political or rational discourse. Stigliano labels all of these actions steps "toward achieving power over their world through magic, coincidence, or self-celebration."[23] As the popular and influential Campbell once lamented nostalgically: "The democratic ideal of the self-determining individual . . . [and] the scientific method of research have so transformed human life that the long-inherited, timeless universe of symbols has collapsed."[24]

With this background on perennialist philosophy in hand, we analyze, in the next chapter, its pivotal role in the Maya 2012 end of the world episode. The offspring of perennialist philosophers have been criticized as much as the parents from whom they acquired their metaphysical predilections. Most Mayanists fail to grasp any evidence to support the notion of Maya perfectionism; for example, like most trained in the field, archaeologist Prudence Rice views the development of the Maya calendar as a tool of self-aggrandizement, employed by elites in an ongoing drama of political posturing, economic opportunism, and struggles for power.[25] In other words, the carved stelae that look back at us in the great plazas of their ruined cities were *not* part of a program for drastically altering conditions in a historically terrorized world through action arrived at by tapping into the collective unconscious. Rather, they were the products of rulers seeking legitimacy among the citizenry.

Finally, when it comes to romancing the ancient Maya on the issue of environmental purity, the evidence on the ground also proves the Maya were far from perfectionists. As archaeologist David Webster has demonstrated in his exhaustive study of the fall of the ancient Maya, the culture, despite its astronomical, mathematical, and philosophical wisdom, exerted a decidedly negative impact on the ecosphere.[26] Nor were the ancient Maya a united people. Their hieroglyphs tell the story of a decentralized civilization that frequently engaged in warfare. There are sound lessons of history here, but as long as the perennialists choose to turn a deaf ear to the solid evidence that reveals our ancient human ancestors to be as flawed as we, our fantasy-loving, gullible, popular culture will continue to be influenced by their artfully crafted "invented sacred traditions."[27]

12
Ancient Galactic Wisdom and 2012 Mayanism

It has become commonplace that America is in the throes of an unrivaled period of millenarian activity. Even the heyday of the Millerites, Shakers, Mormons, and Oneida Perfectionists in the 1830s and 1840s cannot compare to it, and there is no sign that millenarian anticipation will diminish anytime soon.

—*Political science scholar Michael Barkun*

The specter of catastrophe in Lawrence Joseph's book *Apocalypse 2012*, Roland Emmerich's film *2012*, and other works mentioned earlier coexisted alongside predictions about metaphysical transformations accompanying time's end. We deal specifically with that coincidence in this chapter.

Promoting the descent myth, Maya 2012 prophets frequently cite the last page of the Maya Dresden Codex, one among a few surviving indigenous bark paper documents written in hieroglyphic notation during the century leading up to the Spanish conquest (the document derives its name from the European city where it ended up after European contact). The scene (figure 12.1) depicts an open-mouthed serpent vomiting water. Water also gushes out of celestial glyphs that adorn the body of the serpent. Suspended in space beneath it, an old female deity pours blue-colored liquid out of a pot, while a male warrior god below her hurls darts and spears. As Ernst Förstemann, head of the Dresden Library, wrote in his 1906 commentary on the codex, "This page can denote nothing but the end of the world"—a quote that would inspire many a Maya Doomsday theorist.[1]

Figure 12.1. World destruction by flood or a metaphor about cycles of fertility? (Page 74 of the Maya Dresden Codex. Akad Drück-u Verlag, Graz.)

What did the Maya actually have to say about the flood? The few decipherable glyphs at the top are only partially understood.[2] However, a statement about a great flood is described in one of the Books of Chilam Balam (Jaguar Priest) written during the colonial period shortly after contact. The description of events offers a fitting caption for what we see pictured on Dresden 74:

> And then great Itzam Cab Ain (the caiman sky deity) ascended back then that this deluge may complete the word of the katun (prophecy) series . . .
> One fetching of rain (flood water being poured from a vase)
> One lancing of rain (a possible reference to the deity's spear).[3]

Were the post-conquest Maya simply reiterating, in the language of their conquerors, what already had been written in their ancestral hieroglyphic document? Did they really believe Doomsday was imminent? Other passages might suggest otherwise (note especially the last line):

> And thus the word of this katun may be accomplished
> And then it was given by Dios
> A deluge occurs for the second time
> This is a destruction of the world
> Then this ends
> That Our Lord who is Jesus Christ may then descend[4]

These lines read a lot like the biblical narrative of Noah's flood and the Christian Second Coming. So what are they doing in a book about Maya prophecy? Scholars who have studied texts from colonial Yucatán believe that Maya myths about the destruction of the world and the descent of the gods from heaven were heavily influenced by Roman Catholic ideas about the Apocalypse brought over by the Spanish friars sent to convert the Indians. On the other hand, anthropologist Timothy Knowlton thinks that, far from blindly accepting the religious ideology of the invaders to appease the will of the conqueror, for the Maya at the time of contact the Christian Apocalypse actually might have made sense. He finds that, at a very basic level, indigenous texts do seem to be telling of the destruction and reflowering of the world. But did they mean the whole world? And literal destruction? Or was it more metaphoric? For example, the cyclic destruction-creation process mimics the slash-and-burn agriculture commonly practiced in Yucatán. In essence you need to destroy the old soil to make the new more productive. That may be what the flood story in the colonial Book of Chilam Balam is really all about—how the process of fertility works in cycles of destruction and re-creation. It may have had nothing to do with the annihilation of the entire world as we know it at a terminal point in the Western-derived linear time scale.

Credit José Argüelles, co-originator of Earth Day and founder of the first Whole Earth Festival, with first delivering 2012 Maya prophesy to the forefront of popular New Age culture. It began in earnest with his 1987 volume entitled *The Mayan Factor: Path beyond Technology*. Though his work appeared more than a decade after the Waters and McKenna books, Argüelles nonetheless claimed to have acquired the 2012 Maya connection independently, as early as 1953, from his reading of archaeologist Eric Thompson's works. Argüelles's format follows historian Nicholas Campion's analysis of the basic narrative scheme of millenarian prophesying, discussed in chapter 2: an astronomically timed upheaval is followed by the restoration of a new humanity with enhanced spirituality.

Argüelles started out as an art historian, receiving a PhD from the University of Chicago. As anthropologist John Hoopes has pointed out, Argüelles was both a student of astrologer Dane Rudhyar and an acquaintance of the McKenna brothers.[5] He also partook of psychedelic substances, having experimented with LSD in the 1960s. In an earlier work, *The Transformative Vision*, published in the same year (1975) the Waters and McKenna volumes appeared, Argüelles identified 2012 as the seminal year for spiritual transformation, though he did not specify a date.[6] Following Peter Tompkins's cosmic scenario, he predicted that at the seminal moment a beam of energy emanating from the center of the Milky Way Galaxy would initiate the new era, but not before the prelude to the main event, the Harmonic Convergence, which, he announced in *The Mayan Factor*, would occur twenty-five years before the main event.

Argüelles characterized the Harmonic Convergence as a fundamental shifting point into the final twenty-five years of the "galactic beam." He described time's end as a "climax of matter" and a collective rebirth, a new era of planetary consciousness, its vibes best appreciated by being in the right place—power centers like Mt. Shasta, Machu Picchu, and Egypt's pyramids, not to mention the corner of 83rd St. and Central Park West in Manhattan—at the right time. The prophet labeled these places light centers, or the acupuncture points in the body of Mother Earth. Light centers and radiating beams are frequently employed millennial visionary terms, according to religious studies professor Philip Lucas, who has followed their deployment especially in New Age author David Spangler's work.[7] Spangler defined the New Age as a present-day reality in an alternative dimension. It lies within all of us, implanted like a seed whose presence, if we allow it, is capable of transporting us beyond time. Being near the central hubs, or etheric centers within the Earth body, that radiate the higher frequencies helps, for these special places are the powerhouses that produce the current that connects the network of consciousness of the transcendent Christ.

According to Argüelles's calculations, the seminal date that would lead up to the final beam's end was August 16, 1987. It marked the end of twenty-two cycles of 52 years (1,144 years). These were divided into thirteen "heaven" cycles, which began in 843 CE and ended in 1519, followed by nine "hell" cycles terminating on the day 1 Reed in the Aztec calendar. Argüelles claimed to have based his date-fixing computations on a subcycle of the Aztec calendar.

The 1987 event captured media attention and attracted thousands of participants, though no official UFO sightings corresponded with the hand-holding, humming, and dancing of an estimated 20,000 participants. Media coverage ran the gamut from the *Wall Street Journal* to a series of *Doonesbury* cartoons.

Argüelles claimed his authority as legitimate spokesperson regarding ancient Maya prophecy via messages channeled to him through a vertical stone tube built into the tomb of Kinich Hanab Pakal, the Maya king of Palenque. The conduit connected the king's burial chamber to the surface of the ruler's funerary monument, the Temple of the Inscriptions. Argüelles even crafted his own 13 × 20, or 260-day, Maya calendar, which he named "Dreamspell." It consisted of thirteen 28-day months plus one "day out of time." His time construct bears a distinct resemblance to the World Calendar that had been proposed as an alternative to the Western calendar at the time of the foundation of the United Nations.[8]

In my opinion, Argüelles "13:20-frequency" that makes up the Maya 260-day sacred count is no more natural than the 12:60-frequency base of our own calendar, which he saw fit to attack on the grounds that the latter is mechanized and out of step with nature's synchronic order. Argüelles may have been unaware that the 360-plus-day period of the annual migration of the sun among the constellations of the zodiac had suggested to Babylonian astronomers, as early as the second millennium BCE, that a natural way to keep time would be to use a base-six, or sexagesimal, system for reckoning the year and its divisions—whence our 24-hour day, 60-minute hour, and so on. The number 12 in our calendar harmonizes with nature, too, because it represents the approximate number of lunar months in a seasonal year. Likewise, Maya timekeeping was guided by nature, except that their 13 × 20 = 260-day system responded to a different set of natural phenomena; for example, the human gestation period and the interval of the appearance of Venus in the evening or morning sky both approximate 260 days, and 20 represents the number of fingers and toes on the human body. The 13 in the equation equals the number of layers thought to exist in Maya heaven. One wonders whether, had Argüelles been in closer touch with the history of the calendar he so fervently sought to disrupt, he might have come up with a better hypothesis.

As hinted above, José Argüelles was also responsible for popularizing the *galactic* connection to Maya prophecy. He called his time-keeping device the "Galactic Maya" calendar, with its twenty "solar seals" and thirteen "galactic tones"—the better to attune it to the closing of the great Maya cycle known as the long count. This galactic association would be assigned a central place in the prophecies of those who followed Argüelles (figure 12.2). But before we examine the rationale behind the long-term timing of galactic phenomena, we need to make a brief excursion into how the Maya calendar, in particular the long count, works, so that we can understand its central role in 2012 prophecy.

Sometime in the very early centuries CE a wise Maya daykeeper, likely motivated by the king he served, who wished to emphasize his connection to the ancestor gods, put together a time-reckoning system that had the effect of planting the roots of dynastic history in deep time. We can think of this invention as a kind of temporal odometer. It was built out of cycles upon cycles of days, all arranged according to multiples of 20. Individual days were accumulated into 20-day months and the months into years, except that there were 18 instead of 20 days in the year cycle, almost certainly to arrive at a larger cycle conveniently close to the length of the year. The Babylonians adopted a similar strategy, except that they devised a year of 12 months of 30 days—and so did the Egyptians. Next, years were accumulated into scores of years (20 × 360 = 7,200 days) and then into scores of scores of years (20 × 7,200 = 144,000 days). This process resulted in the long count, a cycle that ran

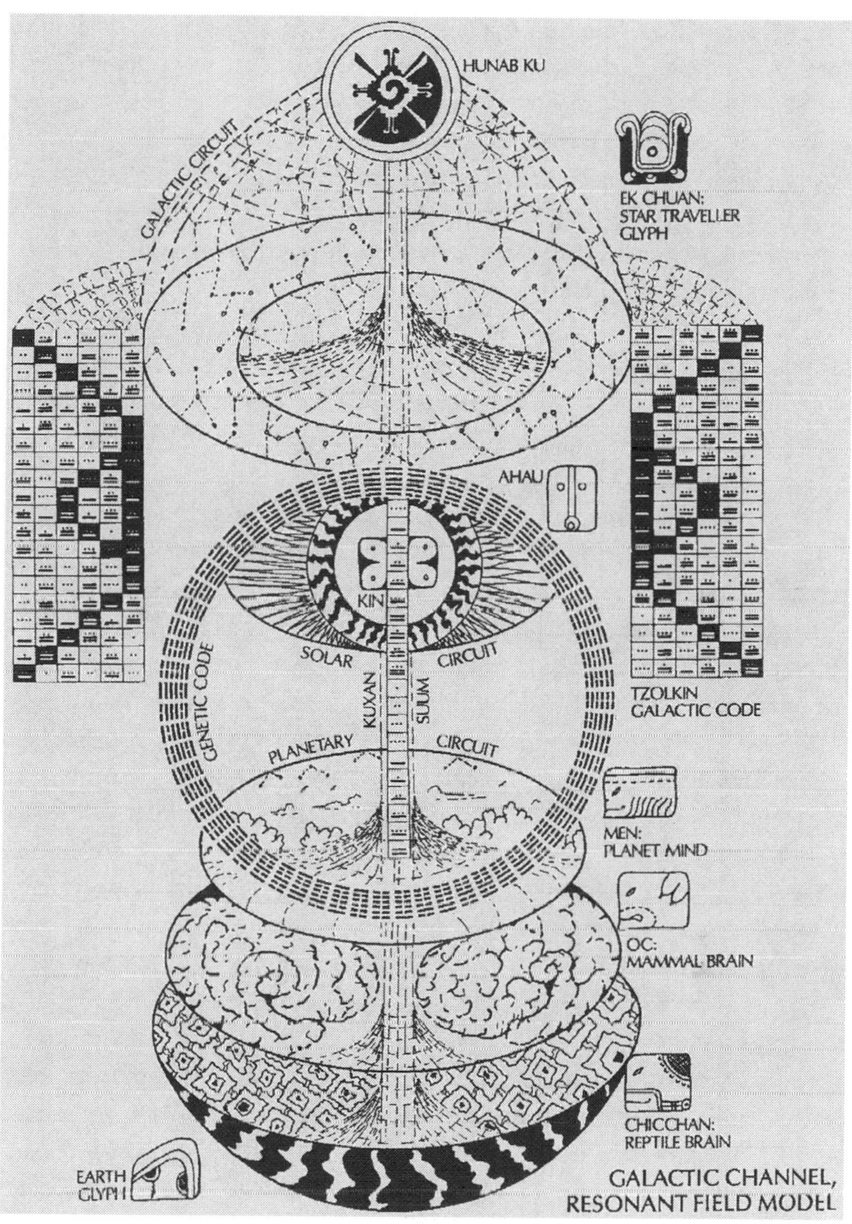

FIGURE 12.2. According to 2012 prophet José Argüelles, the Maya predicted the world would be transformed to a new level of consciousness on a "galactic beam." (Image from *The Mayan Factor* by José Argüelles ©1987. Reprinted by permission of Inner Traditions International and Bear & Company. www.innertraditions.com.)

up to thirteen of the latter units before it returned to zero again. The odometer on your car is an excellent example except that, unlike the deterioration that takes place under the hood, the gearwork of the Maya time clock gets reset at 13.0.0.0.0 and a new long count cycle, 5,125.37 of our years in length, begins afresh. Two small details are worth adding: First, not all experts in Maya studies subscribe to this recyclable version of the calendar. For example, epigrapher David Stuart argues that deep time, as understood in the minds of some Maya elite, rolled on well past the thirteenth *baktun* cycle. A carved date from Palenque, for example, tells of a future event that will happen in the year 4772. The full version of the calendar, according to Stuart, encompasses nearly 72 octillion years.[9] And second, there is no evidence that the Maya constructed clocks, gears, or other such machinery. The word *clock* used to describe Maya timekeeping is purely a metaphor.

Maya computists pinned the foundation date of the present cycle to August 11, 3114 BCE. No one really knows why. I think the best explanation may be that this date corresponded to the anniversary of some quasi-historical event, perhaps the birth of a foundational deity. If this sounds familiar, it may be because our Christian calendar, devised by a sixth-century monk to be reckoned from the putative date of the birth of Christ, operates pretty much the same way—with one major exception. The Western calendar rolls along in a linear fashion, the end of time corresponding to the Second Coming and Judgment Day, after which eternal time exists only in the hereafter.

For biologist turned prophet Carl Johan Calleman the key to the contemporary doorway of awakening to higher consciousness was set to turn on October 28, 2011, between the two rare transits of Venus in 2004 and 2012 across the disk of the sun, which he believed the Maya also knew about. Venus transits are passages of that planet across the disk of the sun. They occur in pairs at eight-year intervals about once a century. Astronomers agree that Venus transits are virtually impossible to view without the aid of a telescope or binoculars. Calleman also looked for a solution to the problem of Maya time conception in the structure of their pyramids. The most important ones, for example, Palenque's Temple of the Inscriptions and the Temple of Kukulcan at Chichén Itzá, have nine levels. This led him to propose his nine-step theory of underworlds. Articulated in *The Mayan Calendar and the Transformation of Consciousness* (2004), Calleman's dispensational thesis parsed out a series of hierarchical levels beginning with the Big Bang, which he set at 16.4 billion years ago (modern cosmology pegs it at 13.8, give or take a half billion).[10] This accelerated scale emanates straight from Blavatsky's morally based theory of human evolution, via the McKenna brothers' time line concept.

Human consciousness, according to Calleman, rested on lower (earlier) levels, such as the occurrence of animal life, the appearance of primates, the use of tools by our ancient ancestors, and so on. As time moves forward, the seminal levels on the pyramid of techno-progress, reached via great advances called "doorways of opportunity" (compare the McKennas' "concrescences"), became more compacted. Calleman charted the breakthroughs that happened the last several times the door was ajar; for example, 1518–1526 (Magellan circumnavigated the world), 1631–1639 (the first national postal services were initiated in Scandinavia [Calleman is Swedish]), and so on. Next, in even more compressed order, came industrialization, the invention of electricity, gene splicing, the ubiquitous A-bomb, and the development of the Internet (1999). Like the McKennas and Helena Blavatsky, Calleman gets to choose the seminal events. He even took a page from José Argüelles's 1987 Harmonic Convergence by organizing a series of "Oneness Parties" to bring people together in select places in order to meditate on the imminent transformation of humanity. When the new consciousness arrives, such human action will help to avert environmental catastrophe, he wrote; and we will take responsibility as cocreator with God—quite an extraordinary elevation in the human condition.

As we learned in chapter 7, aliens from the Galaxy often play the role of transcendent beings. Pastor Miller's angels of the Lord descending from heaven are replaced by secular messengers from extraterrestrial worlds traveling in UFOs. Many contactees relay the message that a higher intelligence oversees all human development. We are thus guided toward the New Age, at which point alien intervention will lift us to an alternate plane of reality, where nature and humanity are one. 2012 prophesying is no different. Extraterrestrials are also a major element of Argüellian transcendentalism; beam's end, for example, is what the Maya, who were legitimate descendants of extragalactic aliens, latch onto in order to convey themselves between extraterrestrial worlds, sowing the seeds of a universal civilization as they go. What will happen at the defining moment, when our ancient Maya forebears return to tend to their "crops"? All our senses will attain new revelations, for then, Argüelles tells us in typical science jargon, we will "reconnect with the heliotropic octaves in the solar activated electromagnetic field."[11]

Whence this enhanced popularity of galactic phenomena in contemporary apocalyptic theorizing? The word *galaxy* comes from *gala*, the Greek word for milk, to which they likened the white luminous band that encircles the sky. Today we know it by its common name, the Milky Way. Astronomers have determined that it is populated by more than 200 billion stars, along with the interstellar gas and dust out of which the stars form. Our Milky Way Galaxy (there are some trillions of such aggregates in the universe at large) makes up the largest "island universe" in the immediate "neighborhood" beyond our solar system. The Galaxy (astronomers refer to it with a capital "G") is unimaginably vast in extent—more than 100,000 light years in diameter. Also it is highly flattened, which means that we here on Earth, being immersed somewhat off center within its plane, see it stretch like a circum-terrestrial alabaster band all the way around the sky.

Though our immersion in artificial light has robbed our eyes of the grand spectacle the Milky Way offers us, when they viewed it in a dark sky, ancient people were very impressed with its glittering, sinuous form, especially on a moonless night. Little wonder they fashioned imaginative stories to account for it. For example, the Egyptians conceived of the Galaxy as the naked body of the goddess Nut (pronounced "noot") stretched over the heavens. The source of divine royalty, she would give birth to the sun god Ra. On the other hand, the Inca of Peru thought of the Milky Way as a river, Mayu, a continuation in the sky of the great river that nurtured humanity here below. The written record tells us that when the ancient Maya looked at the Milky Way they imagined a roadway, a very exclusive one used by the dead to gain access to the sky and the afterworld. So did southern Africans; they regarded the Milky Way as a pathway trod by their ancestors. A body, a river of milk or water, a road or a pathway—all were sensible representations employed by different cultures of the world at different times in their efforts to bring the unfamiliar heavens down to Earth.

Still, why does the word *galactic*—which astronomers now take to apply to vast disk-shaped pinwheels like our Milky Way that make up an even larger universe than cosmologists contemplated just a few generations ago—resonate so strongly with enthusiasts of American pop culture's contemporary end of time philosophy? Why did the prophets of the impending 2012 grand shift of human consciousness imagine the Milky Way to be a source of divine transcendence? As José Argüelles explained: "Amidst festive preparation and awesome galactic-solar signs [here he refers to the alignment of the winter solstice sun with the galactic center, to be dealt with shortly] the human race, in harmony with the animal and other kingdoms and taking its rightful place in the great electromagnetic sea, will unify as a single circuit. Solar and galactic sound transmissions [Is this perhaps a relic of the McKenna brothers' experiments?] will inundate the planetary field. At last, Earth will be ready for the emergence into interplanetary civilization."[12]

I think the common thread that knits together ancient and modern characterizations of an entity so awesome, so incomprehensible as the Galaxy, is deeply woven into the human desire to embrace a phenomenon so vast, remote, strange, and perhaps too terrifying for us to contemplate, by connecting it to something tangible. Only by lending familiarity to the unfamiliar can we find meaning in it. One hopes that in its infinite grandeur, the eye-catching Milky Way skyband that surrounds our world might harbor secrets about human existence.

Astronomer Frank Drake's prediction of the acquisition of an "Encyclopedia Galactica" bequeathed by alien contactees (see chapter 7) is but a short step away from Argüelles's more brazen response to the same question: What can we expect? That question was put to Argüelles on the eve of the 1987 Harmonic Convergence. Like the brothers McKenna, Dane Rudhyar, Helena Blavatsky, and even Cotton Mather before him, Argüelles trotted out the latest scientific terminology to legitimize his impressive (and difficult to decipher) answer (referred to above). Accompanied by "solar and galactic sound transmissions," the Earth will enter true interplanetary civilizations.[13] "They are here with and among us," Argüelles's teacher, astrologer Dane Rudhyar, had explained a decade earlier, "just as Adepts and Masters are with and among us . . . able to radiate waves causing the witnesses to become temporarily attuned, or to *resonate* in their consciousness and even cellular-atomic rhythms to the higher galactic vibrations," just as "a Hindu guru can temporarily arouse psychic vision."[14] In an age of discovery of hosts of exoplanets, these messages channeled from the past wielded even greater impact than they had a generation earlier. As Catherine Albanese suggested in the epigraph to chapter 10, we all seem to be awaiting directions from without.

The contemporary mantle of 2012 psychedelic prophecy making belongs to Daniel Pinchbeck, a British writer and host of a blog promoting New Age ideas and activism. He was influenced by the philosophy of Rudolf Steiner, a follower of Helena Blavatsky, who had developed his spiritualist training to access higher worlds, though without recourse to Eastern mysticism. A disciple of the McKennas, Pinchbeck visited various tribal groups in Africa and the Amazon who ingested psychoactive substances, with which he himself experimented (LSD would ultimately pave his pathway to insight). Pinchbeck became convinced of the validity of alternative realities and the advantage of using chemical means to speed up access them. He once quite confidently told me, on a radio interview panel, that no matter what my knowledge of the ancient Maya might be, it could not possibly reach the elevated plane he had acquired via the drug-induced shamanic states he experienced.

In *2012: The Return of Quetzalcoatl* (2006), Pinchbeck claims, via experimentation with psychic phenomena, to have received 2012 prophecy transmitted directly from the Mesoamerican feathered serpent deity Quetzalcoatl himself.[15] The message seems to be that the world is on the verge of Apocalypse—the fulfillment of both biblical and Maya prophecy. Those of us who have pursued material gains and remained wedded to technology—we who have failed to fight for human freedom and preservation of the environment—will not make the transition, the human ascent to the next plane of consciousness. How to avoid damnation? Accept and receive love and devotion via the "vibrational frequencies that maintain reality."[16] That takes concentration, meditation, contemplation and, according to Pinchbeck, an assist from the plant world. He writes: "Human consciousness is rapidly transitioning to a new state, a new intensity of awareness that will manifest as a different understanding, a transformed realization, of time and space and self . . . that will lead to the rapid development of new institutions and social structures, . . . toward a harmonic, perhaps even utopian, situation on the earth."[17] The transition will culminate in 2012 with the completion of the Maya "Great Cycle" associated with the return of the "Sovereign Plumed Serpent" deity, Quetzalcoatl. Pinchbeck sees this deity as the archetype—he who, according to legend, understands movement in the cosmos, and reveals time and the destiny of humanity.

Pinchbeck spins his fantasy yarn out of threads in the fabric of an old myth. The equation Quetzalcoatl = Jesus, along with the colonial process of the

Christianization of Quetzalcoatl, dates back to the time of the Spanish conquest. It originates, I believe, in the writings of Diego Duran, a Dominican friar sent to convert the Aztecs.[18] Duran was also largely responsible for promulgating the myth that Aztec king Moctezuma II believed Cortez to be one Topiltzin-Quetzalcoatl, the Toltec priest-king who vowed to return to his homeland, from which he had been banished by his people. Duran described him as a "tall man with long straight hair, [who] spent all his time praying in his cell."[19] He slept on the floor next to an altar he built in a temple of his own exquisite design; there he taught his disciples how to pray and how to preach. Drawing on his interpretations of inquiries to his native informants, Duran concludes that "his deeds are of such renown and remind one so much of miracles that I dare not make any statement or write of them."[20] Later in the text, Duran speculates that Quetzalcoatl might have been the apostle St. Thomas, also a master builder, who preached to the Indians of the East: "We read that the glorious apostle St. Thomas was a master craftsman . . . and was a preacher to the Indians but that, having become discouraged there, he asked Christ . . . to send him wherever He wished."[21] Other writers have equated Quetzalcoatl with a Viking and a Chinese explorer.[22]

Syncretism, or the melding of beliefs and practices that conflict—the cross-cultural analogizing of ideas to find unity and to form a common identity, in this case an indigenous holy figure to be equated with the savior—is a common process in the development of world religions. For example, in the medieval period the pagan planetary deities were outfitted with more comfortable Christian clothing. Mercury, the fleet-footed pagan messenger god who travels close to the world, where he could more readily listen in on the affairs of society, becomes a wise scribe. Jupiter, who journeys in the moderate middle ground of the cosmos and moves at temperate speed, is transformed into a judge or a monk.[23] Dressing Quetzalcoatl in Christ's clothing and, as we shall see later, equating the completion of the Maya long count with the Second Coming, is little more than a modern variation on a theme, helped along by images, such as the one we find in pre-contact codices from Central Mexico, that depict the deity descending from heaven on a cotton rope (figure 10.2). A Mormon myth, now largely discarded, also equated Jesus in America with the returning white-bearded deity. Pinchbeck likely acquired his Quetzalcoatl hypothesis from a popular work by Tony Shearer.[24] At least, he credits Shearer with having introduced the Quetzalcoatl prophecy and the Maya calendar cycles to popular readers. Shearer's book had also inspired José Argüelles's cosmic convergence of August 16, 1987.

Historians of anthropology and art history Matthew Restall and Amara Solari offer a different interpretation of the Quetzalcoatl myth.[25] True, the Aztecs did conduct elaborate rituals at key turnover points in calendrical cycles. For example, at the end of a cycle of fifty-two years, when dates in their sacred count of 260 days coincident with those in the agricultural year of 365 days began to repeat, as the Spanish chronicler Bernardino de Sahagun tells us, they put out the fire in the hearth, cast out their mats, and broke their plates. Celebrants climbed the Hill of the Star in Tenochtítlan (Mexico City), the Aztec capital, to make offerings to pay their debt to the gods so that the world would be restored to balance. As they watched the Pleiades star group cross the overhead point at midnight, they lit a New Fire to celebrate the commencement of a rejuvenated time cycle. Then the people carried a portion of this fire back to their hearths. In other words, the New Fire ceremony, like the less elaborate rites that attended the completion of shorter calendrical cycles, had nothing to do with time stopping and the world coming to an end. Quite the opposite, New Fire was a celebration of renewal—a new beginning.

Restall and Solari trace the Mexican version of the millenarian myth to the spin placed on New Testament readings, such as the parable of the banquet in Luke, by millenarian-minded sixteenth-century Franciscan friars in charge of converting natives to the Roman Catholic faith.[26] By means of these parables, wrote one brother, God is hastening us to prepare for "that everlasting feast that will be endless."[27] In effect, the Spanish friars were readying the conquered Aztec people for the Second Coming of Christ. And it was these same holy men who popularized the notion that Cortez was the divine agent sent to open the door to them so that they could perform their task. The story stuck.

Maya chronicler Diego de Landa, first bishop of Yucatán—also a Franciscan—followed a similar course in using biblical texts as propaganda. For example, he took the Virgin Mary, the "woman clothed with the sun, with the moon under her feet and a crown of 12 stars on her head" and referred to as a sign of Doomsday in Revelation, to be an indication that the souls of the Maya needed to be saved in the wake of the impending end of time.[28] This is why her image figures prominently in paintings that adorn Landa's monastic complex next to the ancient Maya pyramid of Izamal in Yucatán. Landa had mounted a campaign of doing away with Maya pagan ideology by destroying every codex and carved monument he could lay his hands on. In his conversion teachings, like those of his brethren in Tenochtítlan, he imposed his own millenarian ideology on Maya neophytes. The imposition becomes evident in colonial native texts such as the Books of Chilam Balam referred to earlier. This brief lesson from history should pose a warning to those who insist on seeking Advent wisdom in the works of non-Western cultures: beware!—you may be peering into a mirror that reflects ideas implanted in your mind from your own culture.

While evidence from the written record goes against the ancient Maya ever having believed in total Armageddon (if they did, one would think they would have conjured up more than the few references we find to the overturn of the 2012 long count carved on their stone stelae), they still may have shared with the Aztecs the idea that times of destruction are followed by periods of re-creation.

Like Frank Waters and Daniel Pinchbeck, José Argüelles also made excellent use of the Aztec myth. He predicted that in 2012 Quetzalcoatl, the Mesoamerican god of peace and love, would descend to commence the dawn of the New Age. But in a curious twist, drawing from the indigenous Aztec Quetzalcoatl descent myth and the Christian Tribulation and Rapture imposed by the Spanish chroniclers on Mesoamerican religious lore, it is actually evil Tezcatlipoca, the dark antithesis of Quetzalcoatl, who will commence to descend down the cotton rope; but then he will morph into his all-good, light-bearing counterpart. We are leaving "the old time of war and conflict, where time is money, and entering a new time of peace and harmony, where time is art," Argüelles once wrote.[29] The new era, he claimed, will be nothing less than post-historic, even post-human, a superhuman phase of evolution. Once again, coming at a time of distrust in American institutions, beginning with Watergate and the host of X-gates to follow (all amply covered by the media), here was a message that bore considerable popular appeal. A handful of establishment scholars gave Argüelles's theories some leeway; for example, anthropologist Robert Sitler, at first a critic of 2012 prophecy, wrote: "The natural world bestowed upon us by the infinitely complex processes of creation, in many very real ways, *is* actually ending. The coincidence between this ubiquitous environmental ruin and the world age philosophy embedded in both Mayan myth and 2012 ideology is irresistibly suggestive."[30] Sitler added his wishes that Argüelles's optimistic visions of humanity's future (of passing into a post-historic, post-human, or superhuman phase of our evolution) would prove true. As we have seen, the same sort of romantic rhetoric once accompanied earlier troubling times, when bizarre alternatives to the woeful state of the world acquired enhanced currency in popular circles.

Following the cosmic road in Argüelles's footsteps, John Major Jenkins invited the world to participate "in the galactic process of Maya cosmogenesis."[31] Jenkins singled out the astronomical event that validates the end of the Maya long count as an alignment of the winter solstice sun with the center of our Milky Way Galaxy. This cosmic lineup, he promised, will open the doorway of opportunity to a "conscious relationship with each other and a creative participation with the Earth process that gives birth to our higher selves."[32]

In the 2012 episode, Jenkins was primarily responsible for conveying the notion that the Maya also were aware of the perennial philosophy; for example, he tells readers that they "possessed an insight into cycle dynamics and conveyed these ideals in their Creation Mythology. At the end of each cycle, a transformation can occur . . . They understood that nature inevitably cycles through phases [and that the] . . . Year 2012 is not about apocalypse, it's about apocatastasis, the restoration of the true and original conditions."[33] According to Jenkins, this is the perfect time for us to act—"to set intentions for the next round of the human endeavor." Critical of Argüelles's communal hand-holding, Jenkins advocated that "each person can choose where they want to be, inwardly, regardless of the circumstances of the outer world."[34]

As anthropologist John Hoopes has pointed out, Jenkins's ideas, as well as those of many postmillennial New Age prophets, also drew heavily on the work of the prolific, influential and, to judge by my only meeting with him, in 1984, extraordinarily charismatic fiction writer turned historian of religion Mircea Eliade.[35] As we learned in the previous chapter, in his *Myth of the Eternal Return* Eliade first made the distinction between sacred and profane time. There he explored the practice of ritual as a mechanism for the renewal of cyclic time, which he describes as a breakthrough process whereby a practitioner returns to a primordial tradition in which the world is pristine (sacred), rather than corrupt (profane). Interpreted in the Christian tradition, the former might correspond to the time before the sinning of Adam and Eve.

What to anticipate on the winter solstice of 2012 is all foretold in the Maya calendar and inscriptions, not to mention alignments at the Maya ruins, argued Jenkins. To his credit, Jenkins took considerable trouble to learn about the elements of the Maya calendar and writing system. Specifically, he posited that the Maya had set up their long count calendar 2,000 years ago with the 2012 alignment as an end date in mind. Jenkins appears to have acquired a portion of his wisdom from a very influential text coauthored by the celebrated epigrapher, artist and art historian Linda Schele. The astronomical elements of that text are worth reviewing briefly in the present context.

Schele spearheaded the Palenque meetings that led to the decipherment of much of the Maya script and, until her early death in 1996, was regarded as the most important contributor to breaking the code of the hieroglyphs. In *Maya Cosmos: Three Thousand Years on the Shaman's Path* (1993), Schele, in collaboration with archaeologist David Freidel and writer Joy Parker, suggested that particular images carved on Maya stelae represented virtual maps of the sky.[36] The authors offered evidence in the form of computer-generated sky maps showing the Milky Way, represented as a "World Tree," or conduit, connecting the upper and lower worlds with the middle realm in which the Maya live. The cosmic tree stood in perfect north-south alignment on the seasonal date of the last Maya creation epoch (August 11, 3114 BCE).[37] Schele shares with readers her personal revelation, prompted by a remark made by Mayanist Matt Looper (then a student in one of her classes). The topic was the iconography of the effigy of the Palenque ruler Pakal depicted on the lid of his sarcophagus. "While I was telling the class about the Wakah-Chan-World Tree being the Milky Way, I heard him [Matthew] murmur from the back of the crowded seminar room, 'That's why he entered the road.' His words exploded like a lightning bolt in my mind. The great image of Pakal's sarcophagus at Palenque . . . shows him at the moment of his death falling down the World Tree into the Maw of the Earth . . . he entered the road, the Milky Way."[38]

Based on earlier references in Maya scholarship, Schele and Freidel repeatedly refer to the World Tree that holds up the sky portion of the cosmic house—the axis of creation, because the Maya First Father raised it up at that time. Though they make no claims to non-Maya references, their idea resonates with one of Mircea Eliade's basic theses: "The sky is conceived as a vast tent supported by a central pillar; the tent pole or the central post of the house [here he refers to the house of people of the Asian and North American Arctic] is assimilated to the Pillars of the World."[39] Recall that this is the pole the shamans climb on their celestial journeys.

In the two decades that have elapsed since *Maya Cosmos* appeared, and despite my own continuing reservations, the concept of some sort of cosmic representation of the World Tree in Maya studies remains alive, if not proven. For example, epigrapher Simon Martin traces it back to the Olmec culture, while iconographer Karl Taube supports the identification of the Panel of the Cross at Palenque as the World Tree.[40] On the other hand, Restall and Solari speculate that the Maya World Tree is a received impression of the Cross of Christ proselytized by Franciscans.

In line with Eliade's studies of shamanism, especially the premise that every human being is capable of reexperiencing ambient spiritual forces inherent in the cosmos, Schele and Freidel remark, almost wishfully, "The wonderful thing about this idea is that it nurtures a sense of belonging to the world and to the cosmos. We need not look up at the night sky or the sun and feel insignificant. Rather, shamanism teaches us that those bright beings are part of a shared history and life-force that belong to all humanity."[41] Then, quite apart from applying it to the Maya, the authors of *Maya Cosmos* appear to endorse and personalize the practice: "We believe that shamanism can function as a guide in complex, civilized societies and that as a way of organizing knowledge it spans the Americas today."[42] And later: "Letting this remarkable record of their minds and hearts speak to us has been one of the most exhilarating experiences of our lives."[43] Rereading *Maya Cosmos* twenty years, later I can better appreciate how much the enthusiasm and admiration of Freidel and Schele for Maya achievements and ways of knowing seemed off-putting to some of their critics (myself included), who might have overinterpreted their findings to be couched in the framework of a universal subconscious archetypal understanding of the cosmos.

In his 2012 prognostications, Jenkins equated the Freidel and Schele sky creation maps with imagery carved on stelae at the early classic ruins of Izapa, a peripheral (non-Maya) archaeological site located on the Pacific coast near the contemporary Mexico-Guatemala border. There he discovered building alignments with the winter solstice sunset position. Jenkins did not subscribe to conventional interpretations of the Izapa monuments by Maya scholars, who regarded them to be focused on the ruler, who is specifically portrayed as an avian creature, rather than on some transcendent cosmic alignment to set up a cyclic turnover that would happen two millennia later.[44] It turns out that Jenkins's alignments are ubiquitous in the early classic Maya period.[45] My own view is that a more practical reason for setting them up may have had to do with the agricultural seasonal calendar and the offering of sacrifice as debt payment for a hoped-for prosperous crop.

Like Argüelles, in a later work Jenkins hedged his bet and prepped followers for a next step in the event that no global transformation took place on December 21, 2012.[46] He placed himself above the New Age rabble by stressing that esoteric ancient Maya knowledge can be used to benefit humanity. *The 2012 Story*, especially the final chapter, becomes a self-help text, advising believers to focus on their personal transformation. After all, Jenkins tells readers with a ring of cognitive dissonance, "the world image is a projected dream of the inner psyche, the burden of successful world renewal lies with the individual."[47]

In their account of the emergence of 2012 mythology out of the New Age philosophy of the 1970s, Kevin Whitesides and John Hoopes discuss how believers overcome cognitive dissonance.[48] How can we reconcile the superior invention of the Maya calendar with the inferior living conditions in which the present-day Maya people find themselves? Answer: by the spiritually revealed existence of a higher advanced culture that descended to contemporary decadence. At another level, devotees resolve the dissonant condition by rejecting what the Maya experts teach us—they are untrustworthy and deceitful while we are insightful. Our beliefs are not pseudo-scientific. They are the real truth, the only path to spiritual enlightenment.

John Hoopes calls the 2012 phenomenon we have been contemplating "Mayanism," "an eclectic collection of beliefs that grow out of what has been variously identified as the eclectic tradition, New Age thought, and metaphysical religion."[49] He regards Mayanism as "a contemporary projection of Western ideas with roots in European and more ancient Jewish and Christian cosmology and eschatology onto the ancient Maya for the purpose of achieving goals of individualized self-improvement and self-actualization," specifically, "wishful thinking on the part of Europeans who seek validation in an enlightened pre-Christian (or at least non-Christian) past."[50] The desacralized version of the return to the Garden of Eden is all a part of the archetypal experience of escaping Eliade's "terror of history." Joscelyn Godwin's definition of occultism as "a term for the pursuit of occult science in deliberate opposition to the prevailing beliefs of scientific materialism" offers a close parallel to Hoopes's definition of Mayanism.[51] Godwin further notes that while conspiracy theory is anathema to the historian, it is an indispensable component in the history of the occult, in the sense that earthly events do not occur only out of material cause and effect but rather are influenced by higher causes. (See also the discussion of occultism in chapter 5.)

CONCLUSION

Contrasting the Signs of the Times

But the persistent presence of a large proportion of hard-core biblical literalists in this country . . . was not anticipated either by freethinkers or by proponents of "rational" religion at the end of the nineteenth century.

—*Author Susan Jacoby*

There are curious parallels between end of the world narratives where our story of romanticized versions of the past started—with the October 22, 1844, prediction—and where it ended, on December 21, 2012. Before I enumerate them, let me run down an apocalyptic checklist by reviewing basic beliefs held by the most influential contemporary prophetic timekeepers we've discussed.[1] First, there is a preoccupation with nuclear annihilation, environmental destruction, and other disasters; second, the crisis is imminent; third, believers share in a loss of confidence in American institutions, especially science and government; fourth, evil conspiracies abound; fifth, there is a yearning for salvation amid a feeling of helplessness in the face of threatening external forces. Yet there is hope: history unfolding may all be part of a wondrous grand plan. If you pay attention you'll see the signs and you'll know the time; the final chapter of human history will be written when those who keep the faith arrive in paradise—here or elsewhere.

The signs of the times, the prophetic arithmetic, the adjusted calculations, the replacement of the sudden ending or transformation of consciousness by a more gradual coming-of-age scenario that transpires as end-time nears or even passes—all of these aspects characterize both the 1844 and 2012 apocalyptic scenarios. For example, take the "heavenly pickup." In the 2012 myth, Quetzalcoatl and UFOs become the contemporary secular version of the descending Christ in the 1844 episode. Social media played a highly influential role in disseminating both stories. The printing press of the 1840s, with its endless stream of pamphlets and newspapers advertising time's end, is supplanted by today's Internet websites; yesterday's derogatory broadsides become today's online debunkers. Pastor Miller's persuasive promoter Joshua Himes is resurrected in popular influential bloggers like Geoff Stray. And finally, these like-in-kind characteristics and behaviors are all underlain by shared motives that drove the 1844 and 2012 agendas.

As long ago as 1915, the German philosopher Max Weber, one of the founders of the discipline of sociology, wrote that developments such as modern modes of time reckoning and the process of rationalization in the contemporary world had left no place for apocalyptic thinking. Religious ritual had become routinized, and prophecies about the end of the world demystified.[2] This may have been true in Europe, but in America, as we have seen, things were different. The nuclear era and the threat of terrorism, coupled with the nonunified nature of religious denominations in America, have only strengthened apocalyptic leanings. Today, 45 percent of all Christians in America identify themselves as "born again"; this is a significant change in that it demonstrates the spread of evangelism beyond the formal member groups of the Evangelical Association, which itself doubled in population during the 1990s, then doubled yet again during the first decade of the third millennium.[3]

Sociologist Robert Bellah has observed that in today's world the relationship between people and their inquiry into the conditions of their existence has become more complex than it was a century or more ago. The bond between the religious and social orders today has loosened. This freedom of personality—Bellah calls it individualism—that exists now has no historical parallel.[4] But despite the secularized nature of the modern world, people as individuals continue to seek the sacred in a romanticized past.

We had it and we lost it—but we still can get it back. The past was superior to the present. There once were cultures that possessed the spiritual capabilities we all yearn for. They were advanced well beyond civilizations of the present age; but they made the mistake of following the temptation to descend from the spiritual to the material plane. Yet, because humanity is a microcosmic version of the cosmos, the hidden secrets of the universe reside within us. We can return to our once-glorious past. Through discipline and patience, if we endure we can unlock the clues to the true meaning of human existence. We observed these motives and means surfacing in Helena Blavatsky's writings on eastward-leaning theosophical wisdom, in Aldous Huxley's perennial philosophy, and in Mircea Eliade's eternal return—shared ideologies forged by late nineteenth- and early twentieth-century spiritual philosophers who gave birth to contemporary transcendentalism. The New Age prophets of 2012 used their ideas to pattern an end time template.

October 22, 1844, and December 21, 2012, are just two among countless religious- and secular-based predictions of "the end of the world as we know it" spread over the past American century and a half. Older readers may recall Edgar Whisenant's *88 Reasons Why the Rapture Is in 1988*, followed by *89 Reasons Why the Rapture Is in 1989* (by the same author), and so on to 1993 and 1994. The end of the world date-setting business had then been brisk. Remember Y2K? The digital millennium bug was supposed to wreak havoc with data storage. Software wouldn't be able to correctly abbreviate the four-digit year 2000 to two digits. Computers that had stored data in double-digit years might confuse 2000 with 1900. Fear spread that utilities and other infrastructure would fail. Measures were taken by skilled programmers and though there were a few problems—an alarm sounded two minutes past midnight at a Japanese power plant and slot machines stopped working at a racetrack in Delaware—millennial New Year's Day dawned pretty much like any other.

As Y2K receded, pundits predicted a falloff in fearmongering. They figured those who bit the hook would begin to become disillusioned by the bait they tasted. But TV documentaries continued to flourish—especially following 9/11. In 2003, for example, four world-ending predictions received considerable attention. They included the destruction of Los Angeles by an asteroid impact as punishment inflicted on Hollywood for creating too many pornographic movies, and the invasion of the Zetas, space aliens threatening to stop the world from rotating (their mechanism for doing so was never articulated). A banner year, 2006 saw no fewer than fifteen predictions of time's end, among them the "Big One" centered in LA (January 25), a comet collision (May 25), the beginning of the Tribulation (June 6—666, you'll recall, is the "number of the beast" in Revelation), and Israel being wiped off the map (August 22). Glenn Beck, popular spokesperson for conservative political causes, was credited with the last prediction, though on August 23 he announced that he was merely quoting a Middle East scholar. The Lord's Witness and the True Bible Code, a religious group, foretold of the UN Plaza being struck by a nuclear bomb on September 8 or 9 (they had trouble pinning down whether the disaster would occur before or after midnight). The House of Yahweh interpreted signs in the book of Daniel to fix the outbreak of nuclear war at September 12. And finally, a Puerto Rican religious leader targeted the Second Coming of Jesus as December 17—in San Juan.

Jesus had a busy year in 2007. He was booked to appear in Washington, Jerusalem, Baghdad, and Moscow—all at the same time. But a group of "True" Russian Orthodox followers predicted the event would take place in May 2008 (their revelation text consisted of bar codes on processed canned foods, which they read as Satanic symbols). These were two among more than a dozen such predictions for 2007–2008. When the world doesn't end, a common response of those who had alerted us is "Oops, we made a mistake," or "The world really did end and those of us on the higher plane of existence have already experienced it in subtle ways." Members of the first category of prophets form a large collect including, as we have seen, Pastor William Miller himself.

The most recent headline grabber in the Hal Lindsey religious tradition to offer both the "made a mistake" and "it already happened" options has been eighty-nine-year-old engineer and biblical literalist Harold Camping. Camping amassed a fortune in the construction industry. He used his wealth to start his own church in San Diego and to establish Family Radio, a seventy-station network capable of reaching all of the continental United States and parts of Asia and Europe. Camping's faith lay in the precise truth encoded in biblical Scripture. In 1992, after a claimed lifetime of study and calculations based on passages in Genesis and New Testament Revelation (for example, 2 Peter, 2 Thessalonians, and Luke), he laid it all out in a 500-page million seller titled simply *1994?*[5] Camping announced the exact date of the Rapture as September 6, 1994. When that date, year, and several more years passed and God's mathematical cryptic missives continued to prove ineffectual, Camping realized he might have made a mistake. First he explained that it was the Tribulation he'd actually reckoned, and that this was already taking

FIGURE 13.1. A contemporary postmillennial billboard advertising the imminent end of the world. ("Judgment Day 21 May 2011 [English]" by O'Dea at WikiCommons. Licensed under CC BY-SA 3.0 via Wikimedia Commons.)

place—just look at all the wars in the Middle East, famine in Africa, and earthquakes around the world, not to mention the increase in homosexuality. So he revised his chronology: the Rapture would not ensue until 2011—on May 21 at 6:00 p.m., to be precise.

Camping's description of time's end sounds uncannily like Cotton Mather's back in colonial times (see chapter 3).[6] It would commence with an earthquake off the east coast of New Zealand. Tsunamis, then fires would spread across the world. Media attention to the revised date was widespread, helped along by the 5,000 messages on billboards rented by Camping and spread across the United States and thirty other countries (figure 13.1). He also spread the word via his Open Forum website and daily radio broadcasts. CNN, BBC, Fox, even the *New York Times* and Al Jazeera ran stories on Camping's prediction. On May 19, two days before the final inning, Camping shut down his radio station, closed his offices, left his home, and secreted himself and his wife in a hotel to await the sound of the trumpet from the firmament that would signal the descent of the savior.

It is difficult to know how many serious followers Camping had attracted over the years. He claimed 200 million. His radio messages, which were broadcast in tens of languages, were certainly capable of reaching hundreds of millions of people. Significantly, like orthodox Protestants in Miller's day, many Christians say that even though they didn't believe Camping, they tuned in to his broadcasts anyway. Some who had spent their money to help finance Open Forum ads and had given away their possessions were quite annoyed because the world didn't end. Complaints were filed with the FCC. Religious detractors accused Camping of preaching the word of Satan.

How did Camping explain what didn't happen the second time around? Well, again, it did. God *did* return to earth. And the earthquakes happened too. But, as some of Pastor Miller's followers had testified a century and a half earlier, the happenings were spiritual rather than physical. If God had told Camping otherwise, he wouldn't have been taken seriously. Like Miller, Camping corrected his calculations, this time stretching his bandwidth a bit. Judgment, he predicted, will occur over a period of 153 days; and we have just begun to enter that period. It will end on October 21, 2011—then the world *really* will be destroyed. Eighteen days into the countdown, Camping suffered a stroke. Though largely silenced, he did make a brief appearance. Speaking in a slurred voice, once again he hedged his bet slightly: "I do believe we are getting very near the end"; what God started on May 21 "*probably* will be finished out on October 21 in the final end of everything."[7] Finally, in March 2012, at the age of ninety, Camping posted an online open letter admitting he was wrong about predicting the world's end, said he'd never do it again, and asked for forgiveness. He died at the end of the next year.

José Argüelles never lived to see history's Day Omega either. He died in March 2011. But what of the other 2012 prophets? John Major Jenkins continues to research his idea that a December solstice sun and Dark Rift and Crossroads (the point where the Milky Way crosses the ecliptic) alignment, produced by the precession of the equinoxes, lay behind deliberate Maya attempts to target December 21, 2012, as the end date of the long count. He also continues to argue that the perennial philosophy embraced the "core, archetypal, spiritual teachings of the Maya, which are obvious to careful readers of Maya creation mythology."[8] Remaining hostile to critics, Jenkins, emphasizing his position as a nondegreed independent scholar/researcher, views the establishment as incapable of assessing his work. Scholars, he believes, "are not well apprised of one or more disciplines that are necessary for understanding my interdisciplinary synthesis."[9] Jenkins also remains openly critical of other 2012 New Age authors and resents being classified among them by academics. His characterization of himself as one who did his best "to offer clarity, insight, and discernment to a difficult topic . . . , that the marketplace and the pop culture has raped and pillaged and otherwise has had its way with. Now, it's tossed aside and I'm discovering, in recent months, that many of my friends, professional contacts and acquaintances had conflated me so intimately with '2012' that, now that it's passed, I'm no longer on the radar."[10]

Today Jenkins participates in sacred tourism—for example, New Year's Eve in Peru, December 27, 2013, to January 5, 2014—and is billed as "Scholar, Author on Unified Cosmogenesis, Galactic Alignment and Reconstructing the World Myths," whose comprehensive work covers "the crisis of sustainability in the modern world."[11] His talks are said to embrace self-renewal and healing in the Maya-Peruvian tradition, and his tryptagonal poems open consciousness to a larger integrated vision of the world.

Carl Johan Calleman also claims his work has been grossly misunderstood. When asked, "What happened to 2012?" he responded that the idea that everything would revolve around a single date isn't true. The tabloids and media misrepresented him. The Maya message is really more about how *we* change, and that's all shifting because of a divine metaphysical plan. Largely unresponsive to critics, Calleman continues to follow the cosmic dispensationalist notion of long-term shifts in human consciousness that are doled out in steps or levels (recall that there are nine of them—just like the nine levels in Maya pyramids) that more or less follow the McKenna-Argüelles model. In his revised theory he notes that the Mayanists have corrected errors in their decipherment; the ninth and final wave was activated on March 9, 2011, and for the first time since Big Bang creation (which he still places at 16.4 billion years ago) and for the next 5,125 years, humanity can access and download unity consciousness.[12]

Calleman is currently composing his magnum opus, *The Global Mind and the Rise of Civilization*, which he advertises as an intelligent design text. It will be a three-volume work that promises to cover all human history, from how civilization arose to "how our minds are produced by resonance with the globe" in a metaphysical plan that guides us (volume 1), to be followed by a second volume entitled *Consequences: Altered States of Consciousness*, and then a third on how the Maya calendar continues.[13] Calleman insists he's not doing it for the money.

Daniel Pinchbeck appears to have moved past the 2012 morass, but he remains an active advocate of rainforest plant medicine. Of the fashionable ayahuasca he tell us that—when you do it in the jungle and are surrounded by the plant itself—it's as if the plants are speaking or even singing to you.[14] When it comes to clock setting, Pinchbeck says only that humanity is *close* to some kind of transmutation event: "Is it something we'll experience in my lifetime or in your lifetime? Is it a fifty-year process? Is it a never-ending process? Are technology and biology going to merge? Are we going to pursue technologies that accentuate and elevate our psychic abilities? . . . I remain optimistic that we're on the cusp of a deeper level of metamorphosis . . . We're just seeing the beginning of it."[15]

It doesn't take a careful observer to realize that the course of post-2012 prophetic arithmetic closely parallels what happened in the wake of the Great Disappointment of 1844. The development of Seventh-day Adventism, which offered the elevation of humanity to eternal life in an extended time frame, is not unlike the promise of what one might call the secular "church of unity consciousness." As Gordon Melton suggested of Millerism (see chapter 1), denial of failure isn't an option and what outsiders call prophecy, insiders see as success—provided the prophecy gets reinterpreted. Then, as now, failure equals fulfillment.

I have chosen to tell the story of American pop culture's voracious appetite for apocalypse by reflecting on a pair of case studies: the nineteenth-century Millerite version of time's end, which flourished during the Second Great Awakening, and third-millennium Mayanism, a product of secular New Age thinking. Both attracted extraordinary public attention for an extended period of time and the narratives are similar, provided you alter the stage and its cast of characters to set up a storyboard that rings with the times. In the 2012 myth Maya inscriptions replace the biblical texts in Daniel and Revelation. Still, each derives the source of transcendent knowledge from a remote past. Carl Johan Calleman's and the McKenna brothers' theory of the accelerated cosmic evolution of human consciousness, with an imminent endpoint of grand transformation, reads like updated pages out of Helena Blavatsky's *Isis Unveiled* or *The Secret Doctrine*. José Argüelles and the other Y12 prophets who followed in his footsteps emerge as latter-day Blavatskys who, having lost faith in the condition of the world, seek wisdom from afar. Not only are her contemporary counterparts just as charismatic as she, but also much of the message they transmit remains mostly about *them*—their special access to universal truth, and the urgent need they feel to tell the world about it. A century ago exotic Eastern leanings were a major source of distant wisdom. Now prophets tune in to the equally distant ancient cultures of Mesoamerica. Embracing space age technology and science, some reach out even farther—to the stars—for extraterrestrial wisdom.

Wouter Hanegraaff, who has written widely on the popularity of modern science in the New Age movement, views the divergence between establishment science and its occult counterpart in terms of two interpretive views. Critics regard much of New Age science as pseudo-science or, at best in a few instances, borderline genuine science. Defenders shore up their marginality by claiming that *they* are the true pioneers, the ones who are conducting cutting-edge science. They regard traditional science as an enterprise too oriented toward materialism. The New Age worldview relies strongly on *interpreting* research data rather than being involved in acquiring it. Methodologically, though both seek a unified worldview, the main difference between the two, according to Hanegraaff, is that New Age philosophers believe that science can be employed to "shed light on, even explain, the workings of the divine in the cosmos and thus secure a scientific basis for religion."[16]

The medium for conveying the divine message also has changed. The complex mathematical calculations behind fixing the date of the end of the world were worked out with pen and paper and illustrated in Miller's famous creation chart, which accompanied live presentations in packed lecture venues under camp tents. Today the revealed word is conveyed via the Internet—that leveling agent of legitimacy—and via film media. Scientific-sounding warnings of fire in the Earth and erupting volcanoes that once colored Matherian and Millerite rhetoric are replaced by today's magnetic pole reversals, sunspots, and planetary and galactic alignments.

Atop the deeply embedded view of Judeo-Christian Western philosophy, all of the occult elements American popular culture thrives on are present and accounted for in millennial mythmaking: joy in the face of chaos, a sudden moment of world-shattering transformation guaranteed to happen at the very time in which we live, a calculable moment that can become known to us provided we follow the path toward revealed knowledge by perfecting ourselves, and the unshakable faith that, if we can endure our Humpty Dumpty world falling apart, somehow it will all magically come back together again—in the shape of a better world.

And so the end of the world seems never ending.

Notes

Preface

1. Anthony Aveni, *The End of Time: The Maya Mystery of 2012* (Boulder: University Press of Colorado, 2009).

2. Anthony Aveni, *Behind the Crystal Ball: Magic, Science and Religion from Antiquity through the New Age* (New York: Times, 1996). A related term employed in this text that embraces the spiritual world is *gnostic*—especially that acquired intuitively and employed as a way to salvation from the material world. Stephen Hoeller, "What Is a Gnostic?" *Gnosis: A Journal of Western Inner Tradition* 23 (1992): 24–27, identifies *gnosis* with knowledge reserved for elites and passed down through various religious traditions, where it still exists despite conflicting with traditional views.

3. Tomoko Masuzawa, *In Search of Dreamtime: The Quest for the Origin of Religion* (Chicago: University of Chicago Press, 1993).

4. Joscelyn Godwin, *Atlantis and the Cycles of Time* (Rochester, VT: Inner Traditions, 2011), ix.

Introduction

1. Lawrence Joseph, *Apocalypse 2012: An Investigation into Civilization's End* (New York: Broadway, 2007), 13, 33.

2. Sharon Hill, "Ask an Astrobiologist about the 2012 Doomsdate," *Harper's Magazine,* November 2012, 28.

3. The word *millennialism* derives from the Christian biblical idea that events leading up to time's end are parsed out in thousand-year stages.

4. José Argüelles, *The Mayan Factor: Pathway beyond Technology* (Santa Fe, NM: Bear, 1987), 130, 184.

5. Ibid., 159.

6. John Major Jenkins, *The 2012 Story: The Myths, Fallacies, and Truth behind the Most Intriguing Date in History* (New York: Tarcher Penguin, 2009), 164.

7. Ibid., 295.

8. Revelation 6:12.

9. Wikipedia.org/wiki/list_of_Apocalyptic_Films (accessed March 13, 2014).

10. Steve Almond, "The Apocalypse Market Is Booming" *New York Times*, September 29, 2013, 48.

11. Catherine Wessinger, ed., *The Oxford Handbook of Millennialism* (Oxford: Oxford University Press, 2011), 720.

12. Leon Festinger, Henry Riecken, and Stanley Schachter, *When Prophecy Fails: A Social and Psychological Study of a Modern Group That Predicted the End of the World* (Minneapolis: University of Minnesota Press, 1956), 31.

13. John R. Hall, *Apocalypse: From Antiquity to the Empire of Modernity* (Cambridge: Polity, 2009), 2; Richard G. Kyle, *The Last Days Are Here Again: A History of End Times* (Grand Rapids, MI: Baker, 1998), 99.

Chapter 1

1. Michael Barkun, *Crucible of the Millennium: The Burned-over District of New York in the 1840s* (Syracuse: Syracuse University Press, 1986), 21, places the movement between 1835 and 1860. The First Great Awakening occurred in 1730–1745 (23).

2. Francis Nichol, *The Midnight Cry: A Defense of the Character and Conduct of William Miller and the Millerites Who Mistakenly Believed that the Second Coming of Christ Would Take Place in the Year 1844* (Takoma Park, WA: Review and Herald, 1944), 19.

3. Whitney Cross, *The Burned-over District: The Social and Intellectual History of Enthusiastic Religion in Western New York, 1800–1850* (Ithaca: Cornell University Press, 1950), 291.

4. Nichol, *Midnight Cry*, 33.

5. Ruth Alden Doan, *The Miller Heresy, Millennialism, and American Culture* (Philadelphia, Temple University Press, 1987), 32–33.

6. Barkun, *Crucible of the Millennium*, 126.

7. Nichol, *Midnight Cry*, 54.

8. Barkun, *Crucible of the Millennium*, 46.

9. Nichol, *Midnight Cry*, 57.

10. Ibid., 43.

11. Barkun, *Crucible of the Millennium*, 38, 94.

12. David T. Arthur, "Joshua V. Himes and the Cause of Adventism," in *The Disappointed: Millerism and Millenarianism in the Nineteenth Century*, ed. Ronald L. Numbers and Jonathan M. Butler (Bloomington: Indiana University Press, 1987), 36–58.

13. David Rowe, "Comets and Eclipses: The Millerites, Nature, and the Apocalypse," *Adventist Heritage* 3, no. 2 (1976): 10–19; see also Barkun, *Crucible of the Millennium*, 55, 103–12.

14. Barkun, *Crucible of the Millennium*, 136.

15. Ibid., 103–4.

16. Nichol, *Midnight Cry*, 139. The other six admonitions are: lay aside all sectarian views, avoid bringing in any doctrines unconnected with the second Advent while preparing for it, avoid placing too much reliance on impressions, judge no man, be aware of any adversary who will try to overcome us when we are unguarded, and finally, sow our seed and gain our harvest, so long as God gives us time.

17. Ibid., 206.

18. Ibid., 238.

19. Ibid., 239.

20. Hall, *Apocalypse*, 151.

21. Nichol, *Midnight Cry*, 514–15.

22. Ibid., 238–39.

23. Ibid., 458.

24. Ibid., 272.

25. Ibid., 271.

26. Festinger, Riecken, and Schachter, *When Prophecy Fails*, 5, 12–23.

27. Ibid. Festinger uses this example.

28. Ibid., 13.

29. *Signs of the Times*, January 25, 1843, 14.

30. Nichol, *Midnight Cry*, 126.

31. Cross, *Burned-over District*, 312.

32. Nichol, *Midnight Cry*, 455.

33. Jonathan Butler, "The Making of a New Order: Millerism and the Origins of Seventh-day Adventism," in Numbers and Butler, *The Disappointed*, 200.

34. Ibid.

35. Ibid.

36. John Gordon Melton, "Spiritualization and Reaffirmation: What Really Happens When Prophecy Fails," *American Studies* 26, no. 2 (1985): 17–29.

37. Recent scholarship finds the Festinger, Riecken, and Schachter theory of cognitive dissonance wanting on a number of issues and interpretations. Melton, "Spiritualization and Reaffirmation," has outlined a number of ways groups adapt to prophetic failure, most especially by denying failure as a means of asserting that prophecy has been fulfilled. Unlike the case of Keech, that of Miller was bolstered by a comprehensive ideology based on a shared literal interpretation of Scripture, belief in prophecy, and an interactive social community in which prophetic ritual could be performed.

38. Barkun, *Crucible of the Millennium*, 120.

39. Ibid., 51

40. Cross, *Burned-over District*, 319.

41. Ibid., 317.

42. Nichol, *Midnight Cry*, 290.

43. Ibid., 512.

44. Ronald L. Numbers, and Jonathan M. Butler, eds., *The Disappointed: Millerism and Millenarianism in the Nineteenth Century* (Bloomington: Indiana University Press, 1987).

45. Ibid., xv–xii.

Chapter 2

1. Anthony Aveni, *The Book of the Year: A Brief History of Our Seasonal Holidays* (Oxford: Oxford University Press, 2004).

2. Émile Durkheim, *The Elementary Forms of the Religious Life* (Oxford: Oxford University Press, 2001).

3. Mircea Eliade, *The Myth of the Eternal Return; or, Cosmos and History* (Princeton: Princeton University Press, 1955).

4. Jamel Velji, "Apocalyptic Rhetoric and the Construction of Authority in Medieval Islam," in *Roads to Paradise: Eschatology and Concepts of the Hereafter in Islam*, ed. Sebastian Günther and Todd Lawson (Leiden: Brill, 2003).

5. Norman Cohn, *Cosmos, Chaos and the World to Come: The Ancient Roots of Apocalyptic Faith* (New Haven: Yale University Press, 2001), 30.

6. Alexander Heidel, *The Babylonian Genesis: The Story of Creation* (Chicago: University of Chicago Press, 1942), lines 137–40.

7. Luis Valcarcel, *Historia del antiguo Perú* (Lima: Editorial Juan Mejía Baca, 1964).

8. Gil Raz, "Time Manipulation in Early Daoist Ritual: The East Well Chant and the Eight Archivists," *Asia Major*, 3rd ser., 18, no. 2 (2005): 27–65.

9. Ibid., 38.

10. Stephen Bokencamp, quoted in David Ownby, "Chinese Millenarian Traditions: The Formative Age," *American Historical Review* 104, no. 5 (1999): 1519.

11. For further discussion of Chinese millennialism, particularly its Buddhist influences, see Scott Lowe, "Chinese Millennial Movements," in Wessinger, *The Oxford Handbook of Millennialism*, 307–25.

12. Ownby, "Chinese Millenarian Traditions," 1524.

13. David Cook, "Early Islamic and Classical Sunni and Shi'ite Apocalyptic Movements," in Wessinger, *The Oxford Handbook of Millennialism*, 267–83, discusses the complex nature of the Mahdi and his coming.

14. Jean-Pierre Filiu, *Apocalypse in Islam* (Berkeley: University of California Press, 2011), esp. chapter 1 and pp. 28–29.

15. Flynt Leverett, "The Mad Mullah," *Harper's*, November 2012, 53.

16. Hall, *Apocalypse*, 41.

17. For a discussion of these terms, see Catherine Wessinger, "Millennial Glossary," in Wessinger, *The Oxford Handbook of Millennialism*, 717, 720, 722, and especially chaps. 1–4; Norman Cohn, *The Pursuit of the Millennium: Revolutionary Millenarians and Mystical Anarchists of the Middle Ages*, 2nd ed. (New York: Oxford University Press, 1970), esp. 28–29; and Bernard McGinn, *Visions of the End: Apocalyptic Traditions in the Middle Ages* (New York: Columbia University Press, 1979), 2–14.

18. McGinn, *Visions of the End*, 10

19. Géza Vermes, *The Complete Dead Sea Scrolls in English* (New York: Penguin, 1997), 110, 114.

20. 1 Thessalonians 4:16–17.

21. McGinn, *Visions of the End*, 4.

22. Revelation 13:1–3.

23. Revelation 19:13–15.

24. Revelation 13:16–18.

25. Jonathan Kirsch, *A History of the End of the World: How the Most Controversial Book in the Bible Changed the Course of Western Civilization* (San Francisco: Harper, 2006), 126.

26. Elaine Pagels, *Visions, Prophecy, and Politics in the Book of Revelation* (New York: Viking, 2012), 1.

27. Revelation 21:2.

28. Revelation 1:1.

29. This is likely a reference to a mirage known as Fata Morgana (named after the Arthurian sorceress), or "fairy castles." The phenomenon is recognizable as a series of inverted stacked images seen shimmering along the horizon.

30. Daniel 7:25, 12:7; Revelation 11:2–3, 12:6, 12:14, 13:5.

31. Nicholas Campion, "The 2012 Mayan Calendar Prophecies in the Context of the Western Millenarian Tradition," *Proceedings of the International Astronomical Union*, Symposium 278 (2011): 250.

32. Revelation 20:3.

33. 2 Peter 3:8.

34. Richard Landes, Andrew Gow, and David Van Meter, eds., *The Apocalyptic Year 1000: Religious Expectation and Social Change, 950–1050* (Oxford: Oxford University Press, 2003), vii.

35. Ibid., 8.

36. Damian Thompson, *The End of Time: Faith and Fear in the Shadow of the Millennium* (London: Sinclair-Stevenson, 1996), 58.

37. Cohn, *Cosmos, Chaos and the World to Come*, 3–60. See also McGinn, *Visions of the End*, 126–41.

38. Cohn, *Cosmos, Chaos and the World to Come*, 282.

39. Michael Grosso, *The Millennium Myth: Love and Death at the End of Time* (Wheaton, IL: Quest, 1995), 45.

40. Cohn, *Pursuit of the Millennium*, 108–13.

41. *Purgatory* 34:33, quoted in Kirsch, *History of the End of the World*, 160.

42. Part 2, act 5, scene 2, lines 40–42, quoted in Kirsch, *History of the End of the World*.

43. Ruth H. Bloch, *Visionary Republic: Millennial Themes in American Thought, 1756–1800* (Cambridge, Cambridge University Press, 1985), 6.

44. Thompson, *End of Time*, 90.

45. Christopher Hill, *Antichrist in Seventeenth-Century England*, Riddell Memorial Lectures 41 (London: Oxford University Press, 1990).

Chapter 3

1. Herbert Rose, *The Eclogues of Vergil* (Boston, NH: Dole, 1904), IV, lines 5–8; US Department of State Bureau of Public Affairs, "The Great Seal of the United States," 4 (http://www.state.gov/documents/organization/27807.pdf (accessed June 10, 2014).

2. Ron Rhodes, *Reasoning from the Scriptures with Masons* (Eugene, OR: Harvest House, 2001), 25–26.

3. Arturo de Hoyos and Brent Morris, *Freemasonry in Context: History, Ritual, Controversy*, (Lanham, MD: Lexington Books, 2004), 212–13.

4. Michael Barkun, *A Culture of Conspiracy: Apocalyptic Visions in Contemporary America* (Berkeley: University of California Press, 2003), 39–65.

5. Catherine L. Albanese, *A Republic of Mind and Spirit: A Cultural History of Metaphysical Religion* (New Haven: Yale University Press, 2007), 125.

6. Laurence Bergreen, *Columbus: The Four Voyages* (New York: Viking, 2011), 244.

7. Ibid., 245.

8. Grosso, *Millennium Myth*, 114–15.

9. Leonard I. Sweet, "Christopher Columbus and the Millennial Vision of the World," *Catholic Historical Review* 72, no. 3 (1986): 369–82.

10. James Breig, "Eighteenth Century Millennialism," *Colonial Williamsburg* 34, no. 3 (2013): 2.

11. Perry Miller, "The End of the World," *William and Mary Quarterly*, 3rd ser., 8, no. 2 (1951): 171–91.

12. Michael Wigglesworth, *The Day of Doom; or, A Poetical Description of the Great and Last Judgment* (Boston: Green and Allen, 1701).

13. Quoted in Mildred Campbell, "Social Origins of Some Early Americans," in *Seventeenth Century America: Essays in Colonial History*, ed. James Morton Smith (Chapel Hill: University of North Carolina Press, 1959), 87.

14. Kirsch, *History of the End of the World*, 178.

15. Quoted in Thompson, *End of Time*, 96.

16. Pierre Jurieu, *The Strange and Wonderful Predictions of Mr. Christopher Love* (1651; repr., Ann Arbor: University of Michigan Digital Library, n.d.).

17. Jonathan Butler, "The Making of a New Order," 189. The quote and the formula are from anthropologist Kenelm Burridge, *New Heaven, New Earth: A Study of Millenarian Activities* (New York: Schocken, 1909), 105–16.

18. Paul Boyer, *When Time Shall Be No More: Prophecy and Belief in Modern American Culture* (Cambridge, MA: Harvard Belknap, 1992), 73.

19. Ibid., 275.

20. Ibid., 73.

21. Thomas Broman, "Matter, Force, and the Christian World View," in *When Science and Christianity Unite*, ed. David Lindberg and Ronald Numbers, 85–110 (Chicago: University of Chicago Press, 2003).

22. Peter Gay, *The Enlightenment: The Science of Freedom*, vol. 2 of *Enlightenment and Interpretation* (New York: Norton, 1977), 8.

23. Perry Miller, *The New England Mind: The Seventeenth Century* (New York: Macmillan, 1939), 231.

24. Miller, "The End of the World," 178.

25. Breig, "Eighteenth Century Millennialism," 5.

26. John Higham, *From Boundless to Consolidation: The Transformation of American Culture, 1848–1860* (Ann Arbor: W. L. Clements Library, 1969), quoted in Butler, "The Making of a New Order," 190.

Chapter 4

1. Glenn Schuck, "Christian Dispensationalism," in Wessinger, *The Oxford Handbook of Millennialism*, 515–28; Barkun, *Culture of Conspiracy*, 41–42.

2. Matthew 24:21.

3. Boyer, *When Time Shall Be No More*, 95.

4. Ibid.

5. Thompson, *End of Time*, 103.

6. Hillel Schwartz, *Century's End: A Cultural History of the Fin de Siècle—From the 990s through the 1990s* (New York: Doubleday, 1990).

7. *Fun*, January 1901, 22

8. Holbrook Jackson, *The Eighteen Nineties* (London: Penguin Pelican, 1939), 16.

9. Gilbert Seldes, *The Stammering Century* (New York: John Day, 1928), 366.

10. Robert Weyant, "Metaphors and Animal Magnetism," in *Science Pseudoscience and Society*, ed. Marsha Hanen, Margaret Osler, and Robert Weyant (Waterloo, ON: Calgary Institute of Humanities and Wilfred Laurier Press, 1980), 100, 104.

11. Seldes, *Stammering Century*, 327–28.

12. Ibid., 363, 364.

13. Ralph Waldo Emerson, *Nature* (Boston: James Munroe and Co., 1836).

14. Alfred L. Donaldson, *A History of the Adirondacks* (New York: Century, 1921), 1:178.

15. Seldes, *Stammering Century*, 371.

16. Ibid.

17. Albanese, *Republic of Mind and Spirit*, chap. 4, 7, 9–11.

18. Ibid., 7.

Chapter 5

1. For a full account, see Joscelyn Godwin, *The Theosophical Enlightenment* (Albany: State University of New York Press, 1994).

2. Helena Blavatsky, *Isis Unveiled: A Master Key to the Mysteries of Ancient and Modern Science and Theology*, 2 vols. (London: Theosophical Publishing House, 1877). It may be noted that the Theosophical Society, later under the directorship of Annie Besant, was not millennial in its orientation.

3. Godwin, *Theosophical Enlightenment*, 305–6.

4. Blavatsky, *Isis Unveiled:* 1:557.

5. Ibid., 1:552.

6. James Frazer, *The Golden Bough: A Study in Magic and Religion* (New York: St. Martin's, 1990).

7. Aldous Huxley, *The Perennial Philosophy* (New York: Harper, 1945); Eliade, *Myth of the Eternal Return*; Giorgio de Santillana and Hertha von Dechend, *Hamlet's Mill: An Essay on Myth and the Frame of Time* (Boston: Gambit, 1969).

8. Helena Blavatsky, *The Secret Doctrine*, 4 vols. (London: Theosophical Publishing House, 1888).

9. Blavatsky, *Isis Unveiled*, 1:38.

10. Godfrey Higgins, *Anacalypsis: An Attempt to Draw Aside the Veil of the Saitic Isis into the Origin of Languages, Nations, and Religions* (New Hyde Park, NY: University Books, 1965).

11. Ibid., xx.

12. Here I follow the detailed summary in Godwin, *Theosophical Enlightenment*, 81–91.

13. Isaac Lubelsky, *Celestial India: Madame Blavatsky and the Birth of Indian Nationalism* (Sheffield: Equinox, 2012), 11. I owe a debt of gratitude to John Hoopes for directing me to this valuable resource.

14. Ibid.

15. Friedrich Max Müller, *India: What Can It Teach Us?* (Escondido, CA: Book Tree, 1999), 49.

16. Lubelsky, *Celestial India*, 100.

17. Ibid., 233.

18. Blavatsky, *Isis Unveiled*, 1:127.

19. Ibid., 1:377.

20. Blavatsky, *The Secret Doctrine*, 2:56.

21. Richard Frazer, ed., *The Poems of Hesiod, "Works and Days"* (Norman: University of Oklahoma Press, 1983), lines 106–201.

22. Ibid., lines 134–35.

23. Ibid., lines 150–51.

24. Ibid., lines 174–78.

25. Ibid., line 189.

26. Nicholas Campion, *The Great Year: Astrology, Millenarianism, and History in the Western Tradition* (New York: Penguin, 1994), 206.

27. Frazer, *Golden Bough*, 640–41.

28. The math is complicated by the fact that each of these Yugas is preceded and followed by subperiods equal to one-tenth the value of that Yuga; thus, 4,000 + (2

× 400) + 3,000 + (2 × 300) + 2,000 + (2 × 200) + 1,000 + (2 × 100) = 12,000 divine years, and 12,000 × 360 = 4,320,000 human years. Since 100 such intervals constitute the life of Brahma, a year in his life, which represents the interval between successive world creations, amounts to 432,000 years. The last Kali Yuga was determined by Hindu astronomers to have begun on February 17, 3102 BCE, and therefore will end some 427,000 years in the future, the start of the so-called golden age.

29. John North, *An Illustrated History of Astronomy and Cosmology* (Chicago: University of Chicago Press, 2008), 175.

30. Blavatsky, *Isis Unveiled*, 1:560.

31. Joscelyn Godwin, *Atlantis and the Cycles of Time: Prophecies, Traditions, and Occult Revelations* (Rochester, VT: Inner Traditions, 2010), 77.

32. Graham Hancock, *Fingerprints of the Gods* (New York: Crown, 1995); Robert Bauval and Adrian Gilbert, *The Orion Mystery: Unlocking the Secrets of the Pyramids* (New York: Crown, 1994).

33. John Gordon Melton, Jerome Clark, and Aidan A. Kelly, *New Age Almanac* (Detroit: Visible Ink, 1991), 16.

34. For example, Sylvia Cranston, *H.P.B.: The Extraordinary Life and Influence of Helena Blavatsky, Founder of the Modern Theosophical Movement* (New York: G. P. Putnam's, 1993); Peter Washington, *Madame Blavatsky's Baboon* (New York: Schocken, 1993).

35. James Webb, *The Occult Underground* (La Salle, IL: Open Court, 1974), 191–92.

36. Barkun, *Culture of Conspiracy*, 23.

37. Webb, *The Occult Underground*, 192.

38. Barkun, *Culture of Conspiracy*, 25.

39. Ibid.

40. Ibid., 27.

41. Nicholas Campion, *A History of Western Astrology*, 2 vols. (London: Continuum, 2008), 2:230.

Chapter 6

1. Wouter Hanegraaff, *New Age Religion and Western Culture: Esotericism in the Mirrors of Secular Thought*, Studies in the History of Religions (Leiden: Brill, 1996), 98–110.

2. John Hoopes, "Mayanism Comes of (New) Age," in *2012: Decoding the Counterculture Apocalypse*, ed. Joseph Gelfer (New York: Equinox, 2011), 38–59.

3. James Herrick, *Scientific Mythologies: How Science and Science Fiction Forge New Religious Beliefs* (New York: Academic, 2008).

4. In his history of American millennialism, Michael Barkun notes that waves of millennialism during both the 1890s and 1930s, like that which gave rise to Millerism, took place during economic depressions: *Crucible of the Millennium*, 151–52.

5. David Spangler and William Irwin Thompson, *Reimagination of the World: A Critique of the New Age, Science, and Popular Culture* (Rochester, VT: Bear, 1991), 57.

6. Otto Friedrich, "New Age Harmonies," *Time*, September 7, 1987, 62–72.

7. Albanese, *Republic of Mind and Spirit*, 509.

8. Ibid., 510.

9. Mitch Horowitz, *Occult America: The Secret History of How Mysticism Shaped Our Nation* (New York: Bantam, 2009).

10. Marilyn Ferguson, *The Aquarian Conspiracy: Personal and Social Transformation in Our Time* (Los Angeles: Tarcher, 1980), 21.

11. Ibid., 410.

12. Ibid., 30.

13. Matthew Bradley, ed., *William James: The Varieties of Religious Experience: A Study in Human Nature* (Oxford: Oxford University Press, 2012), 291.

14. Ibid., 298.

15. Ibid., 298–99.

16. Ibid., 299. For a brief account of the pursuit of James's pathway to the use of psychoactive drugs, see Dimitri Tymoczko, "The Nitrous Oxide Philosopher," *Atlantic Monthly*, May 1996, 93–101.

17. Ferguson, *Aquarian Conspiracy*, 414.

18. Ibid., 415.

19. For a summary, see Walter Clark, "Religious Aspects of Psychedelic Drugs," *California Law Review* 56, no. 1 (1968): 86–99. See also the earlier study on therapeutic uses by Humphrey Osmond, "A Review of the Clinical Effects of Psychomimetic Agents," *Annals of the New York Academy of Sciences* 66 (1957): 418–34.

20. Bob Morris, "A Strong Cup of Tea," *New York Times Sunday Styles*, June 15, 2014, 1, 11. For a fuller account of ayahuasca, see Ralph Metzner, *The Ayahuasca Experience: A Sourcebook on the Sacred Vine of Spirits* (Rochester, VT: Park St., 2014).

21. Metzner, *The Ayahuasca Experience*, 11.

22. Bradley, *William James*, 401.

23. Thompson, *End of Time*, 201.

24. Ibid., 202.

25. John Gordon Melton, Jerome Clark, and Aidan Kelly, eds., *The New Age Encyclopedia* (Detroit: Gale, 1990).

26. See, for example, the debunking literature by James Randi and Michael Schermer (e.g., James Randi, *Flim-Flam, Psychics, ESP, Unicorns, and Other Delusions* (New York: Thomas Y. Crowell, 1980; Michael Schermer, *Why People Believe in Weird*

Things (New York: Holt, 1997), as well as the secular humanist magazine *Skeptical Inquirer.*

27. Albanese, *Republic of Mind and Spirit*, 514.

Chapter 7

1. Immanuel Velikovsky, *Worlds in Collision* (New York: Macmillan, 1950).

2. Here's a line from my own critique: "While a literal interpretation of catastrophes delineated in the Scriptures seems unorthodox, the attribution of such affairs to short-term cataclysmic events in the recent history of the solar system is heretical and the celestial demolition derby Velikovsky devises to work out the details downright preposterous." Anthony Aveni, "A Marshaling of Arguments," *Science* 199 (1978): 288. See also Michael Gordin, *The Pseudoscience Wars: Immanuel Velikovsky and the Birth of the Modern Fringe* (Chicago: University of Chicago Press, 2012).

3. Keith Thomas, *Religion and the Decline of Magic: Studies in Popular Beliefs in Sixteenth and Seventeenth-Century England* (New York: Scribners, 1971), 89.

4. Richard Locke, "Great Astronomical Discoveries Lately Made by Sir John Herschel, L.L.D., F.R.S., and G.," *New York Sun*, August 25, 1835, 2.

5. George Adamski, *Pioneers of Space: A Trip to the Moon, Mars, and Venus* (London: Leonard Freefield Center, 1949); George Adamski, *The Flying Saucers Have Landed* (London: British Book Center, 1953).

6. George Adamski, *Inside the Spaceships* (London: Arco, 1956).

7. amazon.com/George-Adamski (accessed July 31, 2014).

8. Quoted in Benjamin Zeller, "Apocalyptic Thought in UFO-Based Religions," in *End of Days: Essays on the Apocalypse from Antiquity to Modernity*, ed. Karolyn Kinane and Michael Ryan (Jefferson, NC: MacFarland, 2009), 328–48.

9. George Hunt Williamson, *Secret Places of the Lion* (London: Neville Spearman, 1958).

10. Ibid., 29.

11. Robert Ellwood, "UFO Religious Movements" in *America's Alternative Religions*, ed. Timothy Miller, SUNY Series in Religious Studies (Albany: State University of New York Press, 1995), 393.

12. Edward U. Condon, *A Scientific Study of Unidentified Flying Objects Conducted by the University of Colorado under Contract to the United States Air Force* (New York: Bantam, 1966).

13. Susan Palmer, *Aliens Adored: Raël's UFO Religion* (New Brunswick: Rutgers University Press, 2004), 48.

14. Ibid., 113.

15. Ibid., 46.

16. Revelation 11:3.

17. Ellwood, "UFO Religious Movements," 394.

18. Frank Drake and Dava Sobel, *Is Anyone Out There? The Scientific Search for Extraterrestrial Intelligence* (New York: Delacorte, 1992), 160.

19. Barkun, *Culture of Conspiracy*, 81–82.

20. http://abcnews.go.com/Technology/ufos-exist-americans-national-geographic-survey/story?id=16661311, accessed December 1, 2015.

21. Hanegraaff, *New Age Religion*, gives an interesting discussion of the origin and many meanings of the term *channeler* (see esp. 23–41).

22. Shirley MacLaine, *Out on a Limb* (New York: Bantam, 1983).

23. Shirley MacLaine, *Going Within: A Guide for Inner Transformations* (New York: Bantam, 1989), 69.

24. Ibid., 232.

25. Barkun, *Culture of Conspiracy*, 80–98, esp. 88–89.

26. Carl Jung, *Flying Saucers: A Modern Myth of Things Seen in the Skies* (Princeton: Princeton University Press, 1979), 16–17.

27. Daniel Wojcik, *The End of the World as We Know It: Faith, Fatalism, and Apocalypse in America* (New York: New York University Press, 1997). See also Wojcik, "Avertive Apocalypticism" in Wessinger, *The Oxford Handbook of Millennialism*, 66–88.

28. Grosso, *Millennium Myth*, 253; 1 Thessalonians 4:16–17.

29. Robert Flaherty, "UFOs, ETs, and the Millennial Imagination" in Wessinger, *The Oxford Handbook of Millennialism*, 587–610, esp. 603.

30. Dane Rudhyar, *Occult Preparations for a New Age* (Wheaton, IL: Quest Theosophical Foundation, 1975), 254.

31. Ibid.

Chapter 8

1. See Lee Quinby, "The Days Are Numbered: The Romance of Death, Doom, and Deferral in Contemporary Apocalypse Films," in *The End All around Us: Apocalyptic Texts and Popular Culture*, ed. John Walliss and Kenneth G. C. Newport (London: Equinox, 2009), 96–109, for a sociological analysis of this and other films discussed in the present chapter.

2. Ibid., 102.

3. See Mervyn Bendle, "The Apocalyptic Imagination and Popular Culture," *Journal of Religion and Popular Culture* 11, no. 1 (2005); and Conrad Ostwalt, "Visions of the End: Secular Apocalypse in Recent Hollywood Film," *Journal of Religion and Film* 2, no. 1 (1998): 1.

4. Terrence Rafferty, "This Is the Way the World Ends," *New York Times*, June 17, 2012, 12.

5. Glenn Shuck, "Christian Dispensationalism," in *The Oxford Handbook*, edited by Catherine Wessinger, (Oxford: Oxford University Press, 2011), 515–28, esp. 515.

6. Quoted in Jennie Chapman, "Selling Faith without Selling Out: Reading the Left Behind Novels in the Context of Popular Culture," in Walliss and Newport, *The End All around Us*, 148.

7. Shuck, "Christian Dispensationalism," 523.

8. Hal Lindsey, *The Late Great Planet Earth* (Grand Rapids, MI: Zondervan, 1970).

9. Stephen O'Leary, *Arguing the Apocalypse: A Theory of Millennial Rhetoric* (Oxford: Oxford University Press, 1994), chap. 7.

10. Jeffrey Sheler, "The Christmas Covenant," *US News and World Report*, December 19, 1994, 64

11. Wojcik, *End of the World*, 97.

12. O'Leary, *Arguing the Apocalypse*, 173.

13. Dick Hebdige, *Subculture: The Meaning of Style* (New York: Routledge, 1979).

14. Kevin Sack, "Apocalyptic Trilogy Revitalized by Attacks," *New York Times*, November 23, 2001, 1.

15. John Grant Stauffer, "Apocalyptic Myths and Virtual World Culture" (MS, Colgate University, 2011), 2.

16. Mark Heley, *The Everything Guide to 2012* (Avon, MA: Adams, 2009), 268.

17. "How NBC Inserted Racism into the Trayvon Martin 911 Call," *The Blaze*, 2009, theblaze.com/stories/2012/04/09 (accessed August 18, 2014).

18. Matthew Sutton, "Why the Antichrist Matters in Politics," *New York Times*, September 26, 2011, A29.

19. Christina Wilke, "Wayne LaPierre: More Guns Needed for Hellish World," huffingtonpost.com, February 13, 2013 (accessed February 14, 2013).

Chapter 9

1. Rudhyar, *Occult Preparations*, 130–31.

2. Frazer, *Golden Bough*; see the discussion in chap. 6.

3. De Santillana and von Dechend, *Hamlet's Mill*, 151.

4. Hilda Ellis Davidson, review of *Hamlet's Mill*, *Folklore* 85, no. 4 (1974): 282–83.

5. Ibid., 283.

6. Cecilia Payne-Gaposchkin, review of *Hamlet's Mill*, *Journal for the History of Astronomy* 3 (1972): 206–8.

7. Ibid., 207.

8. Edmund Leach, "Bedtime Story" *New York Review*, February 12, 1970, 36.

9. Ibid.

10. Alexander Marshack, *The Roots of Civilization: The Cognitive Beginnings of Man's First Art, Symbol and Notation* (New York: McGraw Hill, 1971).

11. John Lear, "The Star Fixed Ages of Man," *Saturday Review*, January 10, 1970, 99–109; George Michanowsky, *The Once and Future Star* (New York: Hawthorn, 1977).

12. David Ulansey, *The Origins of the Mithraic Mysteries: Cosmology and Salvation in the Ancient World* (New York: Oxford University Press, 1989).

13. Ibid., 83.

14. Ibid., 125.

15. Bauval and Gilbert, *Orion Mystery*; Robert Bauval, *The Egypt Code* (New York: Disinformation, 2006).

16. William Sullivan, *The Secret of the Incas: Myth, Astronomy, and the War against Time* (New York: Crown, 1996).

17. Ibid., quoted on cover.

18. Richard Atkinson, "Moonshine on Stonehenge," *Antiquity* 40 (1966): 212–16.

19. Sullivan, *Secret of the Incas*, 311.

20. Michael York, "New Age Millenarianism and Its Christian Influences," in *Christian Millenarianism from the Early Church to Waco*, ed. Stephen Hunt (Bloomington: Indiana University Press, 2001), esp. 224.

21. Sullivan, *Secret of the Incas*, 15.

22. Ibid., 280.

23. Percy Shelley, *Ozymandias* (1818), in *The Art of the Sonnet*, ed. Stephen Burt and David Mikics (Cambridge, MA: Belknap, 2010). I am indebted to my colleague Alexei Vranich for directing me to Shelley's poem and for discussing with me ideas about the nature of romantic archaeology.

Chapter 10

1. Terrence McKenna and Dennis McKenna, *The Invisible Landscape: Mind, Hallucinogens, and the I Ching* (New York: HarperOne, 1994).

2. Wouter Hanegraaff, "'And End History. And Go to the Stars': Terence McKenna and 2012," in *Religion and Retributive Logic: Essays in Honor of Professor Garry W. Trompf*, ed. Carole M. Cusack and Christopher Hartney, Studies in the History of Religions (Leiden: Brill, 2010), 291–312.

3. Ibid., 298.

4. The clearest explanation of the nearly incomprehensible McKenna theory of induced enlightenment that I have been able to find is in Hanegraaff, "'And End History,'" on which much of my interpretation is based.

5. Olav Hammer, *Claiming Knowledge: Strategies and Epistemology from Theosophy to the New Age*, Studies in the History of Religion (Brill: Leiden, 2001).

6. The fascinating story of decipherment is recounted in detail in anthropologist Michael Coe's accessible book, *Breaking the Maya Code* (New York: Thames and Hudson, 1992).

7. For a detailed account of these discoveries, see Anthony Aveni, *Skywatchers of Ancient Mexico* (Austin: University of Texas Press, 1980). See also Anthony Aveni, *Stairways to the Stars: Skywatching in Three Great Ancient Cultures* (New York: Wiley, 1997).

8. Erich von Daniken, *Chariots of the Gods? Unsolved Mysteries of the Past* (New York: Putnam, 1970), vii.

9. Erich von Daniken, *Gods from Outer Space* (New York: Bantam, 1973), 5.

10. Frank Waters, *Mexico Mystique: The Coming Sixth World of Consciousness* (Chicago: Sage, 1975); Merle Green Robertson, ed., *Primera Mesa Redonda de Palenque* (Pebble Beach, RI: Stevenson School, 1874).

11. Peter Tompkins, *Mysteries of the Mexican Pyramids* (New York: Harper and Row, 1976); Luis Arochi, *La piramide de Kukulcan: Su simbolismo solar* (Mexico City: Panorama Mexico, 1984).

12. Tompkins, *Mysteries of the Mexican Pyramids*, 389.

13. Frank Waters, *Book of the Hopi* (New York: Viking, 1963).

14. Ibid., 411.

15. Armin Geertz, "Contemporary Problems in the Study of Native North American Religions with Special Reference to the Hopis," *South American Indian Quarterly* 20, nos. 3/4 (1983): 393.

16. Philip Jenkins, *Dream Catchers: How Mainstream America Discovered Native Spirituality* (Oxford: Oxford University Press, 2004), 162.

17. Ibid., 18–19.

18. Waters, *Mexico Mystique*, ix.

19. Ibid., 143.

20. Ibid., 257. Actually it's off by a century and a half.

21. Ibid., 258.

22. Ibid., 408.

23. Daniel 8:14. See also chapter 1.

24. John Eric S. Thompson, *Maya History and Religion*, Civilization of American Indian (Norman: University of Oklahoma Press, 1972). See also Michael Coe, *The Maya* (New York: Praeger, 1966).

25. Coe, *The Maya*, 149. See also Michael Coe, preface to Gelfer, *2012*, viii–ix.

Chapter 11

1. Olav Hammer, *Philosophia Perennis*, 172–73.
2. Ibid., 175.
3. Ibid.
4. Ibid., 319.
5. Carl Jung, *Psychology and the Occult* (Princeton: Bollingen, 1977).
6. Aldous Huxley, *The Doors of Perception* (London: Chatto and Windus, 1954).
7. Mircea Eliade, *The Sacred and the Profane: The Nature of Religion* (New York: Houghton-Mifflin Harcourt, 1959).
8. Jenkins, *Dream Catchers*, 164.
9. Eliade, *Sacred and the Profane*, 36, after Werner Müller, *Weltbild und Kult der Kwakiutl-Indianer* (Weisbaden: Frank Steiner, 1955), 17–20.
10. Eliade, *Myth of the Eternal Return*, 37.
11. Ibid., 35.
12. Ibid., 26.
13. Mircea Eliade, *Shamanism: Archaic Techniques of Ecstasy* (Princeton: Princeton University Press, 1964).
14. Eliade, *Myth of the Eternal Return*, 74–75.
15. Mircea Eliade, *The Quest: History and Meaning in Religion* (Chicago: University of Chicago Press, 1969), 3.
16. Ibid., chap. 4.
17. Eliade, *Myth of the Eternal Return*, 5.
18. Ibid., 7.
19. Ibid., 37.
20. Edmund Leach, "Sermons by a Man on a Ladder," *New York Review*, October 20, 1966, 28–31.
21. Russell McCutcheon, *Manufacturing Religion: The Discourse on Sui Generis Religion and the Politics of Nostalgia* (Oxford: Oxford University Press, 1997).
22. Tony Stigliano, "Fascism's Mythologist: Mircea Eliade and the Politics of Myth," *Revision* 24, no. 3 (2002): 32–38.
23. Ibid., 36.
24. Quoted in ibid., 36.
25. Prudence M. Rice, *Maya Calendar Origins: Monuments, Mythistory, and the Materialization of Time* (Austin: University of Texas Press, 2007), esp. chap. 9.
26. David Webster, *The Fall of the Ancient Maya: Solving the Mystery of the Maya Collapse* (London: Thames and Hudson, 2002).
27. After the title of James R. Lewis and Olav Hammer, eds., *The Invention of Sacred Tradition* (New York: Cambridge University Press, 2008).

Chapter 12

1. Ernst Wilhelm Förstemann, *Commentary on the Maya Manuscript in the Royal Public Library of Dresden*, Papers of the Peabody Museum of Archaeology and Ethnology (Cambridge, MA: Harvard University, 1906), 206.

2. See, for example, Linda Schele and Nikolai Grube, *Notebook for the Maya Hieroglyphic Forum at Texas* (Austin: University of Texas Latin American Studies, 1997).

3. Timothy W. Knowlton, *Maya Creation Myths: Words and Worlds of the Chilam Balam* (Boulder: University Press of Colorado, 2010), 62.

4. Ibid., 113.

5. Hoopes, "Mayanism Comes of (New) Age," 54, note 11.

6. José Argüelles, *The Transformative Vision: Reflections on the Nature and History of Human Expression* (Boulder, CO: Shambhala, 1975).

7. Philip Lucas, "New Age Millennialism," in Wessinger, *The Oxford Handbook of Millennialism*, esp. 578; David Spangler, *New Age: A Guide* (Brownstown, MI: Motor City Books).

8. Elizabeth Achelis, *Of Time and the Calendar* (New York: Hermitage, 1955), 27.

9. David Stuart, *The Order of Days: The Maya World and the Truth about 2012* (New York: Harmony Books, 2012), esp. chap. 8.

10. Carl Johan Calleman, *The Mayan Calendar and the Transformation of Consciousness* (Rochester, VT: Bear, 2004).

11. Argüelles, *The Transformative Vision*, 184.

12. Ibid., 194.

13. Ibid.

14. Rudhyar, *Occult Preparations*, 254.

15. Daniel Pinchbeck, *2012: The Return of Quetzalcoatl* (New York: Tarcher, 2006), 297.

16. Ibid., 368.

17. Ibid., 1–2.

18. Fray Diego Duran, *Book of the Gods and Rites and Ancient Calendars*, ed. Fernando Horcasitas, trans. Doris Heyden (Norman: University of Oklahoma Press, 1971).

19. Ibid., 58.

20. Ibid., 59.

21. Ibid.

22. Brant Gardner, "The Christianization of Quetzalcoatl: A History of the Metamorphosis," *Sunstone* 10, no. 11 (1980): 6–10.

23. Jean Seznec, *The Survival of the Pagan Gods* (Princeton: Princeton University Press, 1953); see also Anthony Aveni, *Conversing with the Planets: How Science and Myth Invented the Cosmos* (New York: Times, 1992), fig. 2.1.

24. Tony Shearer, *Lord of the Dawn: Quetzalcoatl and the Tree of Life* (Happy Camp, CA: Naturegraph, 1971).

25. Matthew Restall and Amara Solari, *2012 and the End of the World: The Western Roots of the Maya Apocalypse* (Boulder, CO: Rowman and Littlefield, 2011).

26. Ibid., 79.

27. Ibid., 82.

28. Ibid., 97.

29. Robert Sitler, *The Living Maya: Ancient Wisdom in the Era of 2012* (Berkeley: North Atlantic, 2010), 18.

30. See Sitler's criticism in ibid., 28n25. For the quotation, see Robert Sitler, "The 2012 Phenomenon: New Age Appropriation of an Ancient Maya Calendar," *Novo Religio* 9, no. 3 (2006): 18.

31. John Major Jenkins, *Maya Cosmogenesis 2012* (Rochester, VT: Bear, 1998), esp. part 3.

32. Ibid., 332.

33. Jenkins, *The 2012 Story*, 353.

34. Ibid.

35. Hoopes, "Mayanism Comes of (New) Age."

36. David Freidel, Linda Schele, and Joy Parker, *Maya Cosmos: Three Thousand Years on the Shaman's Path* (New York: William Morrow, 1993). My critique of this hypothesis appears in "Review: *Maya Cosmos*," *American Anthropology* 98, no. 1 (1993): 22–24.

37. Freidel (personal communication, December 18, 2014) stated that personally he did not think he and Schele had in mind a celestial cycle fixed in the deep past, only an alignment related to the August 11 date; see Schele, Freidel and Parker, *Maya Cosmos*, 95.

38. Schele, Freidel and Parker, *Maya Cosmos*, 76.

39. Eliade, *Sacred and the Profane*, 53. Once again I am indebted to John Hoopes for first pointing out this connection to me.

40. Simon Martin, "First Fruit from the Maize Tree and Other Tales from the Underworld," in *Chocolate in Mesoamerica: A Cultural History of Cacao*, ed. Cameron L. McNeil (Gainesville: University Press of Florida, 2006); Karl Taube, "The Jade Hearth: Centrality, Rulership, and the Classic Maya Temple," in *Function and Meaning in Classic Maya Architecture*, ed. Stephen D. Houston (Washington, DC: Dumbarton Oaks Library and Collection, 1998), 427–69.

41. Freidel, Schele, and Parker, *Maya Cosmos*, 12.

42. Ibid.

43. Ibid., 158. As Freidel (personal communication December 18, 2014) explains, it was he who introduced Eliade's *Archaic Ecstasy*, a treatise on shamanism, to Schele. They were further attracted to the notion of cosmic iconography integrated into myth by the works of anthropologists Gerardo Reichel-Dolmatoff and Johannes Wilbert, who express the view that shamanic knowledge serves as a complement to science in the pursuit of understanding native folkways. It was never his intention to propose that the Maya shared a universal subconscious archetypal understanding of the cosmos, rather that they anchored their cosmology in both the careful observation of nature and in faith-based revelations expressed in art, literature, architecture, and a wide array of archaeological contexts. As he put it: "Admiring a way of thinking about the world (shamanism) is not the same as proselytizing it as a matter of conviction and faith."

44. Julia Guernsey, *Ritual and Power in Stone: The Performance of Rulership in Mesoamerican Izapan Art Style* (Austin: University of Texas Press, 2006).

45. Anthony Aveni and Horst Hartung, "Water, Mountain, Sky: The Evolution of Site Orientations in Southeast Mesoamerica," in *Precious Greenstone Precious Feathers in Chalchihuitl in Quetzalli*, ed. Eloise Quinoñes Keber (Culver City, CA: Labyrinthos, 2000), 55–65.

46. Jenkins, *The 2012 Story*.

47. Ibid., 412.

48. Kevin A. Whitesides and John W. Hoopes, "Seventies Dreams and 21st Century Realities: The Emergence of 2012 Mythology," *Zeitschrift für Anomalistik* 12 (2012): 50–74. Hoopes places his first recognition of the term in a book of the same title published by Dennis Alexander in 2001 (personal communication, March 19, 2015).

49. Hoopes, "Mayanism Comes of (New) Age," 39.

50. Ibid.

51. Godwin, *Atlantis and the Cycles of Time*, 167.

Conclusion

1. Drawn in part from Wojcik, *End of the World*, 8.

2. Max Weber, "The Social Psychology of the World's Religions," in *From Max Weber: Essays in Sociology*, ed. Hans Gerth and Charles Wright Mills (New York: Oxford, 1946), 267–301. I am grateful to Dartmouth anthropologist John Watanabe for directing me to this and a number of other helpful sociological readings that inform these issues.

3. Barry A. Kosmin and Ariela Keysar, "American Religious Identification Survey Summary Report" (Hartford: Trinity College, 2009); Rachel Zoll, "Americans Are Still Religious," *US News and World Report*, December 19, 1994, 64. Splinter organizations that have become new churches in America since the mid-nineteenth century include Jehovah Witnesses, Seventh-day Adventists, Latter-day Saints, and Assemblies of God.

4. Robert Bellah, Richard Madsen, William M. Sullivan, Ann Swidler, and Steven M. Tipton, *Habits of the Heart: Individualism and Commitment in American Life* (Berkeley: University of California Press, 1985).

5. Harold Camping, *1994?* (Grand Rapids, MI: Zondervan, 1992).

6. Cotton Mather, interpreted by Miller, *The New England Mind*, 231.

7. Dan Lee, "After the Rapture," *New Yorker*, October 24, 2011, 28–33, 95–96.

8. John Major Jenkins, "On 2012," *JMJ Website*, 5–6, accessed August 1, 2014.

9. John Major Jenkins, "Approaching 2012: Modern Misconceptions versus Reconstructing Ancient Maya Perspectives," in Gelfer, *2012*, 171.

10. John Major Jenkins, "My House," *JMJ Website*, June 2, 2013 (accessed July 15, 2014).

11. "New Year's Eve in Peru," http://greatmystery.org/SacredTours/peruJMJ.html (accessed July 2, 2014).

12. Carl Johan Calleman, "Some New Reflections on the Mayan Calendar 'End' Date," tweeted December 31, 2012 (accessed April 1, 2014).

13. "The Deeper Meaning of the Shift in Consciousness with Carl Johan Calleman," *YouTube* accessed August 20, 2014).

14. "Conversations," interview with Max Dax, *Electronic Beats*, January 13, 2011 (accessed July 25, 2014).

15. Ibid.

16. Hanegraaff, *New Age Religion*, 64.

About the Author

Anthony Aveni is the Russell Colgate Distinguished University Professor of Astronomy, Anthropology, and Native American Studies, serving appointments in both the Department of Physics and Astronomy and the Department of Sociology and Anthropology at Colgate University, where he has taught since 1963. He has also served as visiting professor at the University of South Florida, the University of Colorado, Tulane University, and the University of Padua, Italy. In 1982, Aveni was voted National Professor of the Year by the Council for Advancement and Support of Education, Washington, DC, the highest national award for teaching. *Rolling Stone* magazine named him one of the ten best professors in the United States in 1991. At Colgate, Aveni has received, among other teaching awards, the Alumni Award for Excellence in Teaching (1997), the Balmuth Teaching Award (2011), and the Phi Eta Sigma National Honor Society's Distinguished Teaching Award voted by the freshman class of 1990.

Aveni is also a prolific scholar and author. He helped develop and now is considered one of the founders of cultural astronomy (archaeoastronomy), in particular for his research on the astronomical history of the Aztec and Maya of ancient

Mexico. He has conducted similar research in North America, Peru, Israel, Italy, and Greece. Aveni has involved his students in his research through thirty-nine years of field research trips to Central America and Peru to study history, hieroglyphic writing, calendars, and architecture. In 2004, he was the recipient of the H. B. Nicholson Award for Excellence in Mesoamerican Studies, given by the Peabody Museum and Moses Mesoamerican Archive of Harvard University. In 2013, he was awarded the Fryxell Medal for Interdisciplinary Research by the Society of American Archaeologists.

Aveni has more than 300 research publications to his credit, including three cover articles in *Science* magazine. Two of his short pieces have been cited as "notable essays" in the volumes *Best American Essays of 2002* and *Best American Science Writing of 2002*. In addition, he has written nineteen books and edited fourteen more. Authored works include *Empires of Time*, on the history of timekeeping; *Conversing with the Planets*, a work that weaves together cosmology, mythology, and the anthropology of ancient cultures by showing how they discovered harmony between their beliefs and their study of the sky; *Behind the Crystal Ball: Magic, Science, and the Occult from Antiquity through the New Age*; *Stairways to the Stars: Skywatching in Three Great Ancient Cultures*; *Between the Lines*; and *Nasca: Eighth Wonder of the World*, chronicling his ten-year research program on the mystery of the ground drawings of Nasca, Peru. Additional books include *Ancient Astronomers*, *Foundations of New World Cultural Astronomy*, *The Book of the Year: A Brief History of Our Seasonal Holidays*, and *People and the Sky: Our Ancestors and the Cosmos*. *Skywatchers*, his revised updated version of *Skywatchers of Ancient Mexico*, has served as a basic textbook in archaeoastronomy. *The First Americans: Where They Came from and Who They Became*, the first of two books for children, received the 2006 Golden Spur Award for Western Juvenile Nonfiction and made the 2006 Children's Top Ten list of the International Readers' Association. *Buried beneath Us: Discovering the Ancient Cities of the Americas* was published in 2013. His memoir on teaching, *Class Not Dismissed: Reflections on Undergraduate Teaching and Learning in the Liberal Arts* appeared in 2014.

With his artist wife, Lorraine, Aveni resides in Hamilton, New York.

Index

Page numbers in italic indicate illustrations.